FOUNDATIONS OF FLAT PATTERNING AND DRAPING

Foundations of Flat Patterning and Draping: For the Female Form provides the foundational tools necessary for success in the techniques of flat patterning and draping clothes and costumes.

This book begins with the basics of taking measurements, preparing the fabric for draping, and preparing the dress form. The following chapters explore flat patterning and draping practices for bodices, skirts, pants, dresses, sleeves, collars, cuffs, and facings through detailed step-by-step instructions, checklists, and numerous diagrams. The bodice drafting instructions in this book, specifically, are a new method that accommodates all bust and cup sizes. There are instructions for small and large cup sizes allowing for a fit that does not gap at the armscye as typically happens with previous patterning methods, and additional sections for bodices and sleeves and how to manipulate them to create alternate looks. The techniques in this book generalize across sizes and shapes making it universally applicable for the student technician, as well as the person the garment is being developed for. Each method of drafting and draping has been class-tested and proven to produce well-fitting garments.

Presented in an accessible format with clear instructions and detailed illustrations, this book is well suited for use as a textbook for the undergraduate college instructor teaching costuming or fashion, as well as for the student or individual learning on their own in the theatre, film, or fashion industries.

Larissa McConnell is Continuing Assistant Professor of Costume Design and Technology at Gustavus Adolphus College in Saint Peter, Minnesota. Originally from Buffalo, New York, she earned her B.S. and B.F.A. at the State University of New York at Fredonia and her M.F.A. at the University of Missouri, Kansas City. Larissa has also worked at various theatres around the country, including the Weston Playhouse Theatre in Weston, Vermont; the Alpine Theatre Project in Whitefish, Montana; and both the Chautauqua Theatre Company and the Chautauqua Opera in Chautauqua, New York.

FOUNDATIONS OF FLAT PATTERNING AND DRAPING

For the Female Form

Larissa McConnell

NEW YORK AND LONDON

Cover image: Cover art by Larissa McConnell

First published 2022
by Routledge
605 Third Avenue, New York, NY 10158

and by Routledge
2 Park Square, Milton Park, Abingdon, Oxon, OX14 4RN

Routledge is an imprint of the Taylor & Francis Group, an informa business

Library of Congress Cataloging-in-Publication Data
Names: McConnell, Larissa, author.
Title: Foundations of flat patterning and draping : for the female form / Larissa McConnell.
Description: New York : Routledge, 2022. | Includes index.
Identifiers: LCCN 2021025472 (print) | LCCN 2021025473 (ebook) | ISBN 9780367900977 (hardback) | ISBN 9780367900984 (paperback) | ISBN 9781003022619 (ebook)
Subjects: LCSH: Costume—Handbooks, manuals, etc. | Sewing—Handbooks, manuals, etc.
Classification: LCC PN2067 .M323 2022 (print) | LCC PN2067 (ebook) | DDC 792.02/6—dc23
LC record available at https://lccn.loc.gov/2021025472
LC ebook record available at https://lccn.loc.gov/2021025473

ISBN: 978-0-367-90097-7 (hbk)
ISBN: 978-0-367-90098-4 (pbk)
ISBN: 978-1-003-02261-9 (ebk)

DOI: 10.4324/9781003022619

Typeset in Univers
by Apex CoVantage, LLC

To my husband, Jeff, who has been so supportive throughout this project.

Contents

Contents

Preface

The goal of this book is to educate and inspire future generations of drapers and drafters. While some of these skills may seem magical for novices, by the end of the book you should have gained enough knowledge to be able to graduate to more advanced skills.

This book also has the intention of being an "all-in-one" source for the basics of drafting and draping; a single book with the information most frequently utilized by those still learning the craft. I have found previously that multiple books were necessary as references, and that many are now out of print, creating a void for those who are building their personal skills and libraries. This book is primarily a textbook, with the intention of filling some of that void.

Another reason I wanted to create this book was to develop systems that work for all body types and can be followed by any level of drafting and draping expertise. These instructions have been tested on sizes 2 through 26, by students with a range of experience, in an effort to confirm the instructions' accuracy and to determine the ease of understanding.

Acknowledgments

The author would to thank the many students who assisted with the process of testing the methods, working the kinks out, and development. Their encouragement and support have been instrumental in getting this book written, especially the assistance of Emilee Mason, whose math skills and collaboration were indispensable, as well as Madison Adams, and Morgan Fuller. These students committed hours upon hours of their time, and for that, she could not be more grateful.

The author would also like to thank those who came before her who have written books on drafting and draping. Their voices have been with the author throughout this process.

Introduction

But what is Flat-Patterning and Draping?

Flat patterning and draping are two methods used to create custom, fitted garments.

Frequently, both methods are used, because flat patterning can be the better method for certain parts of a garment, and sometimes draping is the better method. For example, it may be easier to drape the bodice, but draft the collar and sleeves.

Flat patterning is a mathematical system using measurements to create a two-dimensional technical drafting. This drafting is called a sloper, or a body block. Many people are rather intimidated by this method, but the math is actually more a system of graphing than it is calculus.

Draping is more of an "instant gratification" method of creating a pattern. You pin muslin onto a dress form, which allows you to immediately see whether or not the design is manifesting. If it isn't then you are able to rework the muslin or design lines until it is correct.

Chapter 1: Tools Needed

To be successful with draping or drafting, you will need the appropriate tools. The following supplies are recommended. It is also useful to store smaller items you use frequently on you in a half-apron with divided sections. This will allow you to always have your supplies with you, whether at the dress form, at the drafting table, or the ironing board.

Medium weight muslin is traditionally used in draping.

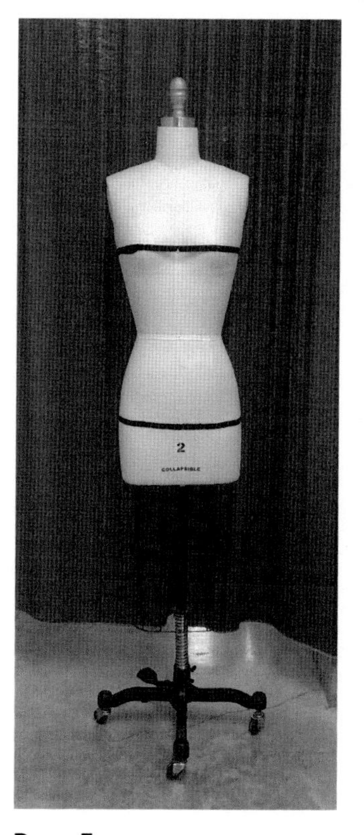

Dress Form

Industrial Iron

DOI: 10.4324/9781003022619-1

Tools Needed

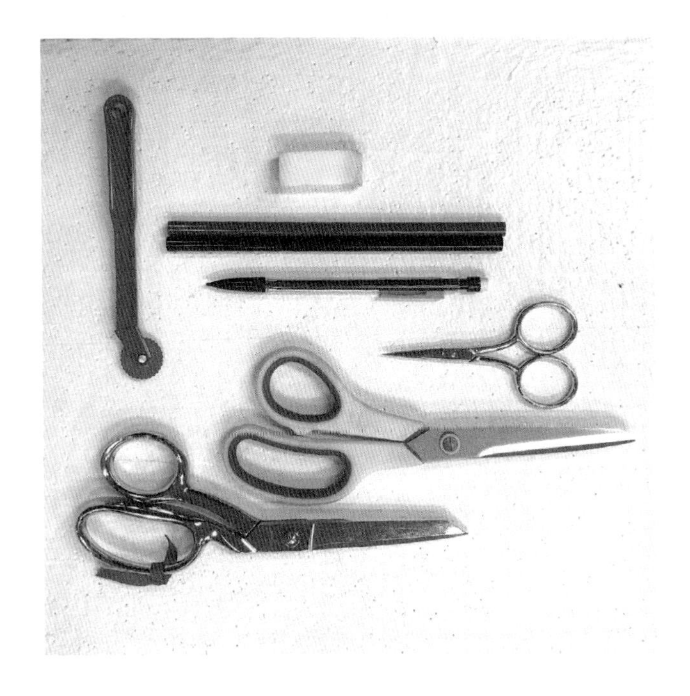

Paper scissors
Fabric scissors
Embroidery scissors/snips
0.7 mm mechanical graphite pencil
White eraser
Tailoring pencils: red and blue
Serrated tracing wheel

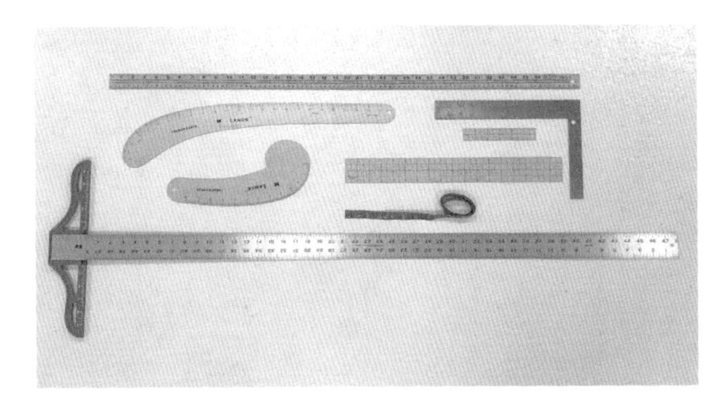

60″ (152.5 cm) measuring tape
2″ x 18″ (5.1 x 45.7 cm) clear grid ruler
1″ x 6″ (2.5 x 15.2 cm) clear grid ruler
36″ (91.4 cm) or 48″ (121.9 cm) metal ruler
24″ (61 cm) aluminum vary curve ruler
12″ (30.5 cm) aluminum vary curve ruler
L-square
T-square

½″ (1.3 cm) black twill tape
Aluminum head ⅝″ (1.6 cm) steel point pushpins
#17 dressmaker pins
Quilter's pins
Pin cushion
Heavy craft paper – painters drop cloth paper found in large home improvement box stores – rolls come in size
35″ (88.9 cm) x 140′ (42.7 m) at some stores
Tailor's ham
Ham stand
Sleeve board
Shoulder pads
Batting
Bias strip

Definitions of Terms

In order to communicate effectively, it is necessary that you are familiar with the terminology. The following terms will provide you with the verbal tools you need. As the Cutter/Draper, you will need to know these terms, but it is just as important for everyone from the Costume Designer to the Stitcher to have knowledge of them so that successful communication can occur.

It is also important to know the hierarchy in a Theatrical Costume Shop. The following are some of the production assignments.

Costume Coordinator/Supervisor/Shop Manager

The Costume Coordinator is responsible for the daily running of the costume shop, including budgeting, purchases, time management of all of the workers, and meetings with the Designer.

Cutter/Draper

The responsibility of the Cutter/Draper is to take the two-dimensional rendering of the costume or garment design and be able to convert it into a two-dimensional pattern or a three-dimensional draping. Through communication with the Designer, and use of the renderings, they will determine the function and design aspects of the garment to be constructed.

They will use flat patterning and/or draping to create the patterns based on the measurements of the person the garment is to be made for. The two-dimensional pattern will be used in the creation of a three-dimensional garment. Usually, a mock-up is made of muslin or other inexpensive fabric that mimics the fashion fabric to be used in the final garment. They will then fit the garment on the person and alter the patterns as needed.

The Cutter/Draper cuts or supervises the cutting of all the fabric for the garment from the pattern. They will have researched the period, style, and techniques necessary to complete the garment to the Costume Designer's specifications. They should also be able to determine the amount of fabric and trims for each garment.

First Hand

The First Hand prepares work for Stitchers, assists the Cutter/Draper in fittings, with cutting, pattern-making, stitching, and alterations. Sometimes they will do the prep work, such as preparing fabrics, gathering notions and trims, etc. They can also supervise and organize the alterations that are needed after fittings.

Stitcher

The Stitcher is the person who sews the garment together. They also have specialized skills that allow them to construct the garment based on the Cutter/Draper's patterning and instructions, and the Costume Designer's design. The Stitcher is supervised by the Cutter/Draper or the First Hand.

Tools Needed

Terms

Apex – the point of the bust.

Arm plate – on the side of the dress form, the metal plate at the place of the armhole. The screw is the midpoint of the armhole.

Bias – on fabric, the 45-degree angle from grain and cross-grain. The bias will stretch and can be used intentionally to create drape on the figure.

Bias tape – a woven fabric cut on the bias to make strips.

Block/blocking – the act of stretching fabric, usually muslin, to create a perfect rectangle with right angles used for draping.

Bodice – the front and back sections for the top half of the figure.

Bust line – the line at the fullest part of the bust.

Bust point – also called the Apex, it is the point of the bust.

Cross grain – the weft thread that runs perpendicularly across the grainline.

Circumference – the measurement that is taken all the way around a part of the figure.

Dart – a section of fabric pinned out when draping, or marked out on a drafting, that creates a more fitted garment.

Dart legs – the lines on the dart that are stitched together.

Draping – a three-dimensional method of creating a garment traditionally using muslin that is pinned to a dress form.

Drafting – a two-dimensional method of creating a garment using the measurements of a figure to technically create graphed patterns.

Dress form – full-scale molded figure used for draping. They also come in ½ scale models.

Ease – additional fabric in a garment to allow for movement.

Facing – in a garment, it is the fabric piece that is sewn to create a clean edge.

Fashion fabric – the fabric used for the final finished garment.

Fashion fabric – the fabric that the final finished garment will be made of.

Grainline – the warp thread that runs the length of the fabric and is parallel to the selvedge. It is the strongest of the thread directions.

Hipline – the line on the figure or dress form, parallel to the floor, that indicates the fullest part of the hip area.

Interfacing – a stabilizing material that is used to stiffen and provide additional structure to garment pieces such as facings, collars, and cuffs. There are many types of interfacing that are for specific uses.

Lining fabric – typically, a lightweight silky fabric that finishes the inside of a garment to make the garment more wearable, long-lasting, and comfortable. It will hide seams and darts and helps make the garment easier to get on and off.

Matching notches – marks placed on patterns to indicate where the pattern pieces line up when stitching. It is traditional to use single notches on the front pattern pieces and double notches on the back.

Mock-up – a full-scale garment created from a pattern traditionally made of muslin or fabric similar to the final fashion fabric. It is created with the intention of testing the pattern's fit for accuracy.

Mummy wrapping – a technique in padding out a dress form that uses bias tape about 1½"–2" (3.8–5.1 cm) wide to wrap the dress form after adding additional padding.

Muslin – a cotton fabric woven with a plain weave traditionally used for draping.

Notions – items used in garment construction such as buttons, snaps, thread, zippers, etc.

Panel – a section of muslin used for draping.

Parallel – runs the same direction as a particular line.

Perpendicular – is at a 90-degree angle to a particular line.

Pivot transfer method – a method of altering a pattern by pivoting the original pattern around the bust point to close or open a dart.

Plain weave – the warp and weft are woven with an up-down pattern. Each weft thread goes over and then under the warp threads alternately. For this weave, the threads are the same weight to give a balanced effect.

Princess line/seam – the line on a dress form or drafted pattern that runs from shoulder to waistline or armscye to waistline but always goes through the bust point. This line divides the center front from the side front.

Rendering – a sketch of a design.

Seam – the edge of a pattern that will be stitched to another edge of a pattern to create the garment.

Seam allowance – an area of fabric that lies next to the seam line that allows the garment to be sewn together.

Selvage (or Selvedge) – the finished, or factory edge, of a length of fabric.

Slash and compress – a method used in drafting to decrease the fullness of a pattern piece. It consists of lines drawn on the pattern that cut and are overlapped to change the shape of the garment. The pattern will shrink in an area creating a narrower look on the finished garment.

Slash and spread – a method used in drafting to increase the fullness of a pattern piece. It consists of lines drawn on the pattern that are cut to flare out the shape of the garment. The pattern will expand in an area creating flare on the finished garment.

Slope – the angle of the shoulder from the base of the neck to the point of the shoulder seam. See the measurements section for directions on how to measure this.

Sloper/body block – the basic pattern or master pattern created by draping or drafting, then converted to craft paper and used to create all other garment designs. It does not include seam allowances.

Straight of Grain – runs the length of the fabric in the same direction as the selvage. It is the strongest thread direction (see Grainline).

Trueing – creating accurate and matching seam lines and grainlines on a sloper so that when the garment is sewn together the seams lines match, the grainline is accurate, and the garment fits as expected.

Twill tape – a ribbon of cotton woven in a twill weave used for marking style lines on a dress form. For the demonstrations in this book, a ½" (1.3 cm) wide ribbon will be used.

Vanishing point – the tip of a dart.

Chapter 2: Measurements

This chapter provides the instructions for taking the measurements you will need to use in the following chapters.

Measurements are the numbers that define the shape of a figure. While measurements can tell you a great deal about how the figure might be shaped, it is helpful to have an image of the person measured so that you know what the numbers actually mean. If you are personally taking the measurements, you may also want a photo of the person being measured for future reference. The numbers taken from a figure can tell you much, but they don't always tell you everything. Does the person carry their weight in the front, or in the back, are they an hourglass, an apple, or a pear shape? These measurements, and the use of them, will give you a good base for your slopers which will, in turn, create the mock-up where alterations may need to take place in order to arrive at the most ideal fit.

It is important to note that you must remain professional during the taking of measurements. Never make a comment or let your face make a comment about a person's measurements or shape. If the person being measured initiates by making a comment, you need to continue with your job and not allow yourself to join in. Many, if not all, people have something about themselves that they might not find to be ideal. Do not be the cause of this insecurity in them. If you have an assistant who will write the measurements on the measurement sheet for you, they also must be aware of how they are conducting themselves.

How to Take Measurements

Tie a thin piece of elastic around the natural waist to assist with the taking of measurements.

(The natural waist can be located by having the person bend slightly sideways – shoulder toward hip – and where the bend occurs is the natural waist.)

The person being measured should wear form-fitting clothing to reduce bulk and allow for the most accurate measurements.

DOI: 10.4324/9781003022619-2

NAME:

MO/YR: month and year that the measurements are being taken. This is a reminder in case the measurements are needed later and to know how current they are.

GRAD YR: when used in an educational setting, this allows for the removal of the measurements from the measurement book after the student has graduated.

ROLE:

PRODUCTION

PHONE:

EMAIL:

SHIRT SIZE: Given as a letter. For example, S, M, L, etc.

BRA: Your bra size is based on the bust and underbust measurements. The underbust measurement is your band size. The difference between your bust measurement and underbust measurement determines your cup size. Each 1″ (2.5 cm) difference is equal to your cup size. For example, an A cup is a 1″ (2.5 cm) difference, a B cup is a 2″ (5.1 cm) difference, etc.

DRESS SIZE: Given as a number.

PANT SIZE: Given as a number.

ALLERGIES: As they pertain to a costume shop. For example: wool, feathers, fur, nickel, latex, spirit gum, etc.

TATTOOS: These may need to be covered, or maybe not, depending on the location of the tattoo, the show, the director's preference, etc.

PIERCINGS: Includes ears, nose, etc. Helpful if earrings need to be worn, etc.

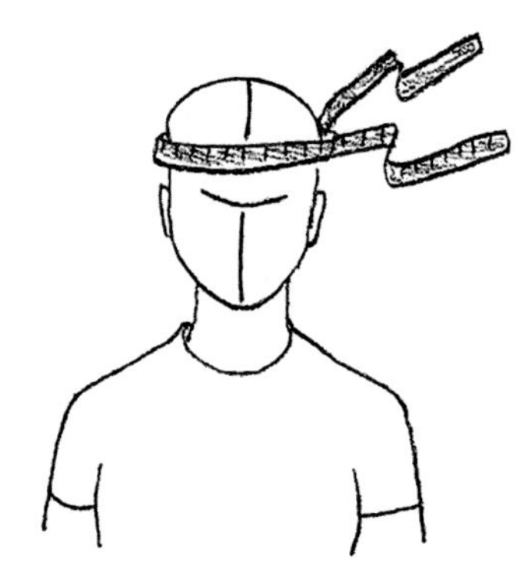

AROUND HEAD: circumference of the head starting at the forehead and going around just above the ears.

Measurements

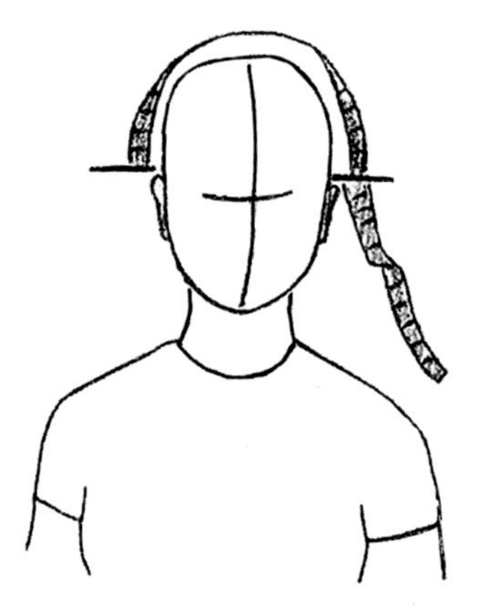

EAR TO EAR: from the top of one ear, across the top of the head, to the top of the other ear.

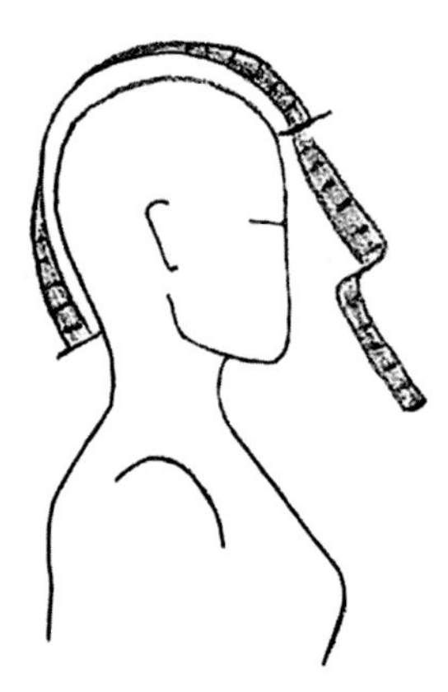

FOREHEAD TO NAPE: from the hairline above the center of the nose, across the top of the head and down to the nape of the neck.

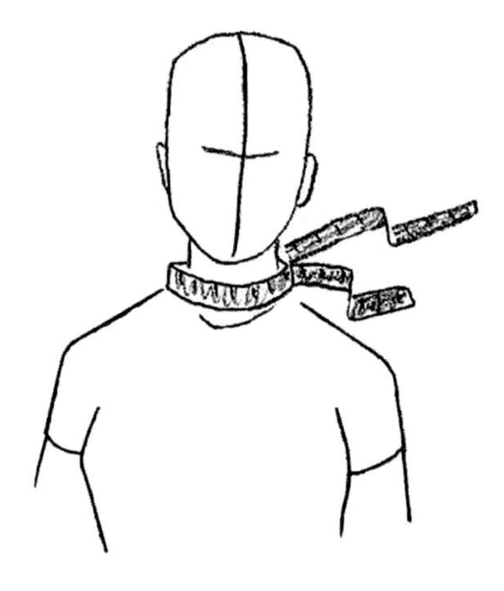

NECK: at the base of the neck.

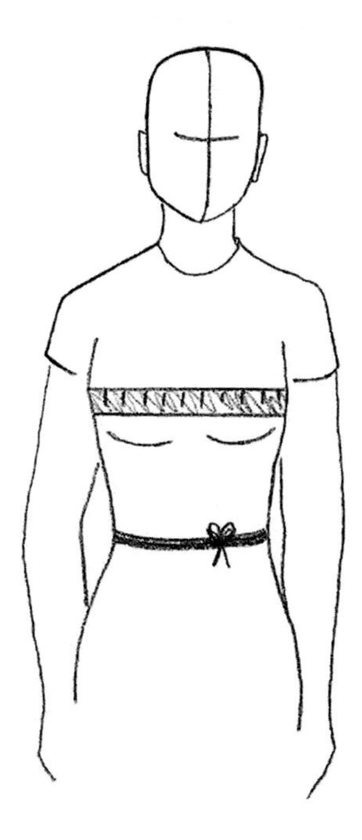

BUST: around the fullest part of the bust with tape measure parallel to the floor.

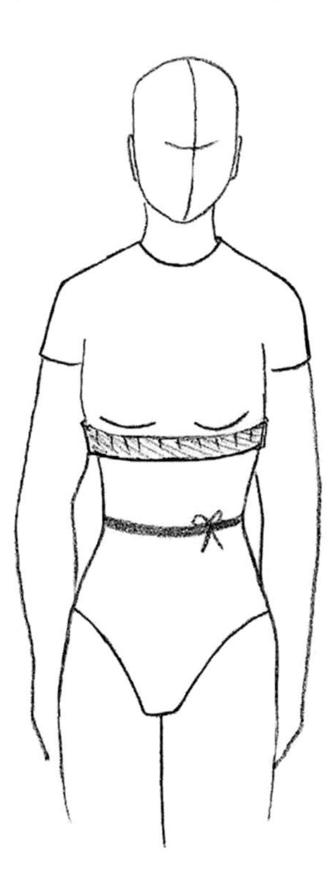

UNDERBUST: directly under the bust where the band of the bra sits.

Measurements

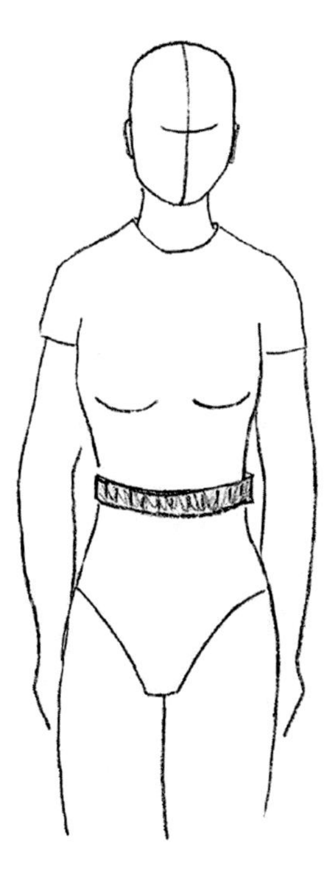

NATURAL WAIST: typically at the narrowest point of the torso, but most importantly, it is where you bend when you bend to the side (not necessarily where you wear your pants).

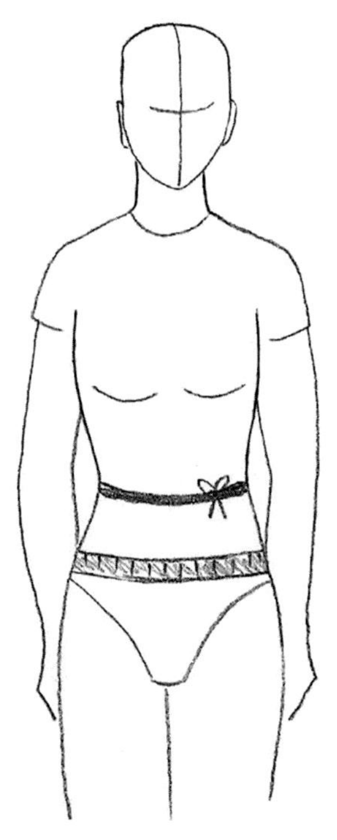

HIGH HIP: at the hip bones between the natural waist and the hip.

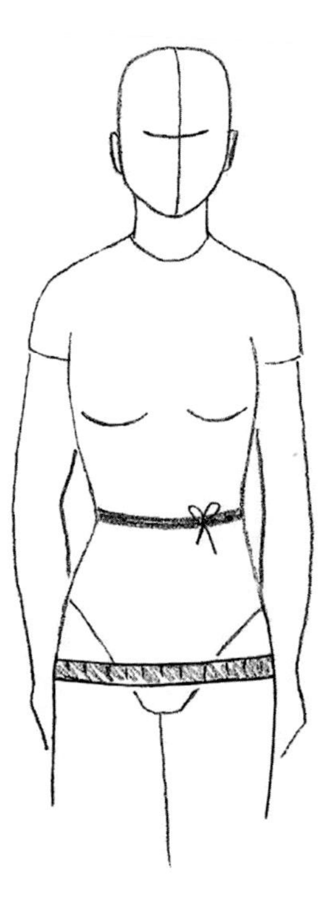

HIP: around the fullest point – it is easier to take this measurement from the side to see the fullness and to make sure that the tape measure is parallel to the floor.

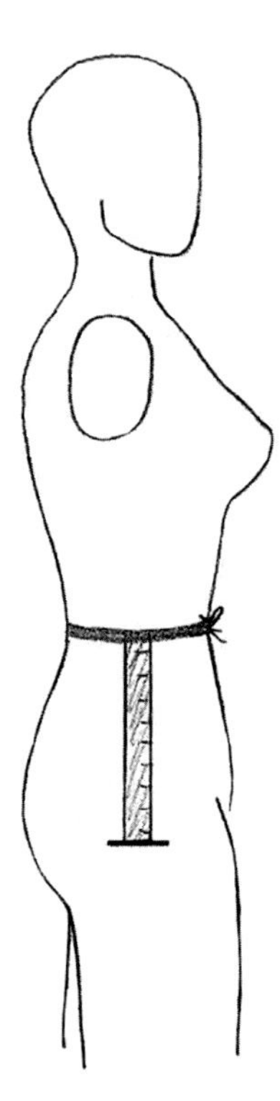

HIP POINT: on the side seam, from the natural waistline to the fullest point of the hip.

Measurements

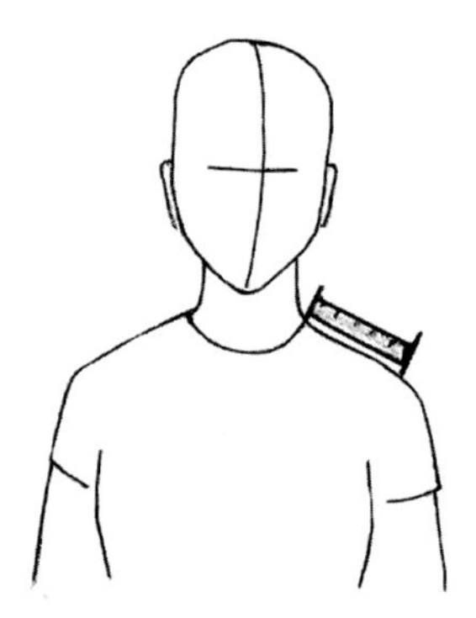

SHOULDER SEAM: from the base of the neck to the point of the shoulder bone.

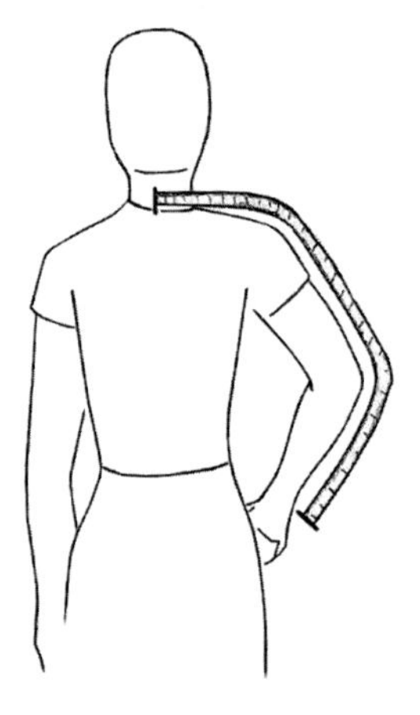

SLEEVE LENGTH: (the hand should be on their hip with their elbow bent away from the body) from the center back at the base of the neck, across the shoulder, down the arm to the elbow and then down to the wrist bone.

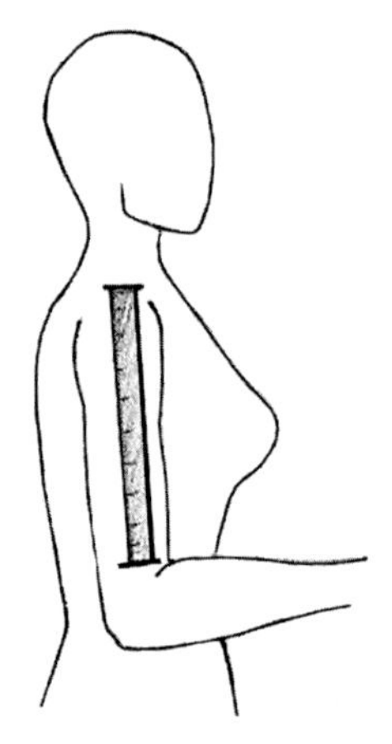

SHOULDER TO ELBOW CROOK: (the arm is against the body, but the elbow is bent at a 90-degree angle so the forearm is parallel to floor) from the point of shoulder bone to the inside elbow to the elbow crook.

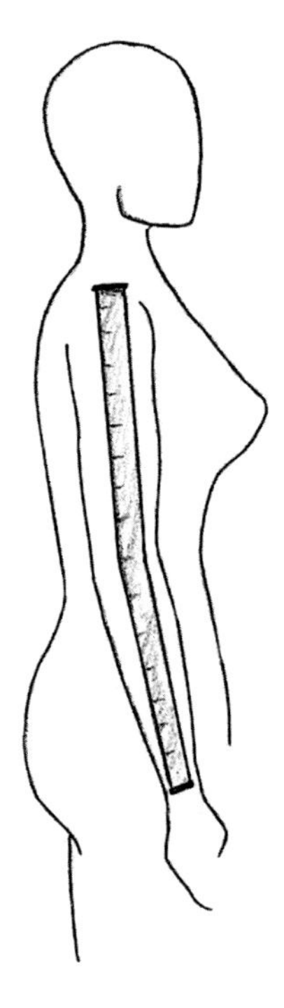

SHOULDER TO WRIST: (the arm is held naturally down against body) from the point of the shoulder bone to the wrist bone.

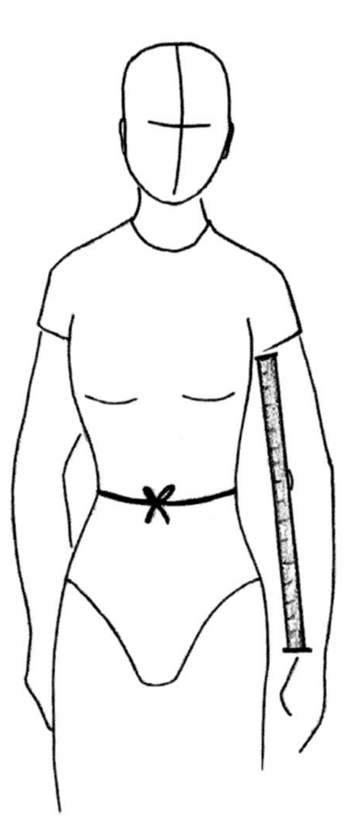

INSIDE ARM: (the arm is held naturally down against body) from the armpit to the wrist.

Measurements

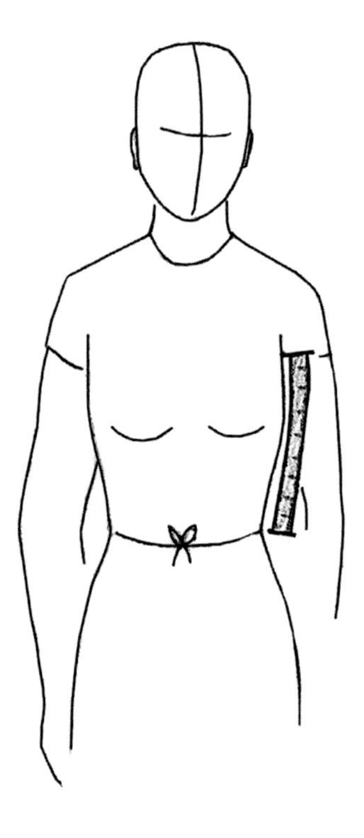

UNDERARM TO NATURAL WAIST: at the side seam, from the armpit to the natural waist.

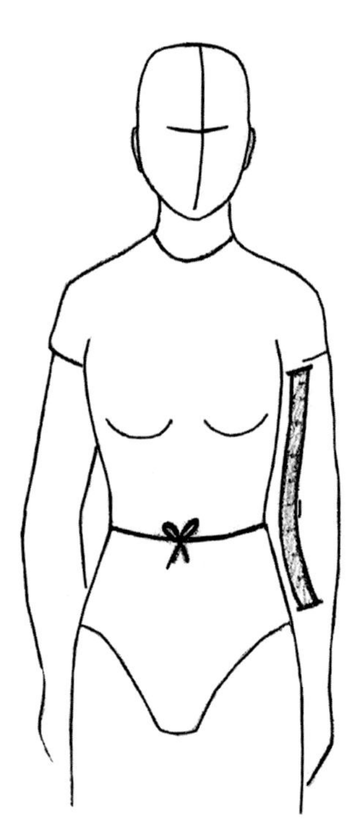

UNDERARM TO HIGH HIP: at the side seam, from the armpit to the high hip.
R OR L HANDED: take measurements on their dominant side.

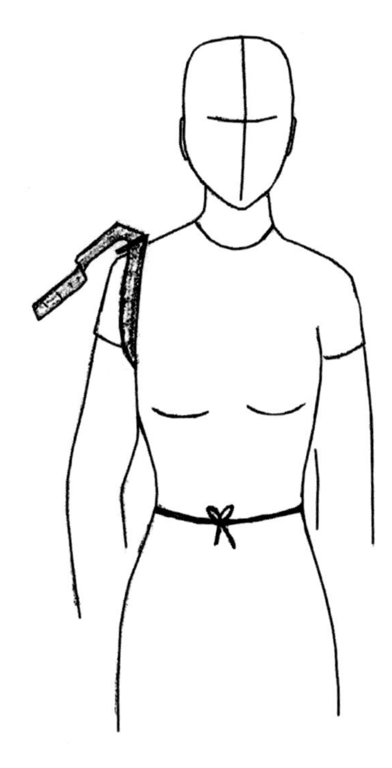

ARMSCYE: lift arm and wrap tape measure around armscye, have them put their arm down, then take the measurement where the tape measure crosses at the shoulder point.

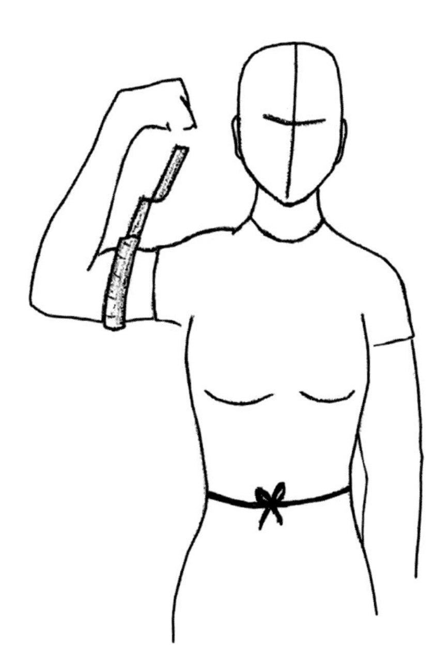

BICEP: have them make a muscle and take the measurement around the fullest point.

Measurements

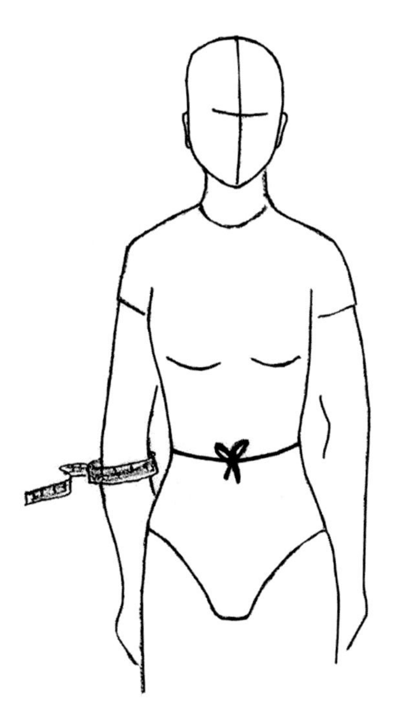

FOREARM: around the fullest point just below the elbow.

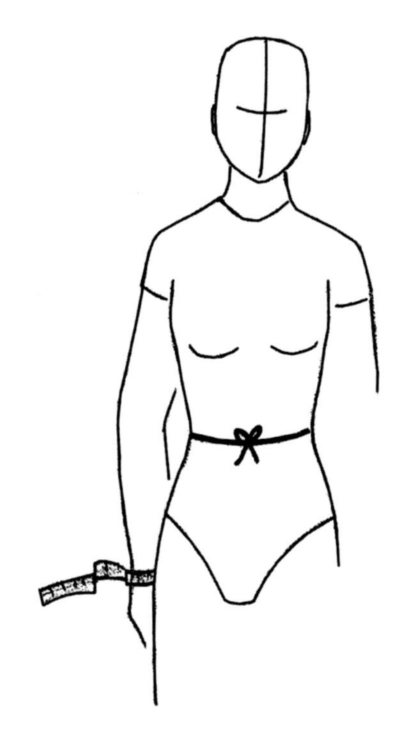

WRIST: over the bones of the wrist.

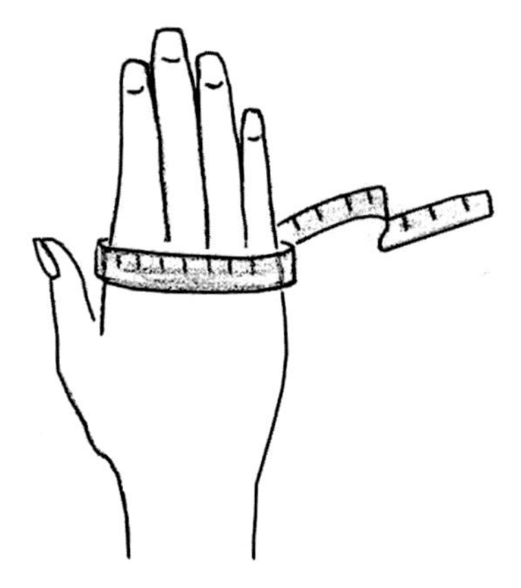

HAND: with fingers together, measure across the base knuckles without the thumb.

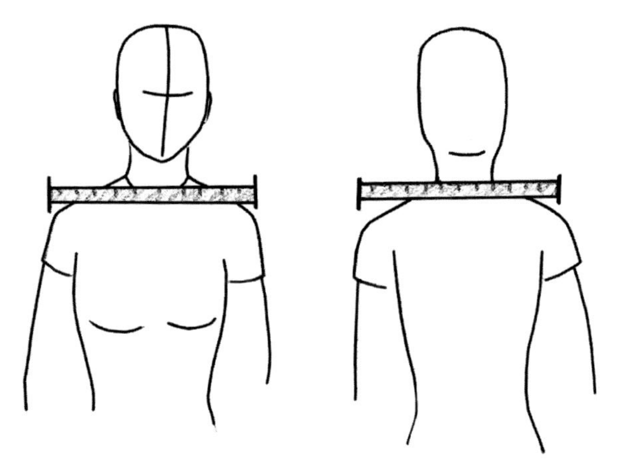

ACROSS SHOULDER FRONT/BACK: from shoulder point to shoulder point.

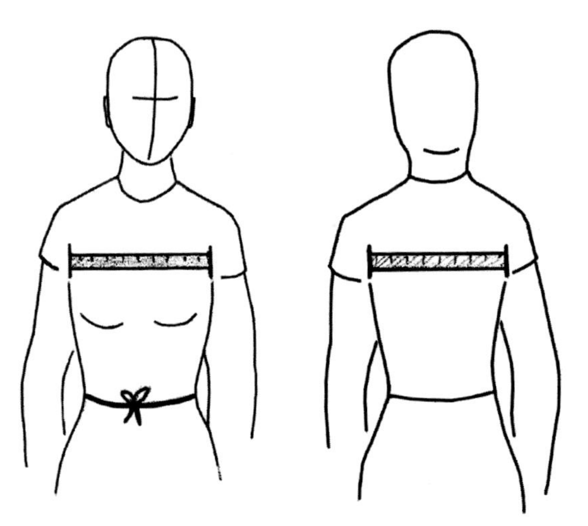

ACROSS ARMSCYE FRONT/BACK: from the crease of the armscye to the other arm's armscye crease.

Measurements

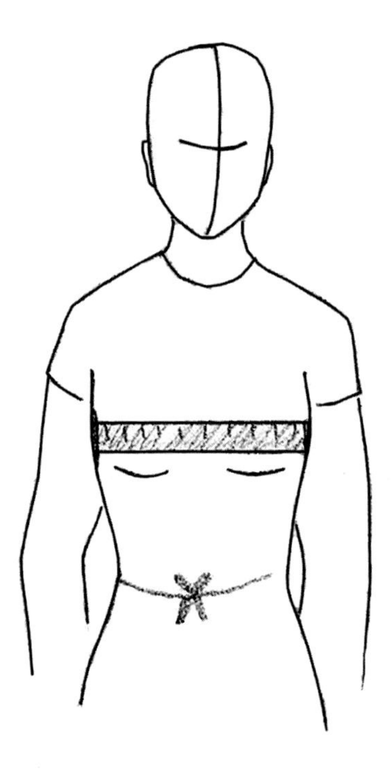

ACROSS BUST FRONT: from under the arm at the side seam, across fullest part of the bust to under the arm at the opposite side seam.

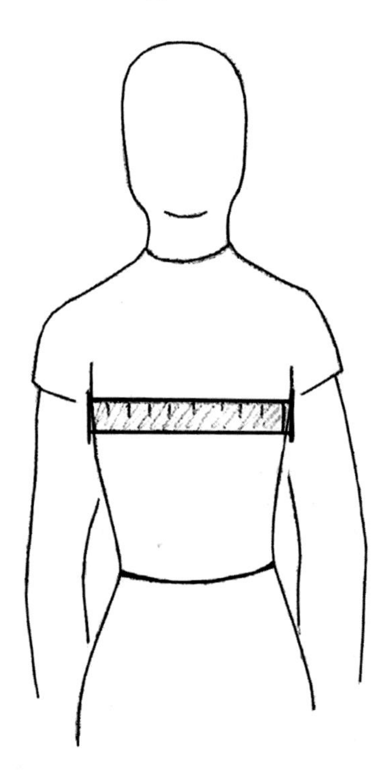

ACROSS BUST BACK: from under the arm at the side seam, across the back along the same line as the bust front, to the under arm at the opposite side seam.

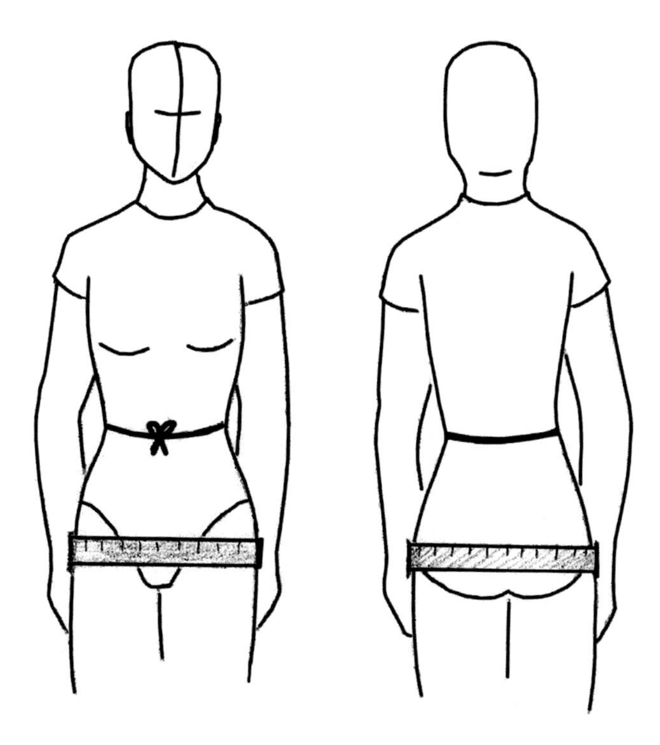

ACROSS HIP FRONT/BACK: from side seam to side seam along hip point line.

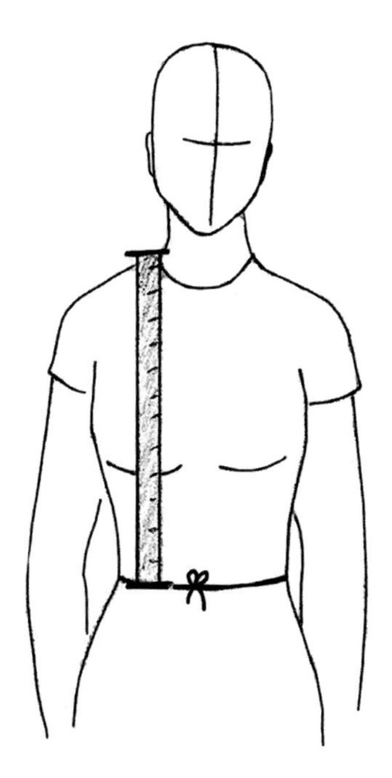

SHOULDER TO WAIST FRONT: from the shoulder at the base of the neck over the apex of the bust and down to the natural waist.

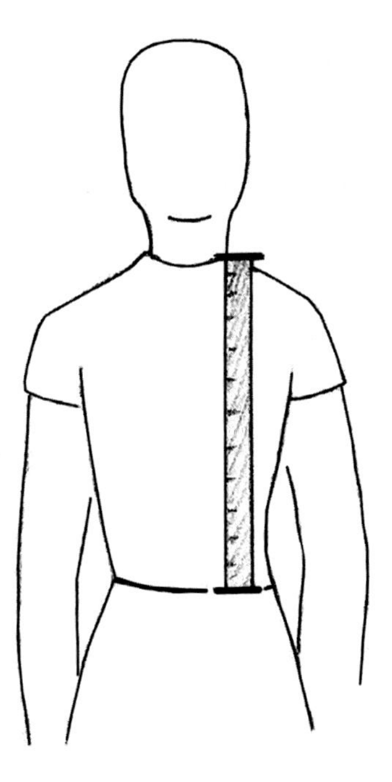

SHOULDER TO WAIST BACK: from the shoulder at the base of the neck down to the natural waist – taken on the same side as the SHOULDER TO WAIST FRONT.

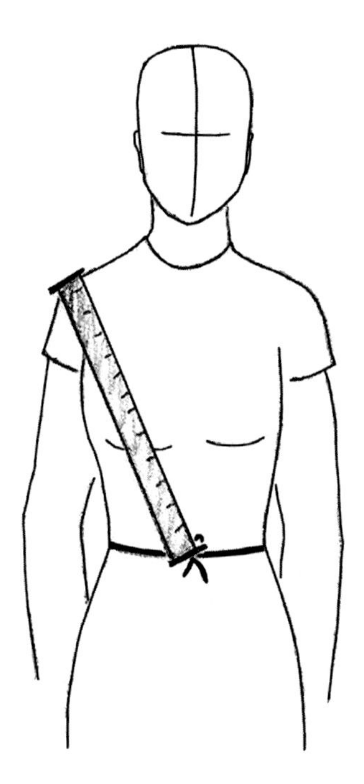

SHOULDER SLOPE FRONT: from the outside point of the shoulder across the apex of the bust to the waist at the center front line – taken on the same side as the SHOULDER TO WAIST FRONT.

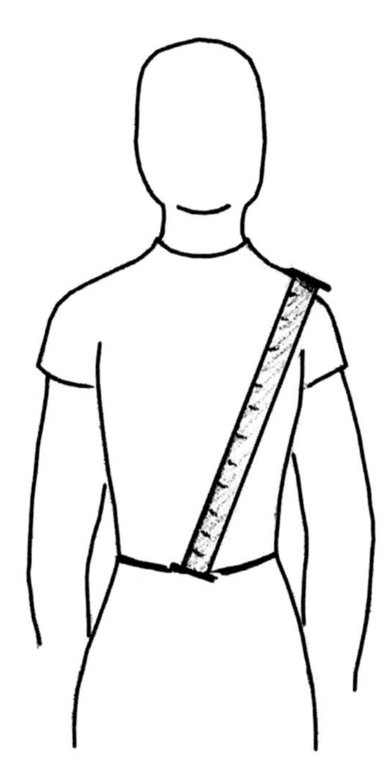

SHOULDER SLOPE BACK: from the outside point of the shoulder to the waist at the center front line – taken on the same side as the SHOULDER SLOPE FRONT.

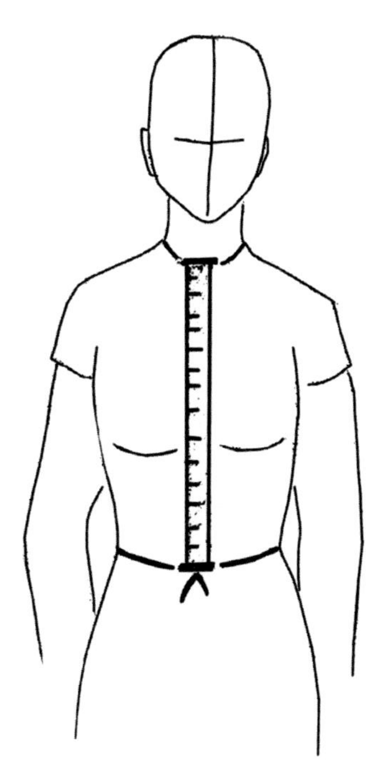

NECK TO WAIST FRONT: from the hollow at the base of the front of the neck to the natural waist down the center front line.

Measurements

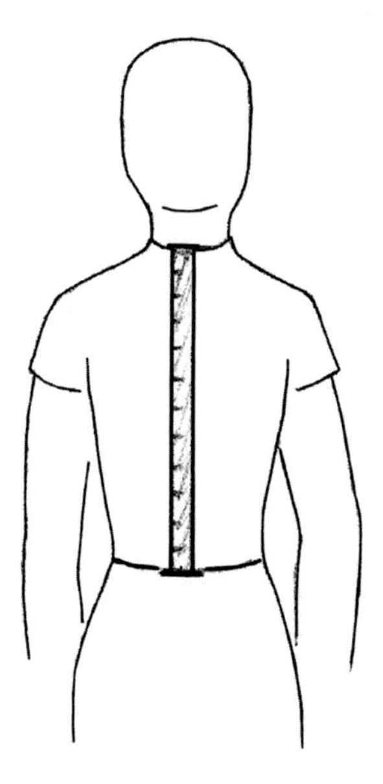

NECK TO WAIST BACK: from the nape of neck to natural waist down Center Back line.

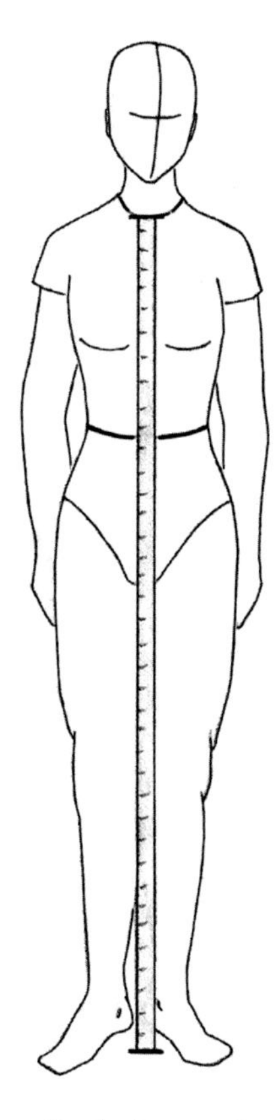

NECK TO FLOOR FRONT: from the hollow at the base of the front of the neck to the floor down the center front line (measurement taken barefoot).

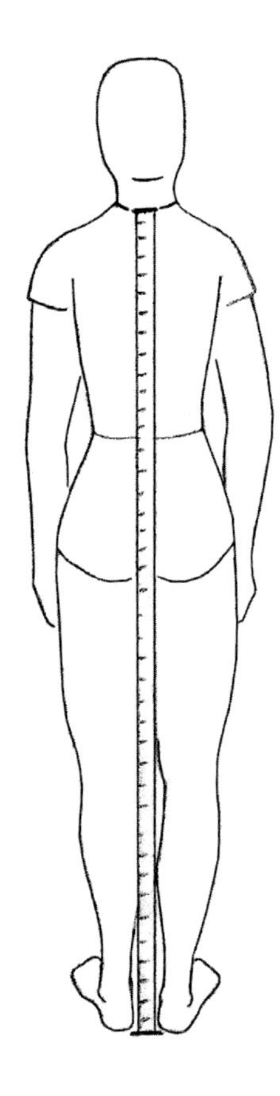

NECK TO FLOOR BACK: from nape of the neck to floor down Center Back line (measurement taken barefoot).

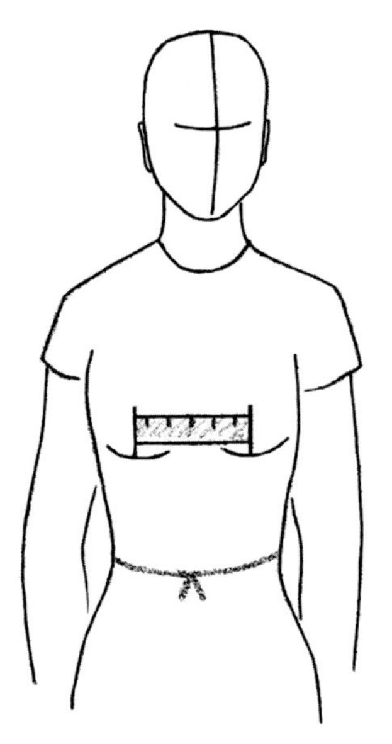

BUST POINT TO BUST POINT: from the apex of bust to the apex of other bust.

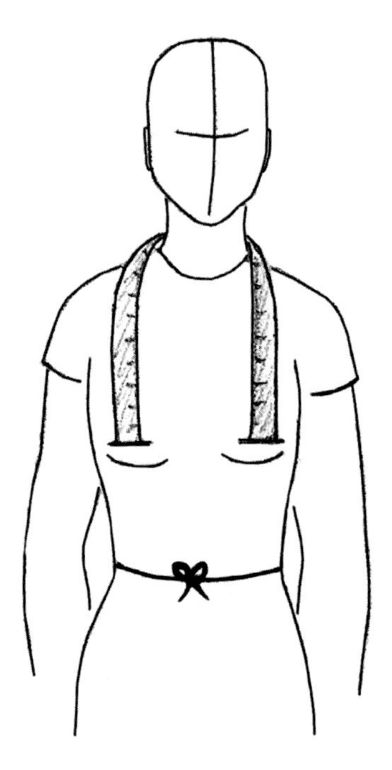

HALTER: from the bust apex, up and around the neck, and down to the other bust apex.

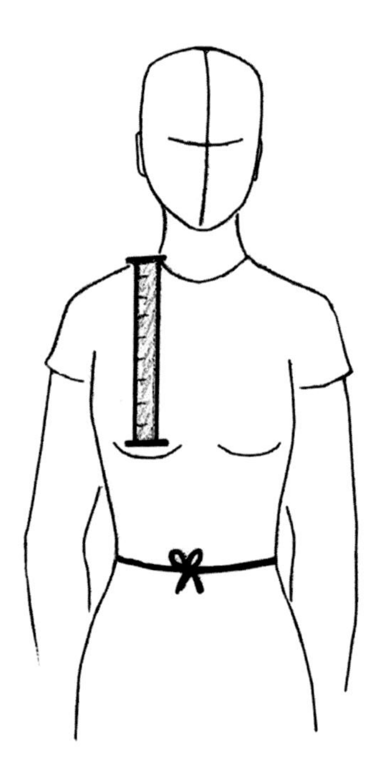

SHOULDER TO BUST POINT: from the shoulder at the base of the neck to the apex of the bust.

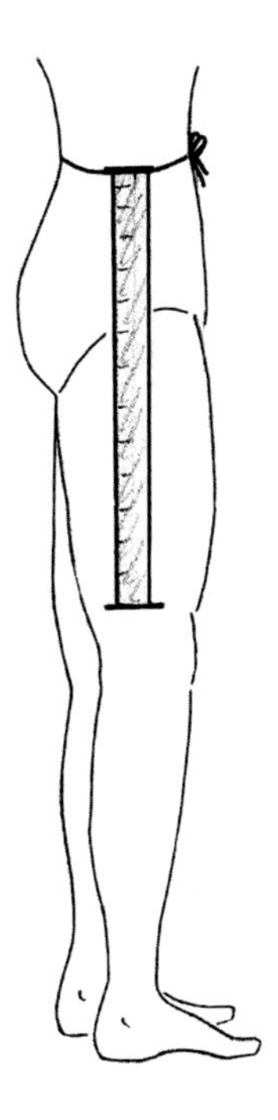

WAIST TO ABOVE KNEE: from the natural waist down the side seam to above the knee.

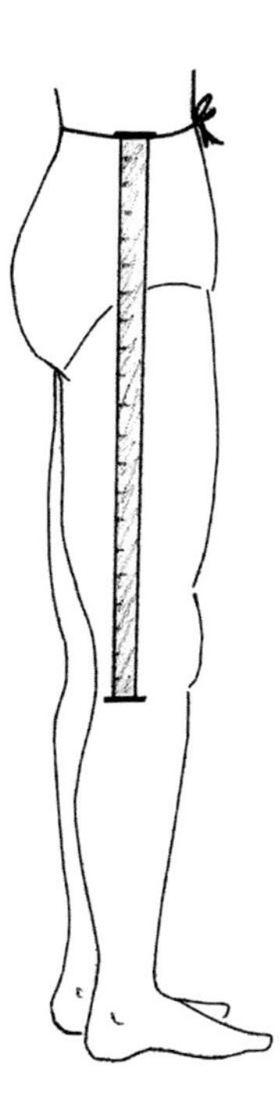

WAIST TO BELOW KNEE: from the natural waist down the side seam to below the knee.

Measurements

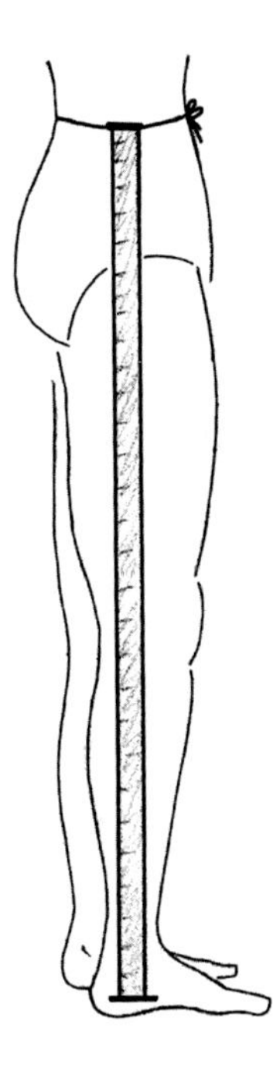

OUTSEAM: from the natural waist down the side seam to below the ankle bone.

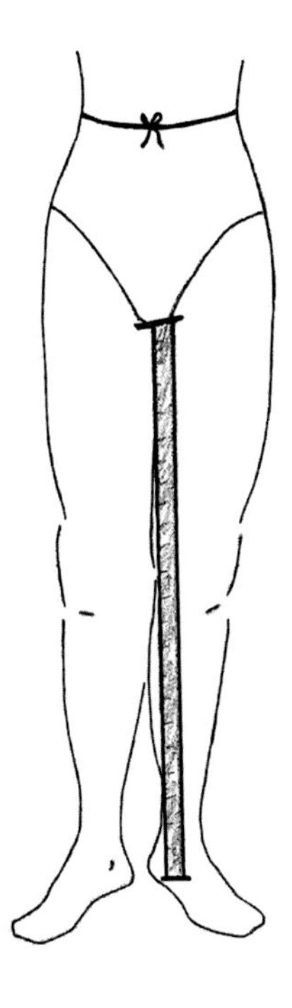

INSEAM: ask the person being measured to place the top end of the tape measure in their upper inner thigh as high up as they can comfortably wear a pant, make sure that their leg is straight, and then measure to below the ankle bone.

CROTCH DEPTH: Outseam minus Inseam = Crotch Depth.

(Taken on the front leg when in a slight lunge.)

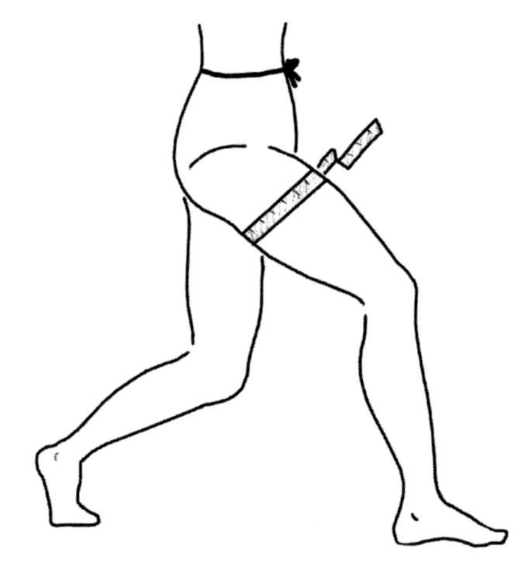

THIGH: taken high up on the leg around the fullest point.

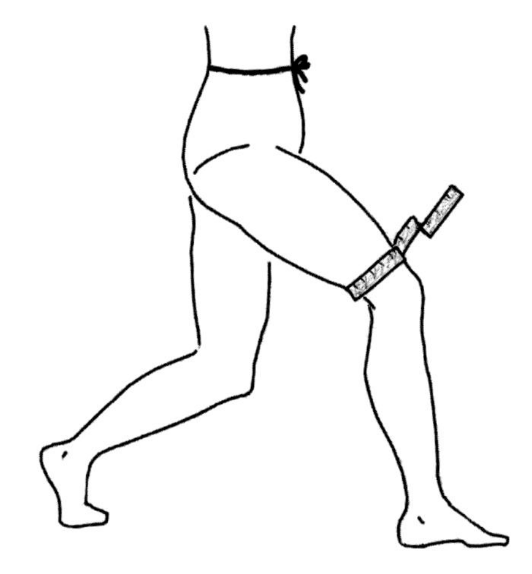

ABOVE KNEE: from just above the bent knee.

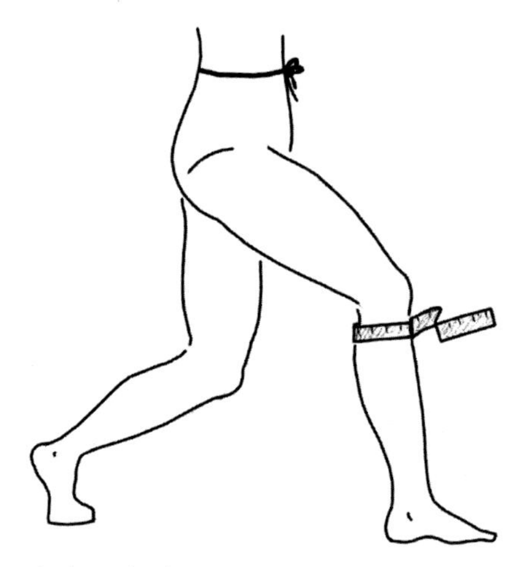

BELOW KNEE: just below the knee.

Measurements

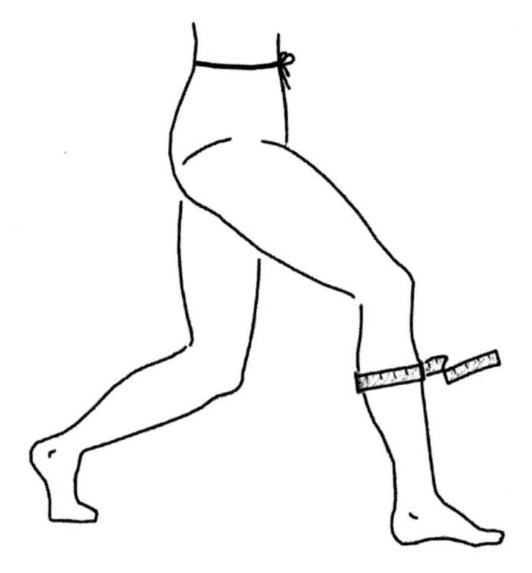

CALF: around the fullest part of the muscle.

ANKLE: around the lower ankle over the bones.

Measurements

Name________________________ Mo/Year ________ Graduation Year ______

Role ________________________ Production ________________________

Phone ________________________ Email ________________________

Height ____________ Shoe Size ____________ Shirt Size ____________

Bra ____________ Dress Size ____________ Pant Size ____________

Allergies ____

Tattoos ________________________ Piercings ________________________

Around Head ________ Ear to Ear ____________ Forehead to Nape ______

Neck ____________ Shoulder Seam____________ R or L Handed ______

Bust____________ Sleeve Length ____________ Armscye____________

Underbust ____________ Shld-elbow crook ________ Bicep____________

Natural Waist ____________ Shld-Wrist ____________ Forearm____________

High Hip ____________ Inside Arm ____________ Wrist ____________

Hip ____________ Underarm to Nat Waist ________ Hand ____________

Hip Point ____________ Underarm to High Hip ________

Shld Front ____________ Back ____________ Bust Pt to Bust Pt ____________

Armscye F ____________ Back ____________ Halter ____________

Bust F ____________ Back ____________ Shoulder to Bust Pt ________

Hip F ____________ Back ____________

Shoulder to Waist F ________ Back ____________

Shoulder Slope F ________ Back ____________

Neck to Waist F ________ Back ____________

Neck to Floor F ________ Back ____________

Waist to Above Knee____________ Thigh ____________

Waist to Below Knee ____________ Above Knee ____________

Outseam ____________ Below Knee ____________

Inseam ____________ Calf ____________

Crotch Depth ____________ Ankle ____________

Chapter 3: Fabric

Definitions for Draping

A textile is a type of material made of natural or synthetic fibers. Also referred to as fabric in the clothing-making industry. It may be created by weaving, knitting, felting, etc.

A woven fabric is any textile formed by weaving.

When referring to woven fabric, there are a few terms that you should know.

Definitions

Selvage: (or "selvedge") the tightly woven edge on fabric that prevents unraveling. It runs the length of the fabric. The threads running the length of the fabric are called the warp threads.

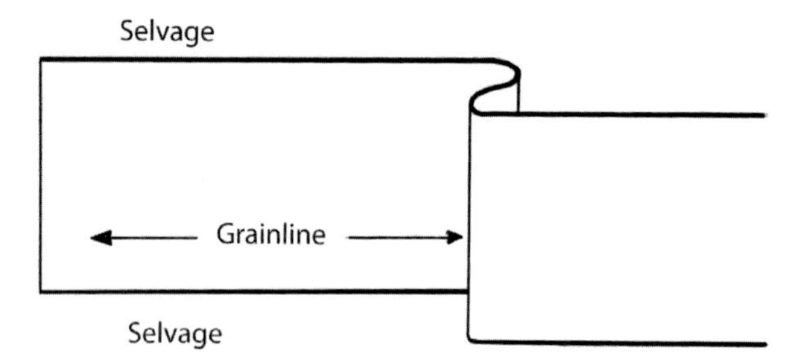

Grainline: the length of the fabric. It runs parallel to the selvedge and is the strongest direction of the fabric.

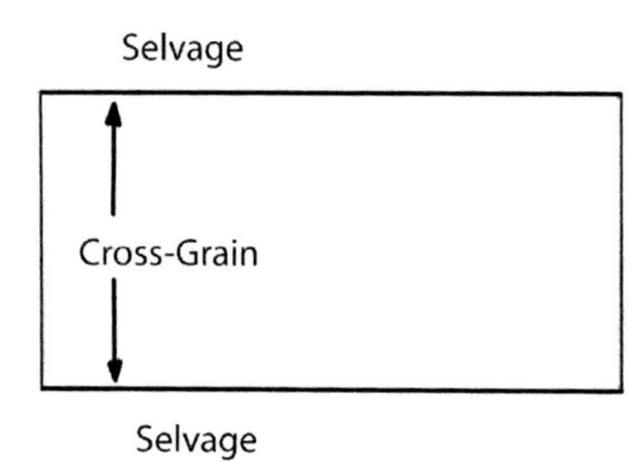

Cross-grain: runs perpendicular to the grainline. It can sometimes have stretch to it. The threads running cross-grain are called weft.

DOI: 10.4324/9781003022619-3

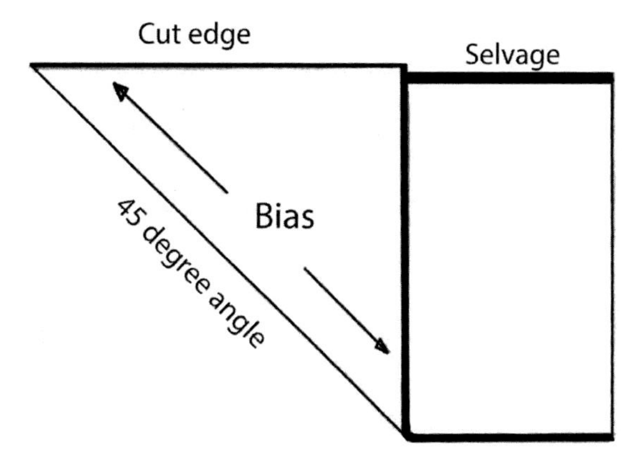

Bias: the 45-degree diagonal on the fabric. It stretches due to the open space between the woven fibers. Can be used intentionally for body hugging garments created without shaping darts.

Muslin: A type of cotton fabric that can be light, medium, or heavy weight, that comes bleached or unbleached, and is made using a plain weave. For the plain weave, the warp and weft are woven with an up-down pattern. Each weft thread goes over and then under the warp threads alternately. For this weave, the threads are the same weight to give a balanced effect. This fabric is what is commonly used to drape on the dress form and to create mock-ups of the drafted patterns to check for fit. It has a strong warp (grainline) and fairly strong cross-grain (weft) which makes it a good choice for beginners who would benefit from a well-behaved fabric to learn draping on.

Muslin is not always the most appropriate fabric for draping though. If your finished garment is going to be made out of a soft, sheer, and flowy fabric, then you should do your draping with a fabric that mimics this. To the contrary, if your finished garment is going to be made out of a stiff heavy fabric, then you should also drape using a fabric that mimics this. And if you are using a knit fabric for your final garment, you should use a knit fabric for draping that mimics your fashion fabric.

Chapter 4: Preparing for Draping

While it may seem that taking a rectangle of fabric off of a roll or bolt is self-explanatory and should be easy, it is usually the case that the fabric is slightly off grain. It is important that you do not cut the fabric into a rectangle, but that it is ripped and then reshaped. Ripping the fabric ensures that it is on grain and cross-grain.

Draping is traditionally done in a fabric that mimics the finished garment fashion fabric. So, for example, if your finished garment fashion fabric is a stiffer fabric you may choose to use muslin to do your drape, but if it is soft and flowy, or a knit, then you would not want to choose muslin since it will not behave correctly and will mislead you in how the finished garment will look.

For the following examples, you will be given instructions for using muslin. Muslin behaves well and is inexpensive making it a good choice for beginners.

There are two methods to finding cross-grain in fabric. One is to **rip** the fabric and the other is to **thread-pull.**

1. For **ripping** fabric across the cross-grain, you will need to clip the selvage into the fabric a small amount. Then take the fabric in your hands and pull on the cross-grain ripping the fabric until you reach the other selvage. Clip the selvage on the other side.
2. For **thread-pulling** (being demonstrated with linen fabric so that you are able to see the steps more clearly) you will literally pull a thread to find grain or cross-grain. You will need to clip the selvage, if you have it, into the fabric a small amount. Then separate a single thread that goes cross-grain.

DOI: 10.4324/9781003022619-4

- Pull on this thread so that the fabric gathers.

- If the thread breaks, which it frequently does, remove that thread and smooth the fabric out with your hands. You will see a gap in the fabric where the thread used to be. Cut along this line to the place in the fabric that the thread broke off.

- Start pulling on this thread again and continue cutting until you reach the other selvage.

- Look for the gap in the fabric where the thread used to be and cut along this line. You should now have a cut edge that is on grain or cross-grain.

Preparing for Draping

Note: Muslin, due to being a plain weave, will rip on grain, as well as across on cross-grain. Once you have these raw edges, you will need to block the fabric.

Directions

- Remove the selvage from the muslin panel by clipping it with your embroidery scissors and tearing along the grainline. You may choose to indicate on your fabric which edge is on the straight of grain. The straight of grain should be used vertically as you drape as it is the strongest direction of your fabric.
- Use embroidery scissors to clip and tear a piece of muslin so that it measures 4–6″ (10.2–15.2 cm) longer and 4–6″ (10.2–15.2 cm) wider than the section you wish to drape.
- Your fabric should now have four ripped edges.

Blocking the Muslin for Draping a Bodice

"Blocking the muslin" is a phrase used to indicate that the muslin panel is free of distortions and will lay as a perfect rectangle with 90-degree angles.

Press the muslin to make it square. (Lay the muslin panel on the corner of a table or use an L-square to determine if the muslin is square.)

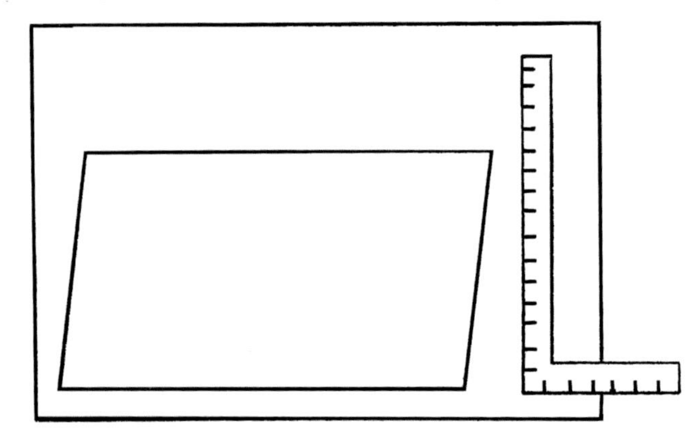

If the muslin is not square, pull opposite corners until the cross-grain is perpendicular to the grainline. Re-press, using steam, to set the desired shape.

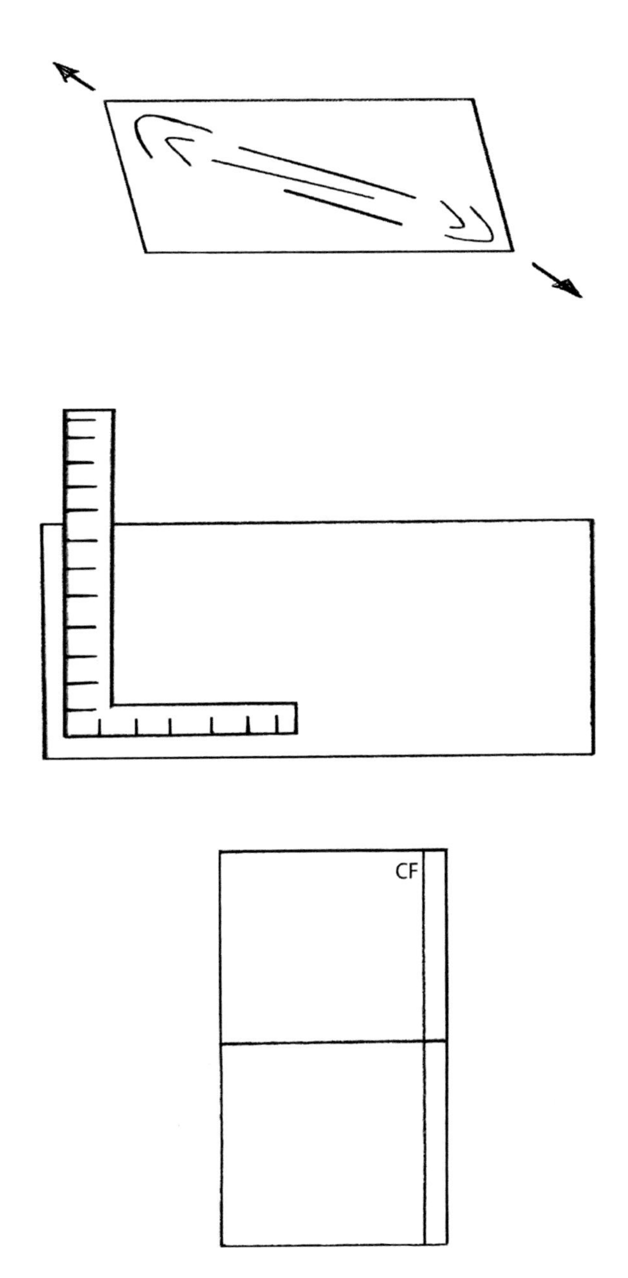

For the **Front,** mark the muslin using your grid ruler to draw a line parallel to the grainline 1″ (2.5 cm) in from the long edge. This is your CF (center front) line. You can press under on this line to make it easier to align it to the dress form's CF. (The CF line and fold should be on your right side of the fabric.)

- Using an L-square, draw a line perpendicular to the 1″ (2.5 cm) guideline about halfway down from the top of the fabric. This is your Bust line.

Preparing for Draping

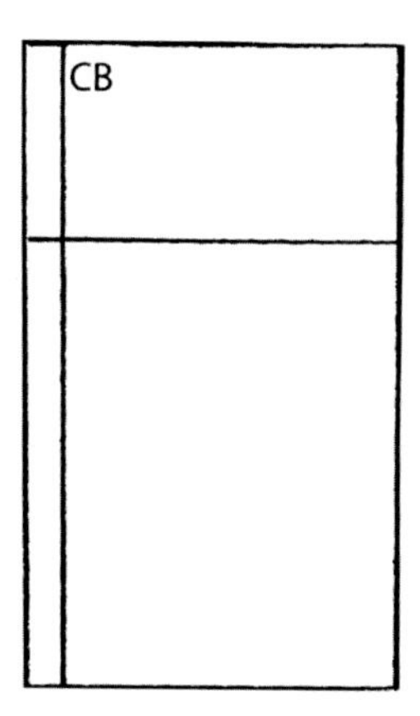

For the **Back**, mark the muslin using your grid ruler; draw a line parallel to the grainline 1″ (2.5 cm) in from the long edge. This is your CB (center back) line. You can press under on this line to make it easier to align it to the dress form's CB. (The CB line and fold should be on the left side of the fabric.)

- Using an L-square, draw a line perpendicular to the 1″ (2.5 cm) guideline about 8″ (20.3 cm) down from the top of the fabric. This is your Shoulder Blade line.

If You Are Making a Princess Bodice Draping

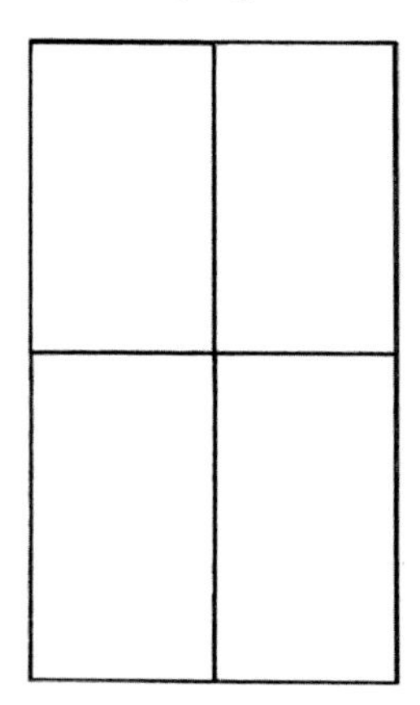

For the **Side Front**, to mark the muslin use your grid ruler to draw a line parallel to the grainline down the *center* of the fabric.

- Using an L-square, draw a line perpendicular to the center line you just drew halfway down from the top of the fabric. This is your Bust line.

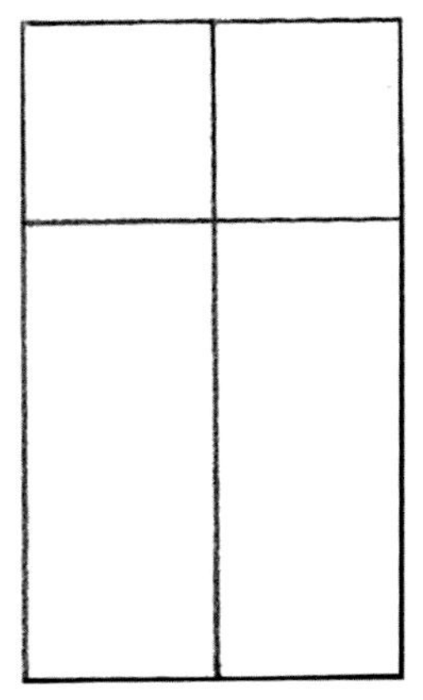

For the **Side Back**, to mark the muslin use your grid ruler to draw a line parallel to the grainline down the *center* of the fabric.

- Using an L-square, draw a line perpendicular to the 1" (2.5 cm) guideline about 8" (20.3 cm) down from the top of the fabric. This is your Shoulder Blade line.
- Your fabric is now ready for draping bodice projects (that are not on the bias).
- It is helpful to prepare all panels of muslin prior to draping.

Preparing the Dress Form

To most effectively drape a garment, it is important that the dress form be as close to the measurements of the person being draped for. Sometimes the dress form is close enough as is, but sometimes the dress form must be "padded out" to accommodate the differences.

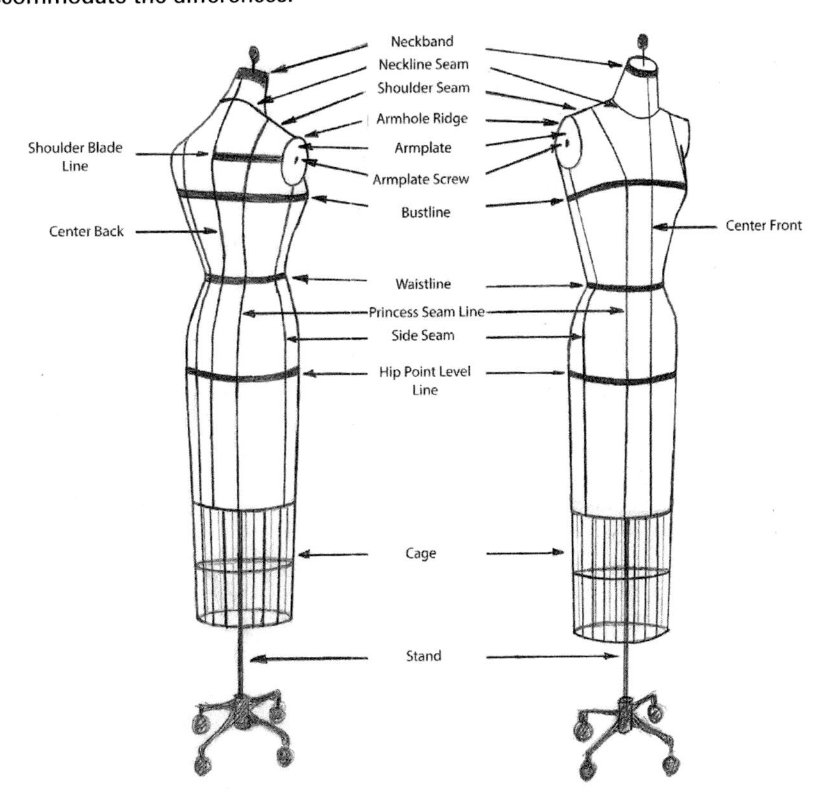

Anatomy of a Dress Form

Padding Out the Dress Form

- Determine the measurements needed based on the difference between the dress form and the figure measured. It is easiest to pad out the waist and hips rather than padding out the bust, so you should determine if there is a dress form that is close in measurement to the figure's bust measurement. You will also need to check the underarm to waist measurement, and hip point measurement.

*You should pad the dress form symmetrically to achieve the desired total measurement even though you will only be draping on the one side of the dress form.

- To pad an area that needs adjusting, place your tailoring shoulder pads at that location and pin so that the heads of the pins face away from the center of the pad, creating tension on the pad so it doesn't pull off.

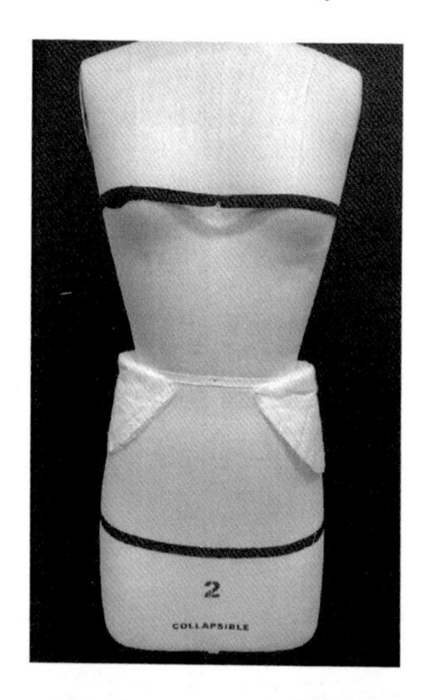

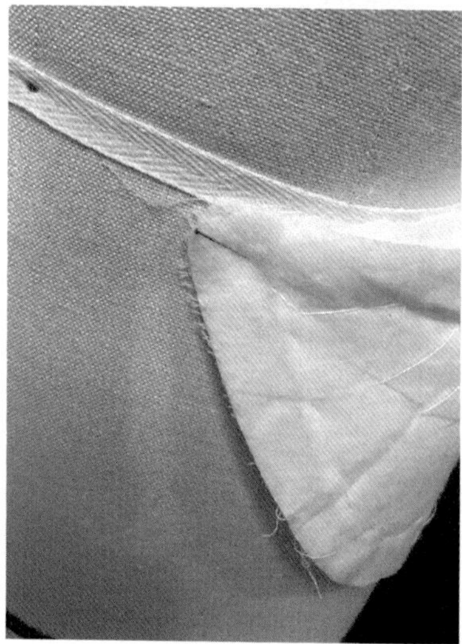

- Place the shoulder pad with the fullest part in the area that needs the most padding and with the thin edge fading out.

You want to make sure that there are no ledges or abrupt edges but a smooth transition between the padding and the dress form.

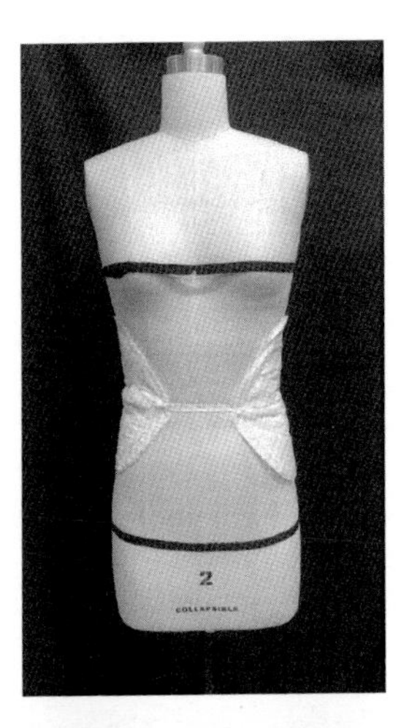

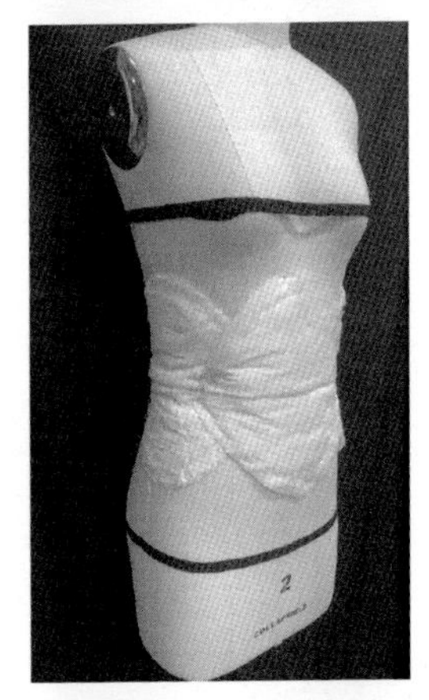

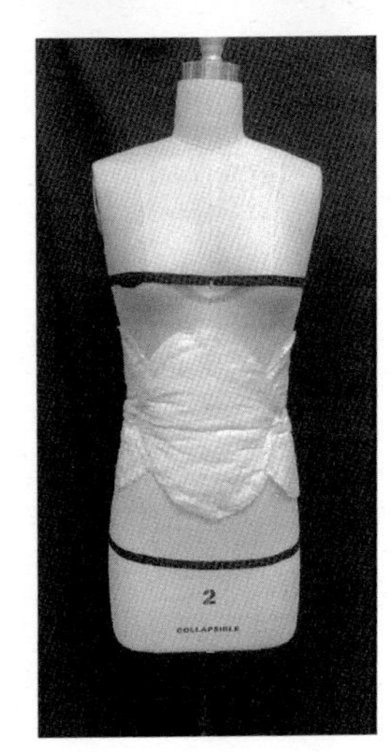

Preparing for Draping

Using quilt batting that isn't too thick, wrap the dress form with layers to smooth out the shoulder padding. Do not leave a ledge, but place another thin layer over.

You will need to pad out the dress form until it measures out at least 2–3" (5.1–7.6 cm) larger than the desired measurement at that location due to the shrinking that will happen when mummy wrapped.

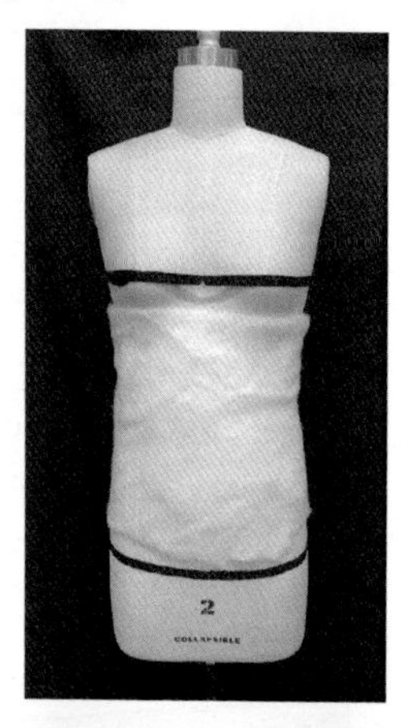

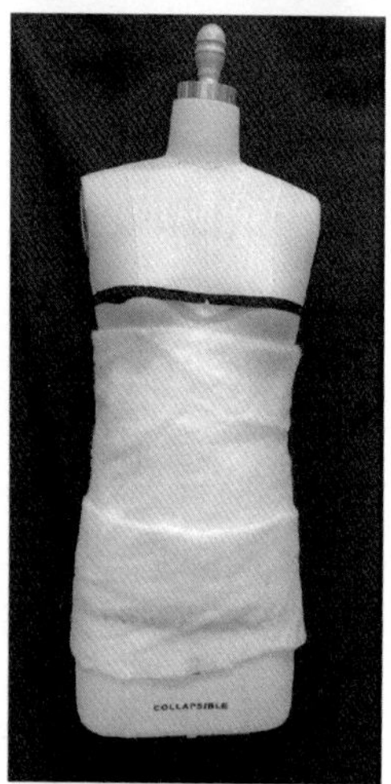

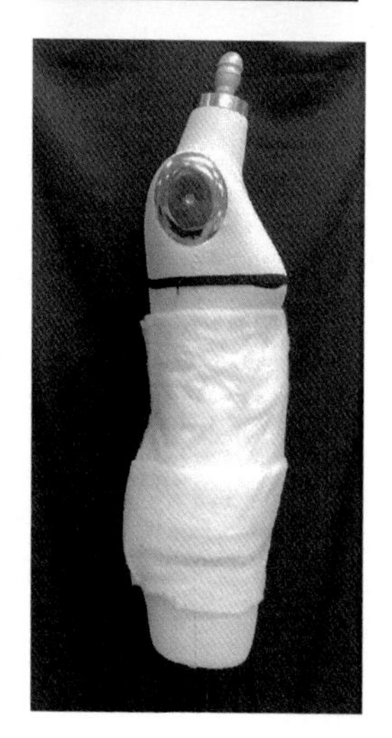

Mummy wrapping: You will need to cut bias strips that are about 1½"–2" (3.8–5.1 cm) wide. Using your bias strips, you will start wrapping over the non-padded area to achieve a smooth transition from dress form to padding. Start pinning the end of the bias strip with the heads of the pins facing away from the direction you are wrapping to create tension on the strip and prevent it from unwrapping. It is suggested that you use dressmaker's pins and not quilter's pins due to the large ball on the head on the quilter's pins. These will be lumpy under your wrapping which is inconvenient for a smooth wrap.

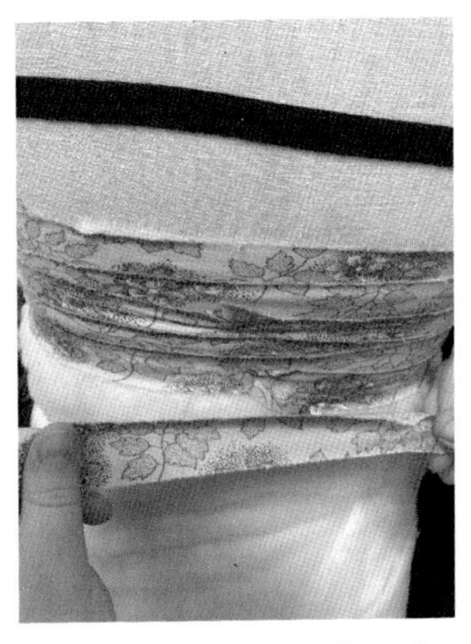

- It is recommended that you wrap from the top down from bust to waist, and then wrap from below the hips up to the waist making sure to overlap in the middle. This allows for the wrapping to stay smooth and not lift off the dress form.
- Overlap your wrapping as you go so that there are no gaps and the padding doesn't pop out in between. Place pins in the strips as needed to anchor them with the heads of the pins facing away from the direction you are wrapping to create tension on the strip and prevent it from unwrapping.
- When you get to the end of your bias strip and you need to start a new one, make sure to overlap them by at least 3" (7.6 cm) so that there aren't any gaps.

When you are done wrapping, the padding should be similar in feel to the dress form – meaning that the mummy wrapping is taut and isn't too squishy. Double check your measurements and make adjustments as needed.

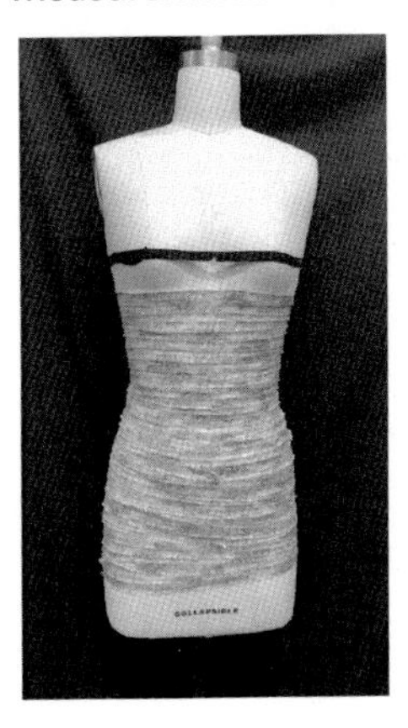

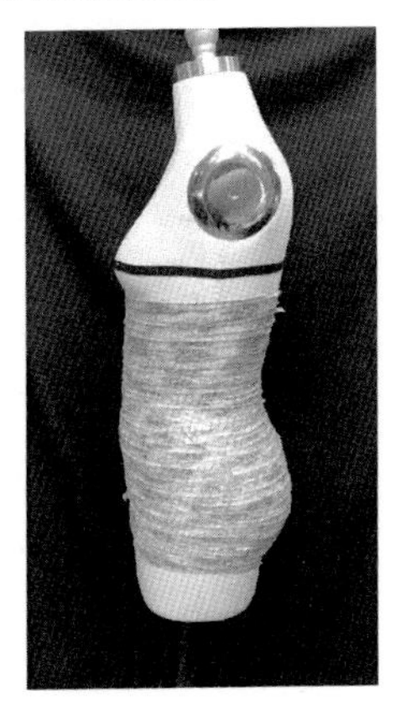

Taping the Dress Form

***(Half muslins are traditionally draped on the dress form's right side if you are right-handed, and on the left if you are left-handed.)

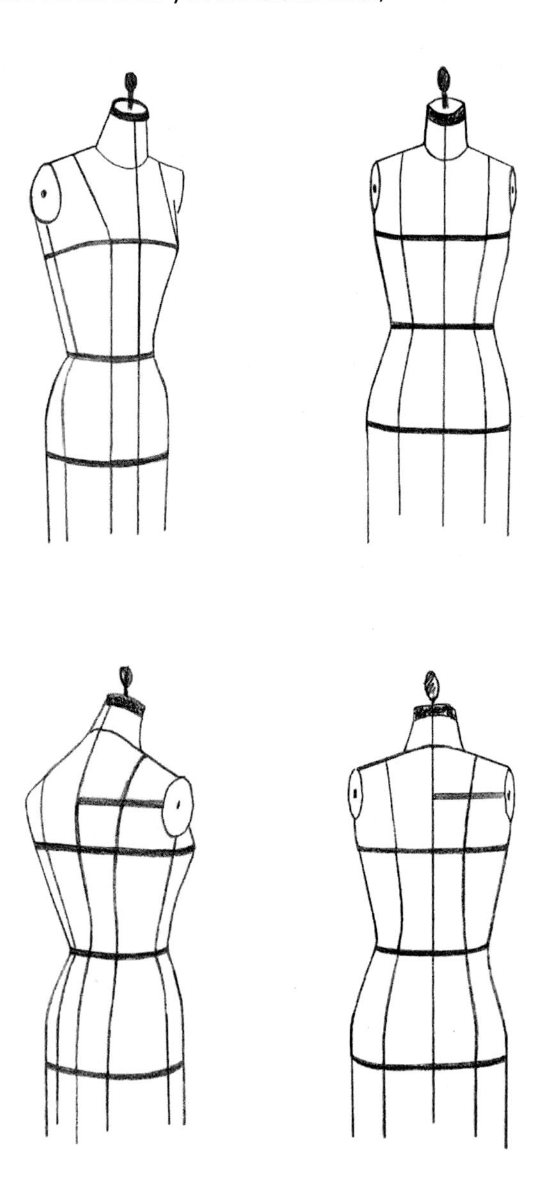

Bust Tape:

- Measure out a piece of black twill tape to go around the fullest part of the bust of the dress form adding an inch or two (2.5–5.1 cm) extra for overlap. Start pinning at one bust point, with pins going through the dress form at a low angle and with the head of the pin facing away from the direction that the tape is pulling. The tape should be centered over the apex. Bridge across to the other bust point and continue around the body being careful that the tape stays parallel to the floor.

Hip Tape:

- Measure from the center of the waist tape down center front 8″ (20.3 cm) (or to the hip point measurement of the person you measured). Pin the tape at this point on the CF seam with the tape centered over the measured point. With pins at low angles and with the head of the pin facing away from the direction that the tape is pulling, continue pinning the tape around the dress form parallel to the floor until reaching the CF and overlapping the tape once again.

Shoulder Blade Line Tape:

- This tape is only placed on the back of the dress form. Measure from the center back of the dress form out towards the armscye ridge so that the tape will be parallel to the floor and is about the height of the screw in the center of the arm plate. Pin the tape with the end turned under about ½″ (1.3 cm) at this line starting at center back with the pins going through the dress form at a low angle and with the head of the pin facing away from the direction that the tape is pulling. Continue pinning the tape across the back of the dress form parallel to the floor until you reach the armscye ridge. Turn the end of the tape under and pin.

DRAPING CHECKLIST:

☐-prepare the muslin – block it to make it square – rip it larger than section to be draped

☐-draw grainlines and crossgrains

☐-pin fabric to the dress form's right side
  -grainline is CF on Front
  -grainline is CB on Back
  -grainline is down centers of SF and SB sections

☐-create design lines (do it in pins or black twill tape first - especially for necklines)

☐-mark design lines in pencil

☐-draw matching notches

(leave on dress form)

☐-continue with next sections - when done, the right half of the dress form should be covered

When done draping, true pattern:
☐-remove pattern pieces from dress form

☐-lay flat on table (do not iron- do not stretch)

☐-true pattern - make sure all lines are smooth and clean and same lengths as matching pieces - alter darts if necessary

☐-transfer to craft paper – use tracing wheel (and tracing paper, if needed)

☐-transfer all markings – grainline, darts, matching notches, etc

☐-label what it is - whose is it, what piece is it (Front, Side Front, etc), date created, etc.

☐-cut out carefully

☐-check trueing of pattern for accuracy
  -adjust if necessary

If pattern is trued and labeled:
☐-cut mockup – adding seam allowances for stitching mockup

Chapter 5: Skirts

This chapter will demonstrate how to drape and draft the basic skirt, drape the flared skirt, introduce you to grainlines and how they affect the hang of a skirt, and give general guidelines for a circular skirt.

How to Drape the Basic Skirt

The Basic Skirt shape is straight, with side seams parallel to the center front and center back, although a very slight flare at the hem is acceptable. The waistline has shaping darts, which, if desired, could be converted into gathers or pleats.

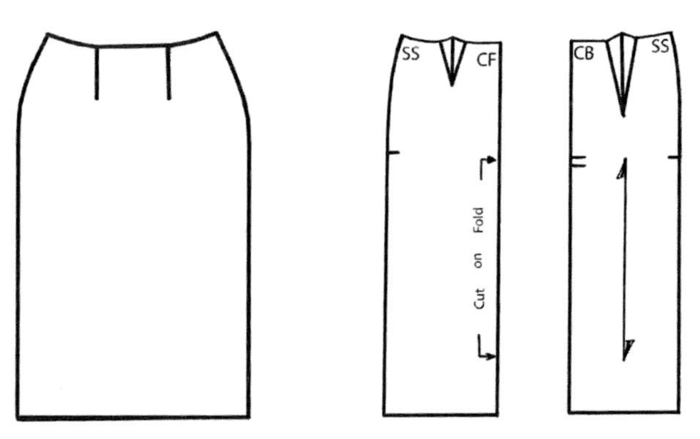

Anatomy of the Basic Skirt

Preparing the Fabric for Draping

(See Chapter 4 on Preparing the Muslin for Draping, and Blocking the Muslin)

- The length of the panel must be on the straight of grain.
- Measure the length for the front and back panels from the waistline to the desired hem length and add 6″ (15.2 cm).
- For the muslin panel, 2″ (5.1 cm) goes above the waistline and 4″ (10.2 cm) is below desired hem length.
- Measure the width of the front panel at the hip point level (marked by the twill tape) from CF to side seam, and add 4″ (10.2 cm).
- Repeat this for the back panel.
- Mark the 1″ (2.5 cm) guidelines for the CF and CB panels along the grainline edge. (CF should be on the right side of the fabric and CB should be on the left side of the fabric.)

DOI: 10.4324/9781003022619-5

Skirts

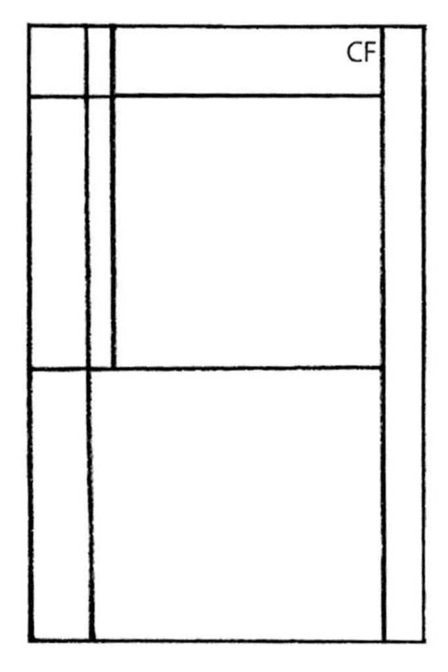

Front

- From the center front line on the front panel, draw a horizontal line at 2″ (5.1 cm) down from the top edge to indicate the waistline.
- Using your L-square, at 8″ (20.3 cm) down from the 2″ (5.1 cm) marking, (or 10″ [25.4 cm] down from the top edge of the fabric) draw a horizontal line across the fabric perpendicular to the CF guideline.
- On your dress form, measure across the hip level line from CF to side seam. Add ½″ (1.3 cm) of ease to this measurement.
- Using this measurement (hip front), draw a side seam line on your front panel parallel to the CF guideline.
- At ¾″ (1.9 cm) in from your side seam line, toward your CF guideline, and from the hip level line up only, draw another line parallel to the CF guideline and side seam line.

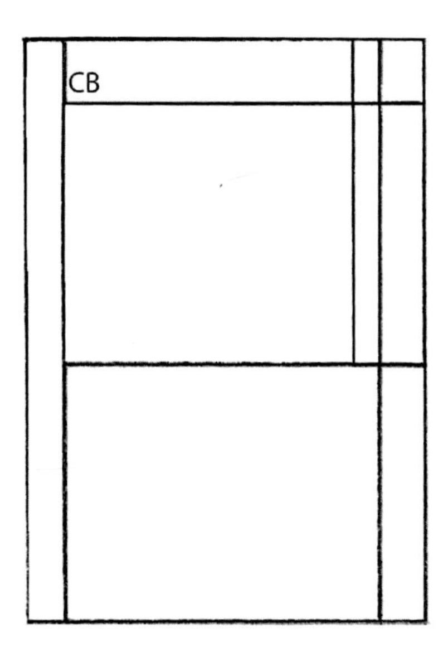

Back

- At the center back line on the back panel, draw a horizontal line at 2″ (5.1 cm) down from the top edge to indicate the waistline.

- Using your L-square, at 8″ (20.3 cm) down from the 2″ (5.1 cm) marking (or 10″ [25.4 cm] down from the top edge of the fabric) draw a horizontal line across the fabric perpendicular to the CB guideline.
- On your dress form, measure across the hip level line from CB to side seam. Add ½″ (1.3 cm) of ease to this measurement.
- Using this measurement (hip back), draw a side seam line on your front panel parallel to the CB guideline.
- At ¾″ (1.9 cm) in from your side seam line, toward your CB guideline, and from the hip level line up only, draw another line parallel to the CB guideline and side seam line.

Directions for Draping

Basic Skirt Front

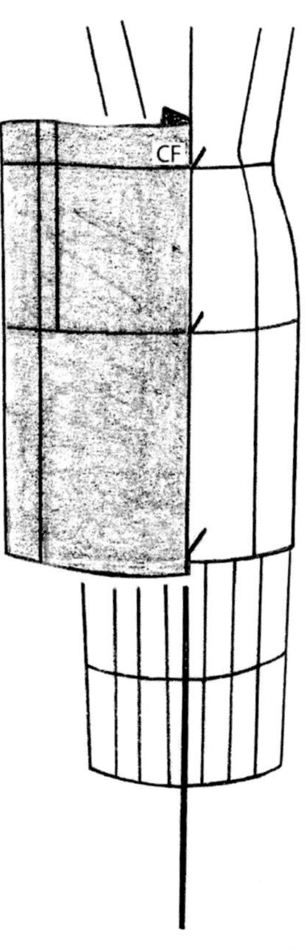

- Pin the front panel to the dress form, matching the CF guideline to the CF line of the dress form, the waistline marking, and the hip level line.

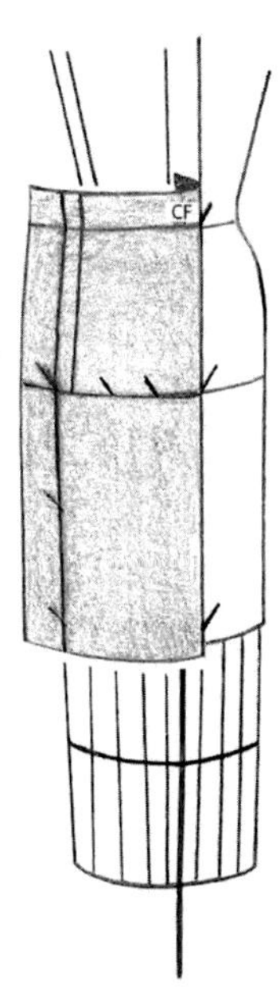

- Smooth across the hipline, matching the long side seam line to the dress form's side seam, and pin at the hip level line at the side seam.
- Distribute the ease evenly along the front hip level line and pin, making sure the cross-grain stays parallel to the floor.
- Pin the side seam to the dress form below the hip level line.

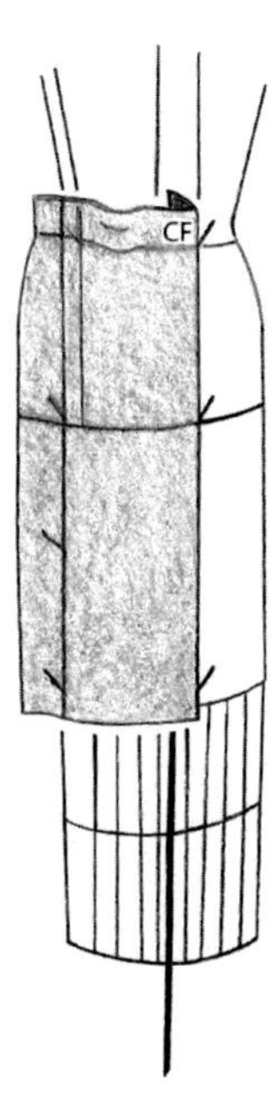

- Pin the short side seam line to the waistline/side seam line. You will have excess fabric across the front waistline.

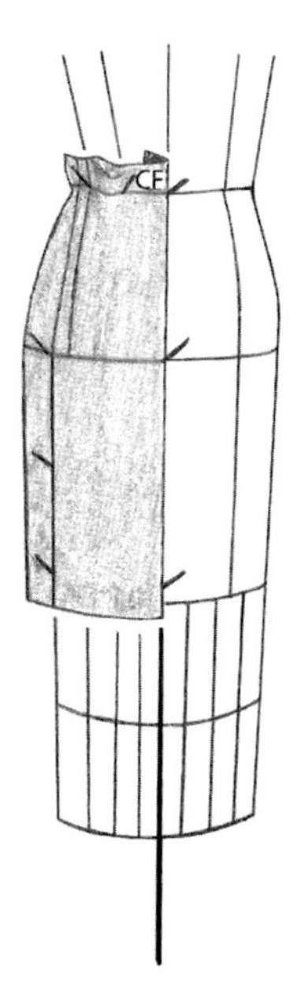

– Smooth the fabric from the CF to the princess line and place a pin at that point.

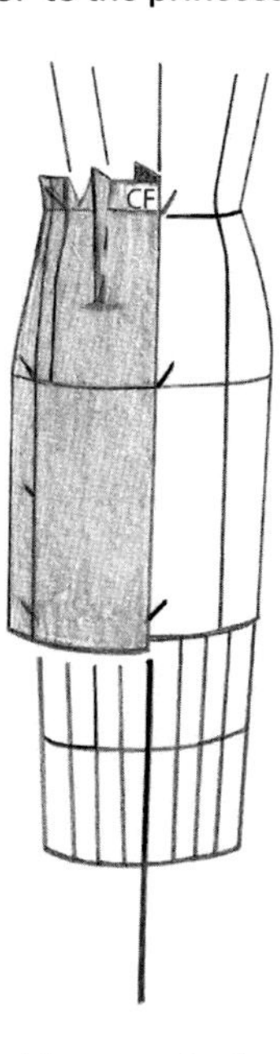

– Smooth the fabric from the side seam to the princess line, clipping the fabric above the waistline as needed to ease the pulling, being careful to only cut to, but not through the waistline.

(Cut to, but not through. Clipping too aggressively is very easy to do. Think of clipping as if you were to clip only to the intended future stitching line within the seam allowance. If you clip too much you will end up in the body of the garment. If you do clip too far, you can mend a small cut with some masking tape placed on the top and underneath the area.)

Skirts

- Remove the pin at the princess line and create a dart at the princess line allowing for ¼″ (0.6 cm) ease at the waistline.
- Taper the dart down toward the hipline to a vanishing point about 3″ (7.6 cm) long, and pin the dart with the pins running the length of the dart.
- Mark the vanishing point with a horizontal pin.
- (The dart may be off-grain and too long but this will be corrected in the trueing.)

Basic Skirt Back

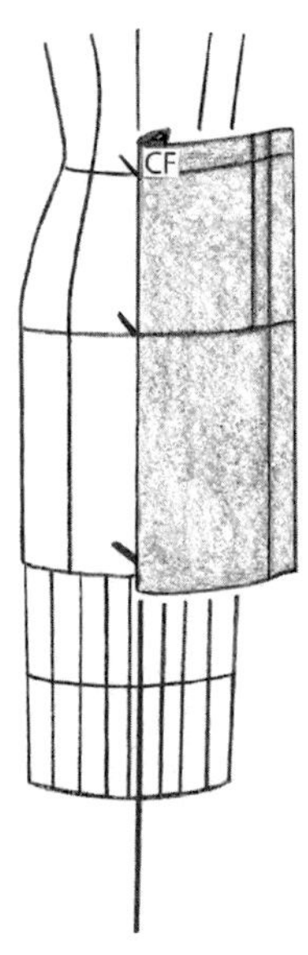

- Pin the back panel to the dress form, matching the CB guideline to the CB line of the dress form, the waistline marking, and the hip level line.

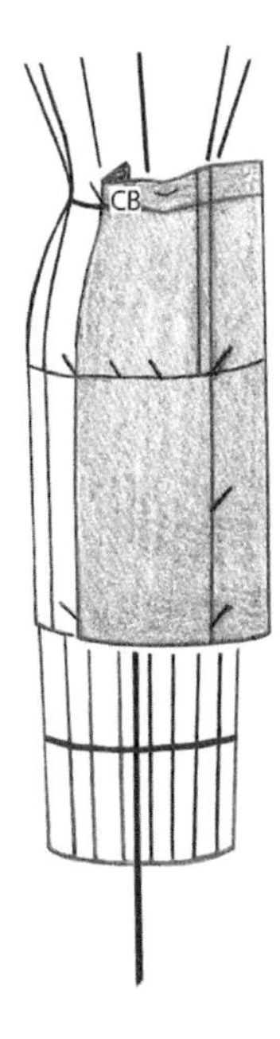

- Smooth across the hipline, matching the long side seam line to the dress form's side seam, and pin at the hip level line at the side seam.
- Distribute the ease evenly along the back hip level line and pin, making sure the cross-grain stays parallel to the floor.
- Pin the side seam to the dress form below the hip level line.

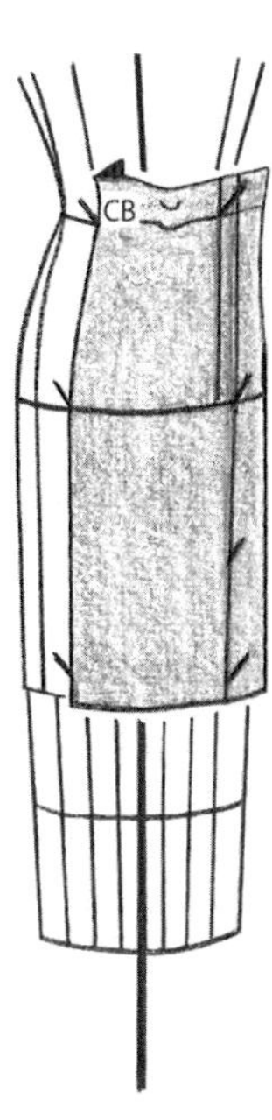

- Pin the short side seam line to the waistline/side seam line. You will have excess fabric across the front waistline.

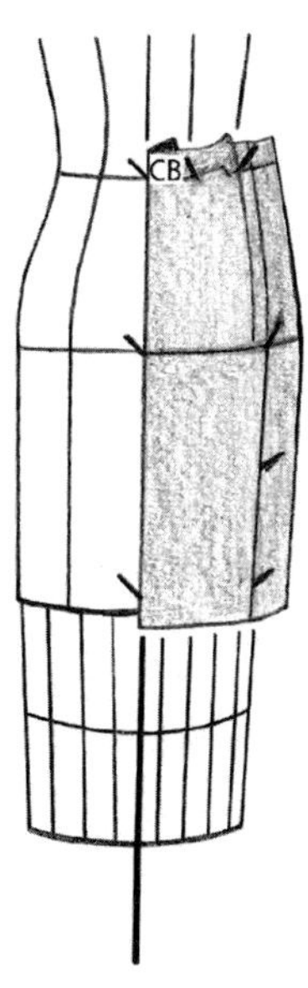

- Smooth the fabric from the CB to the princess line and place a pin at that point.
- Smooth the fabric from the side seam to the princess line, clipping the fabric above the waistline as needed to ease the pulling, being careful to only cut to, but not through the waistline.

Skirts

- Remove the pin at the princess line and create a dart at the princess line allowing for ¼" (0.6 cm) ease at the waistline.

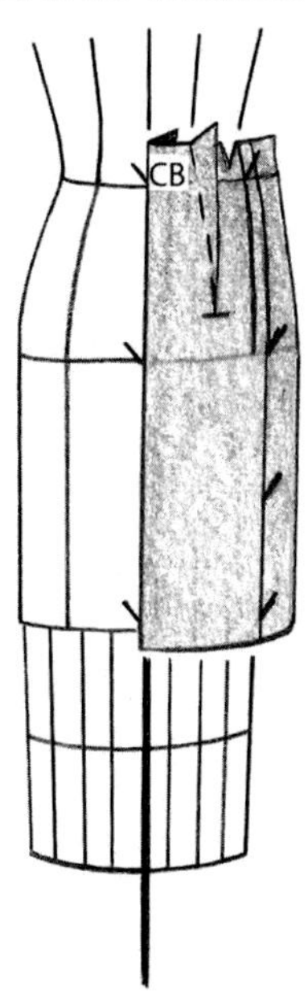

- Taper the dart down toward the hipline to a vanishing point about 2" (5.1 cm) above the hip level line and pin dart with pins running the length of the dart.
- Mark the vanishing point with a horizontal pin.
- (The dart may be off-grain and too long but this will be corrected in the trueing.)

Marking the Muslin

- Draw dashed lines along the center of the twill tape at waistline and at the side seam.
- Create cross marks on either side of the darts where they intersect the waistline, and mark the vanishing points.
- Create cross marks at the side seam where it intersects the waistline.

Combining Front and Back Skirt Pieces

- Trim the front and back side seams to 1" (2.5 cm)
- Trim waistline to 1" (2.5 cm)
- With the skirt pinned together at the side seams below the hip level line, mark on the CB line the desired length.
- Draw a hem from this mark parallel to the hipline.

After Trueing (Follow Directions: "Trueing the Basic Skirt")

– Fit Check

- Pin the skirt to the dress form at waistline CF, CB, and side seam.
- Front and back grainlines should be straight without twisting or pulling.
- Cross-grains should be parallel to the floor.
- Side seam should align with the side seam of the dress form.
- Darts are pinned shut to vanishing points.
- Darts are smooth without twisting. (Twisting happens in the pinched-out area of the dart. If twisted, it will not be a smooth flat dart, but will exhibit a

contorted "twist" which means that the grainline is off within the dart. The grainline of the dart should be parallel to the grainline of the center front of the skirt. The center line of the dart should follow the grainline.)

Trueing the Basic Skirt

(On the actual skirt drape)

Trueing is a term used to describe the process of creating accuracy on a draped or drafted sloper. When the muslin is still on the dress form, it may seem as if the sloper fits well and matches the other sections. It is only when the muslin is removed that the accuracy can be determined. Trueing can be done directly on the draped muslin pieces, or on craft paper. The following instructions will be on the draped muslin pieces. After trueing the muslin, then the pattern can be transferred to paper.

- After removing the skirt from the dress form, with front and back separate and all pins removed, lay the fabric flat on your table.
- The following locations require a 90-degree angle:
- CF waist for ½" (1.3 cm) from CF
- CB waist for 1" (2.5 cm) from CB

(These 90-degree lines allow for a smooth curve when making a full garment. Otherwise you will end up with either a V shape or a ^ shape at those points.)

(Dart Lengths: Front darts are about 3" (7.6 cm) depending on the size and shape of the figure. Back darts are longer, usually about 6" (15.2 cm) but do not extend beyond 2" (5.1 cm) above the hipline).

Front

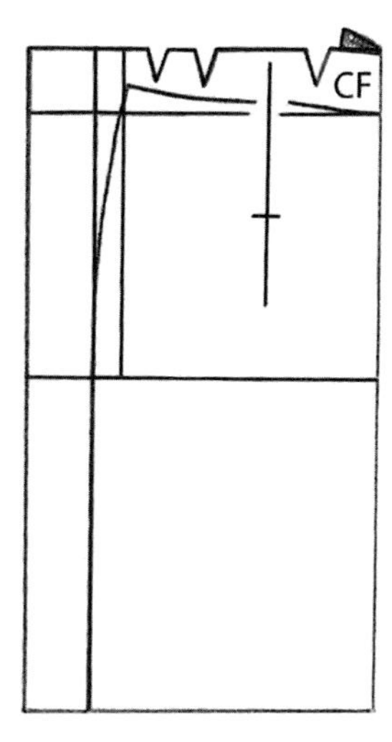

- For the front waist dart, measure the width of the dart at the waistline.
- Divide this measurement in half to determine the center line of the dart. Place a mark in the center of the opening on the waistline.

- Using your straight ruler, draw a line parallel to the grainline through this center point.
- Extend the length of the front dart from the waistline to the vanishing point 3" (7.6 cm) down.

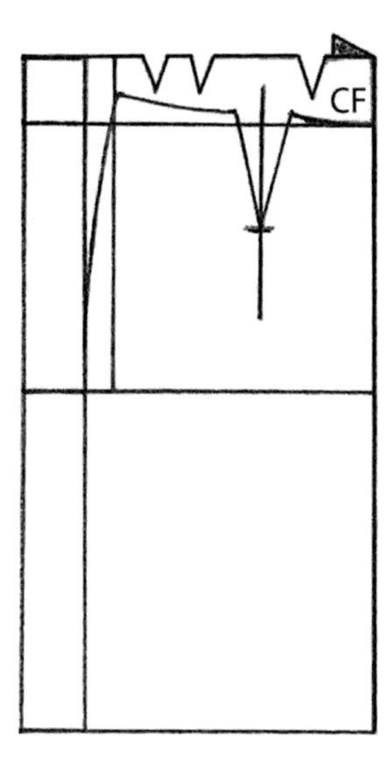

- Mark points on the waistline on either side of the center line that equal half of the dart opening measurement.
- Using your straight ruler, draw in the dart legs from the vanishing point to the new points you marked at the waistline.

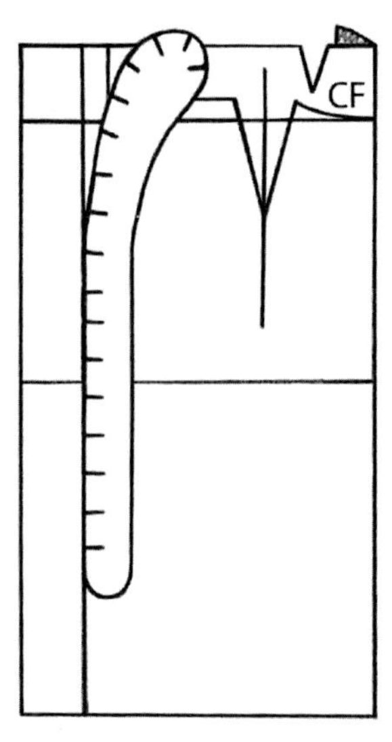

- For the front side seam, use your curved ruler with the curved end up at the waistline and the straight end down toward the hem to finesse your side seam line.

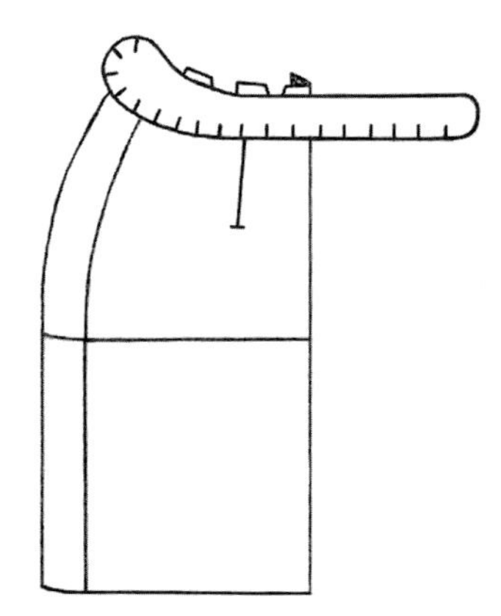

- For the front waistline, fold and pin the waist dart.
- Correct your waistline using your curved ruler with the curved end toward the side seam and the straight end toward the CF.

Back

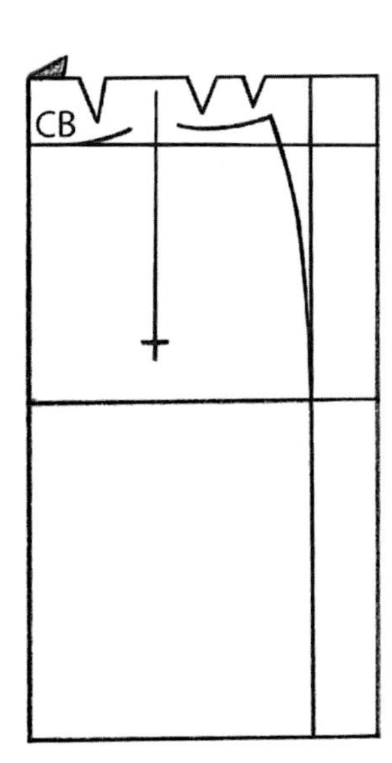

- For the back waist dart, measure the width of the dart at the waistline.
- Divide this measurement in half to determine the center line of the dart. Place a mark in the center of the opening on the waistline.
- Using your straight ruler, draw a line parallel to the grainline through this center point.
- Extend the length of the back dart from the waistline to the vanishing point 6″ (15.2 cm) down, or no more than 2″ (5.1 cm) above the hip level line.
- Mark points on the waistline on either side of the center line that equal half of the dart opening measurement.

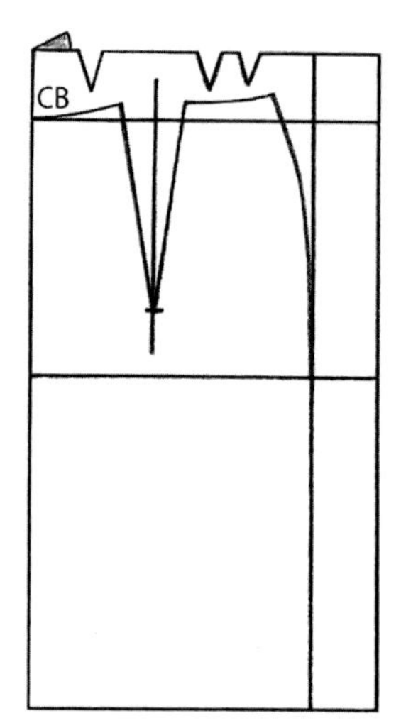

- Using your straight ruler, draw in the dart legs from the vanishing point to the new points you marked at the waistline.

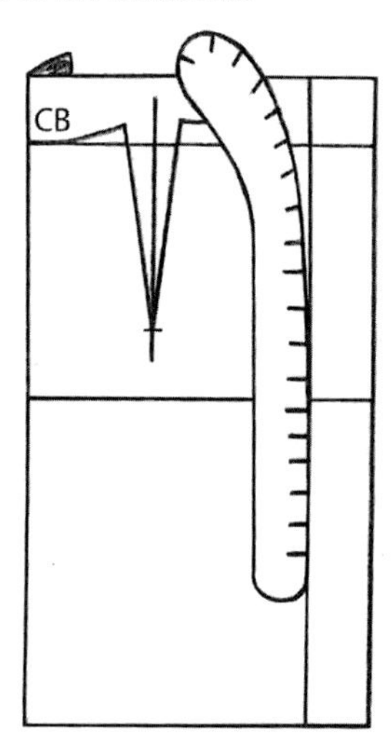

- For the back side seam, use your curved ruler with the curved end up at the waistline and the straight end down toward the hem to finesse your side seam line.

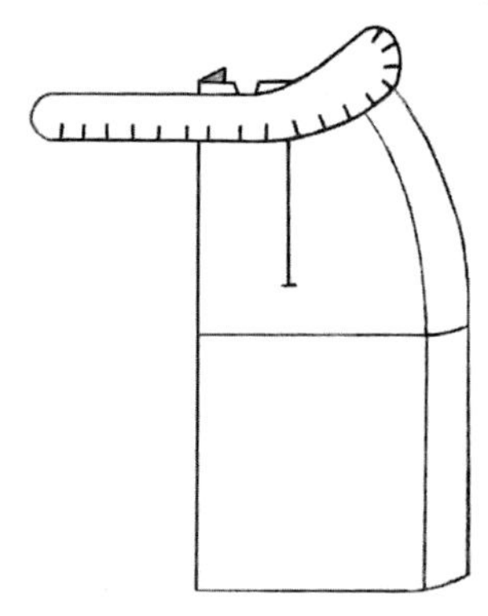

- For the back waistline, fold and pin the waist dart.
- Correct your waistline using your curved ruler with the curved end toward the side seam and the straight end toward the CB.

*True the darts at the waistline by following the directions in the Appendix for Trueing Darts.

Fit Check

- Pin the front and back together at the side seams from the hip level line to hem.
- Using your flexible straight grid ruler, place the ruler on its edge and measure from the waistline to the hip level line for front and back side seams from hip level line to waistline. The measurements should be the same.
- If the measurements are off, then adjust the back side seam to match the front side seam.
- If the measurements are off by more than ⅝" (1.6 cm), then you will need to check the drape to correct for this.
- Now pin the darts closed and check the waistline shape for a smooth curve.
- Leaving the side seams pinned, but removing the dart pinning, draw the hemline in.
- Mark the desired length of the skirt at the CB and draw a line parallel to the hip level line across to CF.

How to Drape a Flared Skirt

The A-line Skirt

The flared skirt, also referred to as the A-line skirt, kicks out at the hem and has a smooth waistline with no shaping darts.

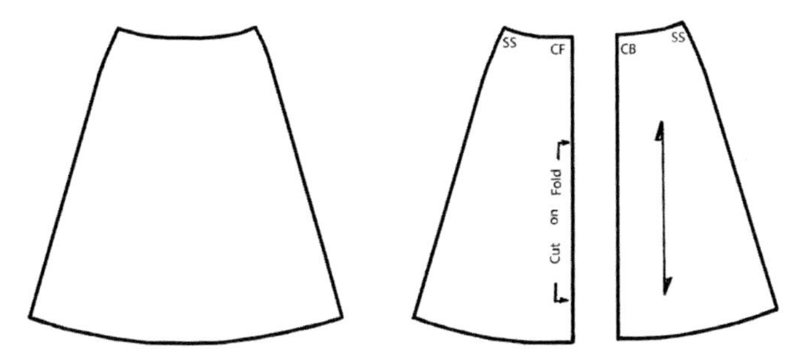

Anatomy of the Flared Skirt

Preparing the Fabric for Draping

(See Chapter 4 on Preparing the Muslin for Draping, and Blocking the Muslin.)

- The length of the fabric must be on the straight of grain. The straight of grain runs the length of the fabric, parallel to the selvage.
- Measure the length for the front and back muslin panels from the waistline to the desired length of the skirt + 5" (12.7 cm).
- Measure the approximate width of the front panel at the hem for the fullness plus at least 4" (10.2 cm).

- Repeat this for the back panel.
- Mark the 1″ (2.5 cm) guidelines for the CF and CB panels along the grainline edge. (CF will be on the right side of the fabric, and CB will be on the left side of the fabric.)

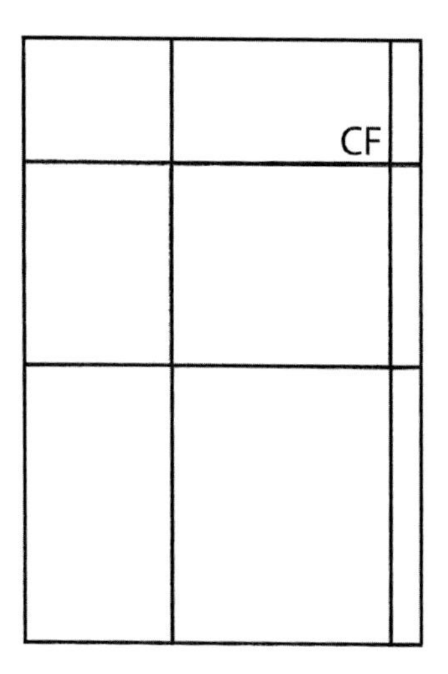

Front

- From the center front line on the front panel, draw a horizontal line at 5″ (12.7 cm) down from the top edge to indicate the waistline.
- Using your L-square, at 8″ (20.3 cm) down from the 5″ (12.7 cm) marking (or 13″ [33 cm] down from the top edge of the fabric), draw a horizontal line across the fabric perpendicular to the CF guideline. This is the hipline.
- On your dress form, measure across the hip level line from CF to side seam. Add ½″ (1.3 cm) of ease to this measurement.
- Using this measurement (hip front), draw a side seam line on your front panel parallel to the CF guideline.

Back

- On the back panel, using your L-square, at 13″ (33 cm) down from the top edge of the fabric, draw a horizontal line across the fabric perpendicular to the CB guideline. This is the hipline.

- On your dress form, measure across the hip level line from CF to side seam. Add ½" (1.3 cm) of ease to this measurement.
- Using this measurement (hip back), draw a side seam line on your front panel parallel to the CF guideline.

Directions for Draping

Flared Skirt Front

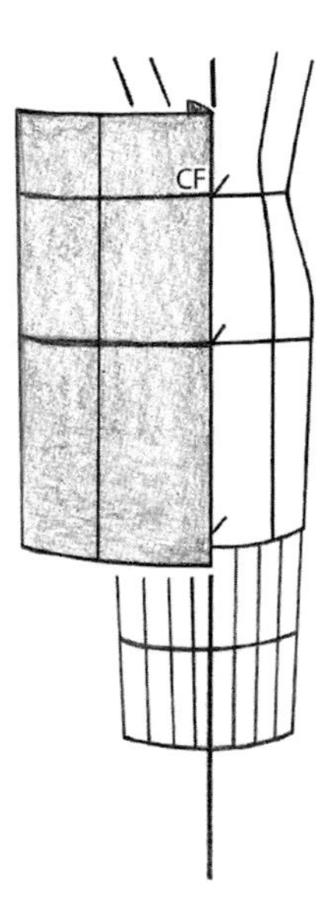

- Pin the front panel to the dress form, matching the CF guideline to the CF line of the dress form, the waistline, and the hip level line.

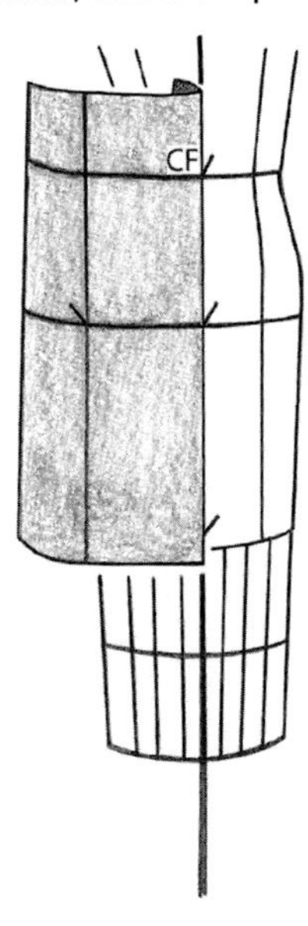

- Smooth across the hipline, matching the long side seam line to the dress form's side seam, and pin at the hip level line at the side seam.

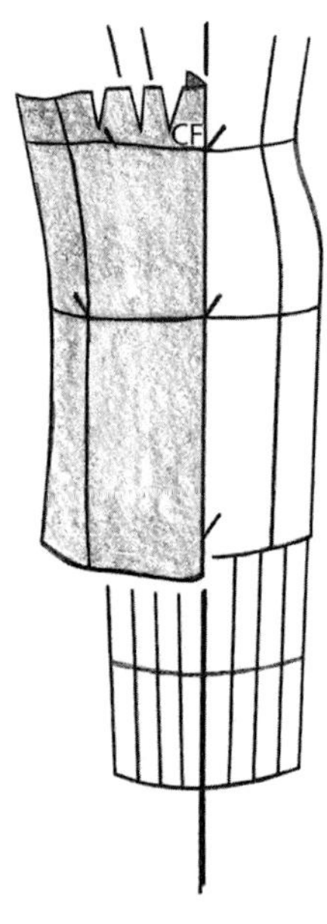

- At the waistline, smooth the fabric from the center front, letting it fall off grain. Clip the fabric from the top edge to the waistline being careful to only cut to, but not through that line.
- Pin the side seam at the waistline.

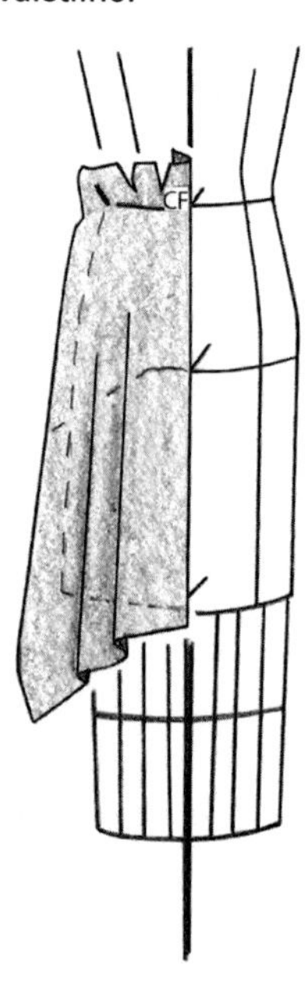

- Remove the pin at the hip level line at the side seam and allow the fabric to fall into flares from the waistline.
- Using a dashed line, mark the waistline, the side seam, and the hem by either using the dress form, or a hem marker.

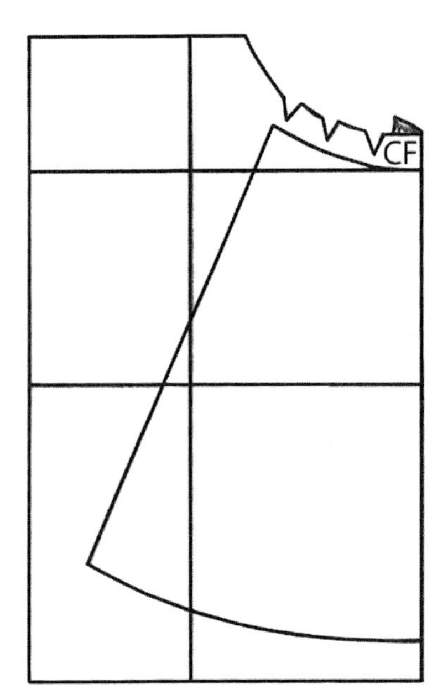

- Remove the skirt panel from the dress form and true the pattern.

Flared Skirt Back

- The skirt back is drafted using the skirt front.

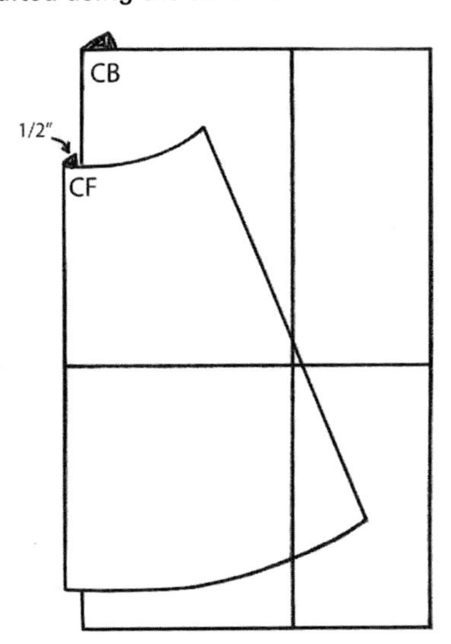

- Lay the skirt back fabric flat on the table and place the skirt front panel over it, lining up the cross-grain line of the hip level, but extending the CF ½" (1.3 cm) past the CB. This allows for the difference in the waist front and waist back measurements.
- Pin the layers together to prevent shifting.
- Trace the skirt front pattern onto the back panel, noting that the back waistline will be redrawn when placed back on the dress form to check for a final fit.
- True up all panels and check for fit.

Trueing: The back pattern is created from the front pattern so trueing should not be necessary.

Fit Check

- Pin the side seams from waistline to hem.
- Place back on the dress form, pinning along front waistline to side seam.
- Adjust the placement of the CB waistline so that the skirt hangs properly and the side seam of the skirt follows the side seam of the dress form.
- The new CB waistline marking will be lower than the trued marking.
- Mark the new back waistline in a contrasting color.

How to Draft a Basic Skirt

The basic skirt shape is straight, with side seams parallel to the center front and center back, although a very slight flare at the hem is acceptable. The waistline has shaping darts, which, if desired, could be converted into gathers or pleats.

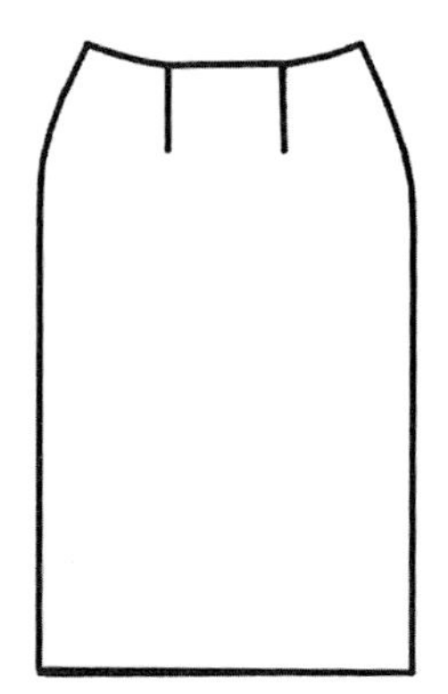

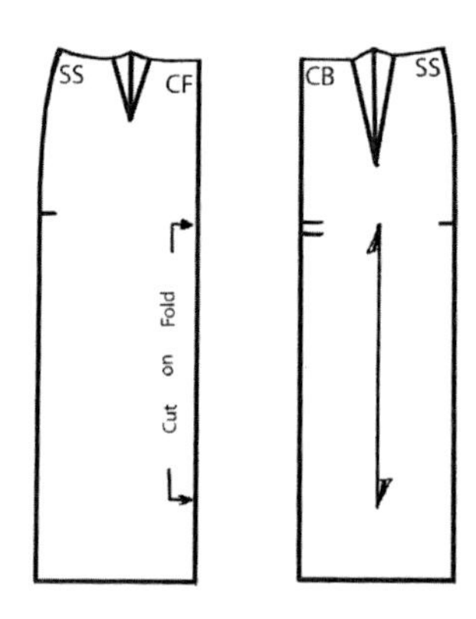

Anatomy of the Basic Skirt

Measurements Needed:		
Waist:	Hip Front:	Bust Point to Bust Point:
Hip:	Hip Back:	CF length of skirt:
Hip Point:		

NOTE: Your Hip Front measurement and Hip Back measurement should equal your Total Hip measurement.

Dart Length

- Darts in the skirt front usually extend 3″ (7.6 cm) in length depending on the size and shape of the figure.
- Back darts are longer at about 6″ (15.2 cm), but do not extend beyond 2″ (5.1 cm) above the hipline.

Note

- For the Basic Skirt, the hem is usually a straight line down to the hip point line, but it can flare to a maximum of 2½″ (6.4 cm).
- If flare is added below the hip point line only, the skirt is still considered a fitted skirt, but if the darts are closed and fullness is added above the hipline, then it is considered a flared skirt.
- The left side will be Skirt Back, and the right side will be Skirt Front.

Directions

- Paper size = Height of the paper should allow for the Center Front Length measurement + 4″ (10.2 cm), and width should allow for ½ Hip measurement + 4″ (10.2 cm).

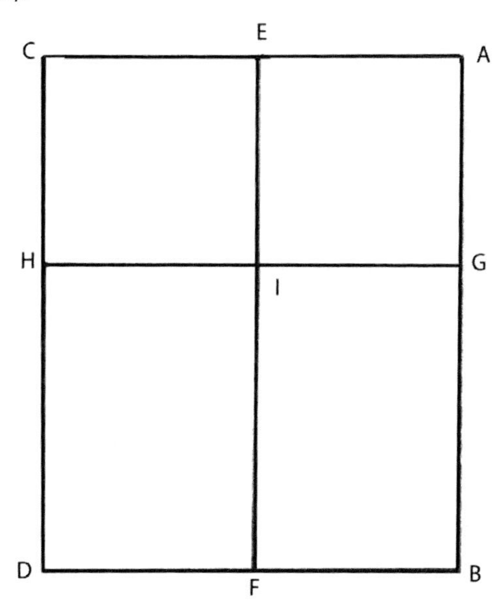

- Draw a vertical line, A-B, 2″ (5.1 cm) in from the right side of the paper, where A-B = the CF length of the skirt.
- From A, draw a horizontal line perpendicular to line A-B toward the left to new point C, where A-C = ½ Total Hip measurement + ½″ (1.3 cm) ease.
- From B, draw a horizontal line perpendicular to line A-B toward the left to new point D, so that A-C = B-D.
- Using your straight ruler, connect C to D.
- From A, mark point G on line A-B, where G = Hip point measurement.
- From G, draw a horizontal line across to new point H. G-H is your hip point line or hip level. (C-H should equal A-G.)
- From point A, on the A-C line, label point E, where E = ½ Hip Front measurement +¼″ (0.6 cm) ease.
- From E, draw a vertical line to new point F, so that B-F = A-E.
- At the intersection of lines E-F and G-H, mark point I.

Waistline

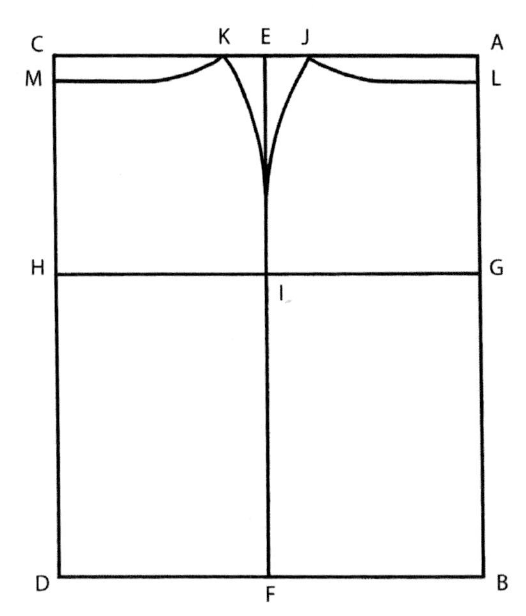

- From point A, measure and mark point J, where J = ¼ Waist measurement + dart measurement from chart* (see below).
- From point C, measure and mark point K, where K = ¼ Waist measurement + dart measurement from chart* (see below).
- Using your curved ruler with the straight edge toward the skirt hem and the curved edge at J, draw a curved line to a vanishing point above point I.
  (The vanishing point is determined by gauging the curves of the figure that was measured. If the figure has more distinct curves, then there would be a more abrupt curve from the waistline and a vanishing point closer to J and further away from the hip point line. If the figure is less curved, then the line from the waistline would also be less curved and the vanishing point would be further from J and closer to the hip point line.)
- Flip your curved ruler, keeping the straight edge toward the skirt hem and the curved edge at K, draw a curved line from K to the same vanishing point determined for the Skirt Front.
- From point A, on the A-B line, mark point L ½″ (1.3 cm) down.
- At point L, and using your straight ruler, draw a perpendicular line out from L ½″ (1.3 cm). This is to create the smooth line across CF when combined with the other half.
- Using your curved ruler with straight edge at L and the curved edge at J, connect J to L.
- From point C, mark point M ½″ (1.3 cm) down on C-D line.
- At point M and using your straight ruler, draw a perpendicular line out from M ½″ (1.3 cm). This is to create the smooth line across CF when combined with the other half.
- Using your curved ruler with straight edge at M and the curved edge at K, connect M to K.

Adding Darts

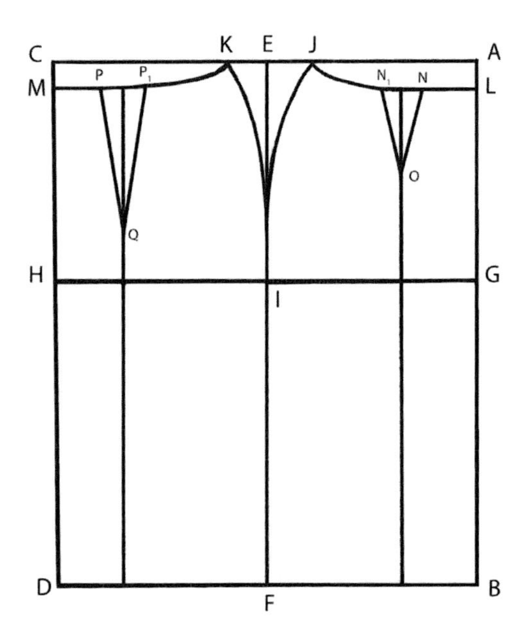

Front

- From L, measure and mark point N, where N = ½ the Bust point to Bust point measurement. N is the top point of the first leg of the dart.
- Mark point N_1 at the dart measurement determined earlier from the Dart Chart.
- Mark the center of the dart between N and N_1. Draw a vertical line from this point to a new point 3" (3.8 cm) down from the waistline, and mark point O. O is the vanishing point of the dart.
- Connect the legs of the dart by drawing lines from points N and N_1 to point O.
- Extend the vertical line from the center of the dart, through O, and down to connect to line B-D. This is your grainline.

Back

- From M, measure and mark point P, where P = 3" (7.6 cm). P is the top point of the first leg of the dart.
- Mark point P_1 at the dart measurement determined earlier from the Dart Chart.
- Mark the center of the dart between P and P_1. Draw a vertical line from this point to a new point 6" (15.2 cm) down from the waistline and mark point Q. Q is the vanishing point of the dart.
- Connect the legs of the dart by drawing lines from points P and P_1 to point Q.
- Extend the vertical line from the center of the dart, through Q, and down to connect to line B-D. This is your grainline.

*True the darts at the waistline by following the directions in the Appendix for Trueing Darts.

Dart Chart:

*-To estimate the amount you need for darts, subtract your waist measurement from your hip measurement.

- If the difference is 11″ (27.9 cm) or more, use 2″ (5.1 cm) darts
- If the difference is 9″ to 11″ (22.9–27.9 cm), use 1½″ (3.8 cm) darts
- If the difference is 7″ to 9″ (17.8–22.9 cm) use 1″ (2.5 cm) darts
- If the difference is less than 7″ (17.8 cm) use ½″ (1.3 cm) darts

How Grainline Affects the Hang of a Skirt

Grainline is a very important aspect of how a skirt will hang. The design and style of a skirt is determined by how the finished garment is influenced by grainline. How does grainline affect hang? When cutting a skirt, or other garment, you should consider the grainline and how you plan to use it.

The lengthwise threads of the fabric (the warp) that are the grainline, are stronger than the cross-grain threads (the weft). The lengthwise threads fall and drape better when they run up and down the body since they stretch less than cross-grain threads.

Cross-grain can be used as grainline in some cases but may eventually stretch out of shape since they aren't as strong as grainline threads.

Bias stretches considerably more than grain or cross-grain and can be used intentionally to drape smoothly along the figure.

*These guidelines are for a four-gore skirt, meaning a skirt with two front panels and two back panels.

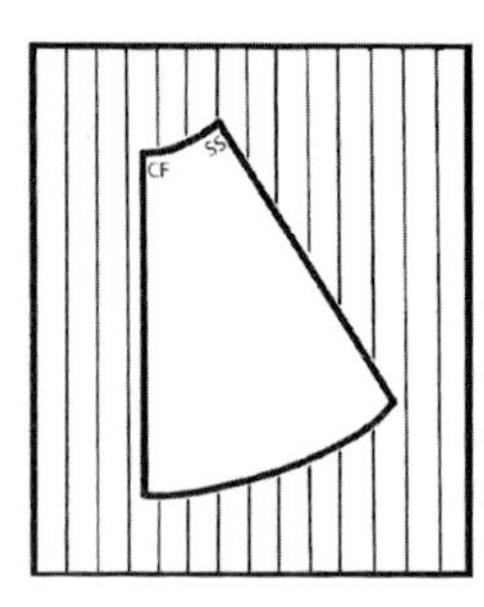

Grain on Center Front

- The center of the front of the skirt will hang straight with the fullness hanging at the sides in folds. Since the side seams are on the bias, the hemline may end up hanging less evenly.

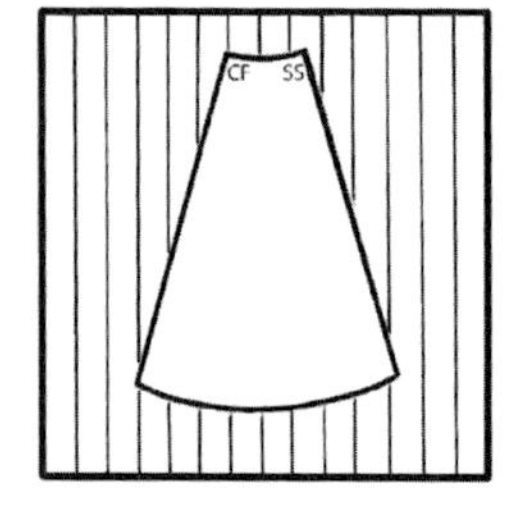

Grain in the Center of a Gore

- The fullness hangs evenly across the entire gore and therefore the skirt, so the hemline will remain more even.

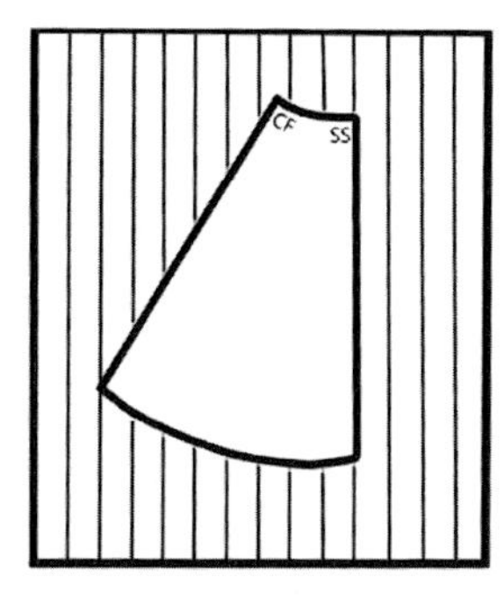

Grain at the Side Seam

- The side seams of the skirt will hang straight with the fullness hanging at the center front. Because the centers of the gores will be on the bias, the hemline may end up hanging less evenly.

Sewing Suggestion

- For a gored flared skirt, sew gores from the hem to the waistline (wide to narrow) to sew with the grainline and to prevent stretching on the bias.

Circular Skirts

The circular skirt has a smooth waistline with no shaping darts, and the hem is a full circle.

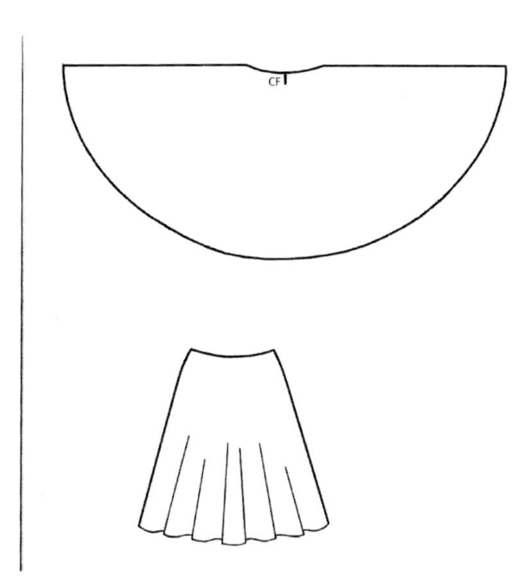

Anatomy of the Circular Skirt

- Circular skirts are made from either a single circle on 72″ (1.8 m) wide fabric, such as felt, or with seams on narrower fabric.
- You need to determine the location of the waistline opening, because this will determine where the seams are to be placed.

Skirts

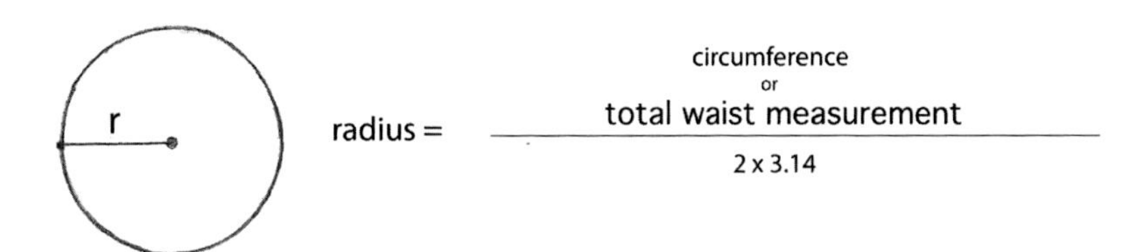

- The waistline circumference follows the mathematical formula:

radius = circumference or total waist measurement
2 x 3.14

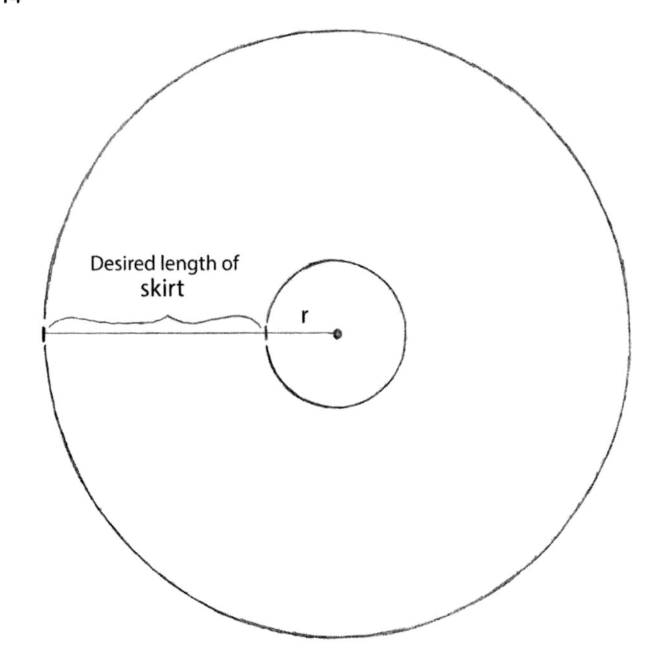

- Determine the length of the skirt for the measurement from waistline to hem.
- Add seam allowance to these numbers for cutting. Seam allowances should be added for the hem at the outer edge of the circle, and for the waistline to the inner, smaller circle.
- If adding seams to create gores, or if you require a center back seam, make sure you add the seam allowances when doing the original math. You should determine how many seams you are going to have and add seam allowance for each side of the seam. For example, if you have decided to have only a center back seam then you would use the waistline circumference + the seam allowance for the two edges that will be sewn. If you decided that you wanted two back gores and one front, then you would use the waistline circumference + the two center back seam allowances, and four side seam seam allowances (two for each side seam).

Chapter 6: Bodices

How to Drape the Basic Bodice

The Basic Bodice sloper is a generic shape of a bodice. Once you have created these sections of the bodice, you are able, through pattern manipulation, to create other styles.

Manipulating fabric while draping is a valuable skill that requires experience and is usually not successfully achieved at the first attempt. You will need to understand the habits of the fabric and know when you, or the fabric, should be relaxing and letting the other take control. This may sound odd, but there are times that the fabric behaves a certain way and you need to allow it to do so, otherwise you will continue to fight its natural characteristics. You cannot force the fabric to do something that it doesn't naturally want to do, because after removing the drape from the form, the fabric will try to restore itself and the result will be an odd fitting garment.

Keep in mind that when draping a flat piece of fabric over the front of the female form, the excess fabric will radiate from the highest point of the bust. This fabric may be arranged in any position as long as it is radiating from the bust. These draping instructions will give you a sloper with front waist and shoulder darts, and back waist and shoulder darts.

These darts can be manipulated into other design styles by combining them into one large dart, dividing them into pleats or tucks, or converted into gathers. They can fall anywhere on the bodice front as long as they radiate back toward the bust point (see Chapter 7).

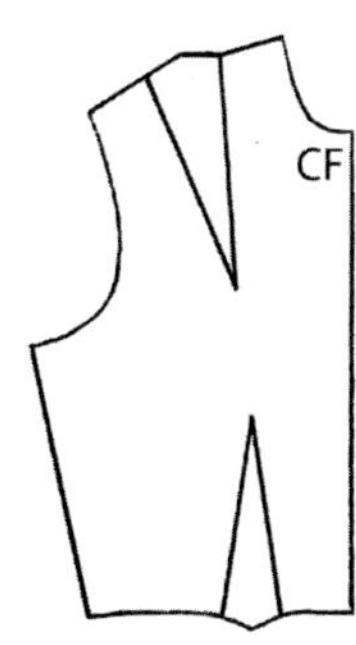

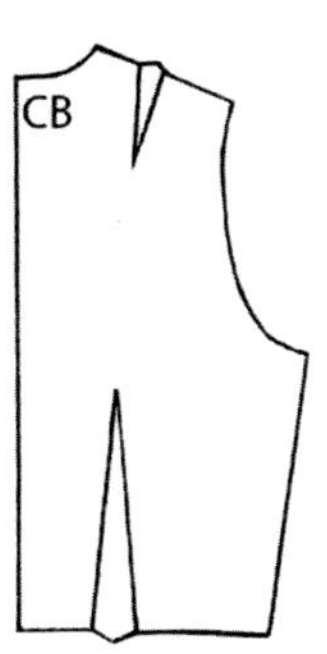

Anatomy of the Basic Bodice

DOI: 10.4324/9781003022619-6

Bodice Front – With Shoulder and Waist Darts

- Prepare the fabric for draping.
  (See Chapter 4 on Preparing the Muslin for Draping and Blocking the Muslin.)

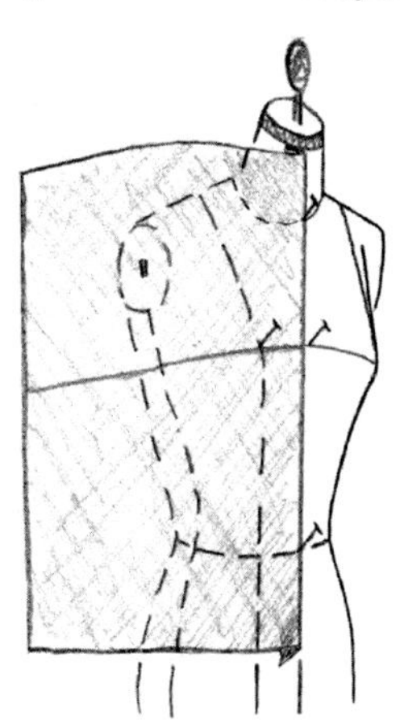

- On your dress form, pin the prepared muslin so that the cross-grain line is centered over the bust tape, with about 3–4" (7.6–10.2 cm) of fabric extending above the neckline seam. The fabric should drape over the shoulder seam.
- The center front line of the muslin should line up with the center front of the dress form.
- Place the pins into the dress form at a low angle with the head of the pin facing away from the center of the muslin (this is so that if you pull the fabric to draw it taut, the fabric is anchored and doesn't slide off the dress form).
- Place pins along center front at the neckline and the waistline.
- Place a pin on the cross-grain line at the bust point.

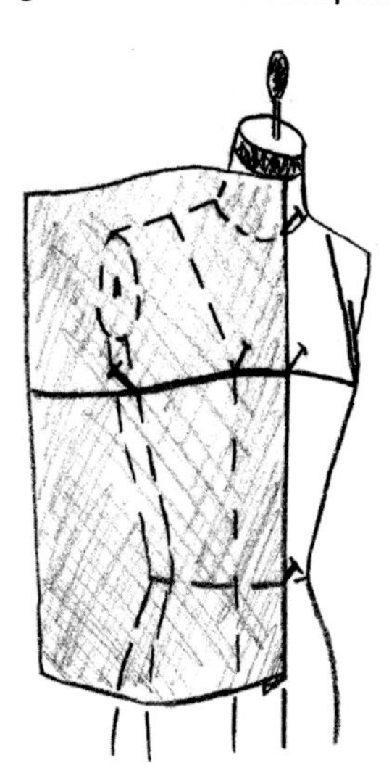

- Smooth the fabric over the bust line to side seam. At the side seam, ½" (1.3 cm) of ease should be added by creating a ¼" (0.6 cm) pinch. Distribute the ease evenly along the bust line and then pin.

Neckline

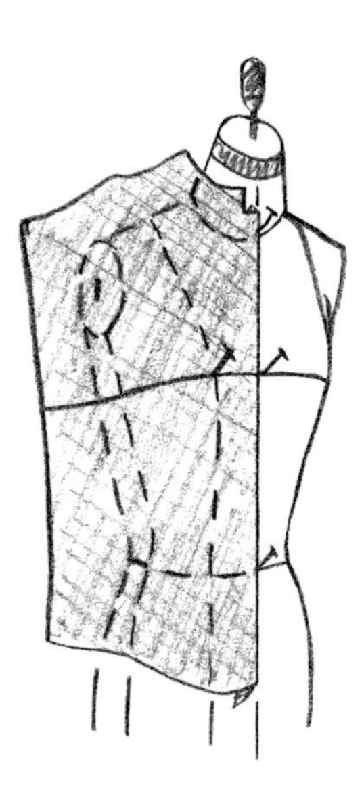

- To smooth around the neckline, make a cut perpendicular to center front line on the muslin about 1" (2.5 cm) above the neck seam on the dress form.

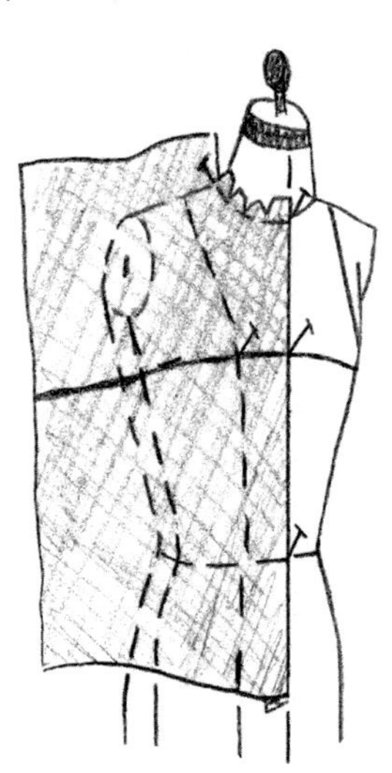

- Cut down to the neckline seam while continuing to smooth around the neck and up to the shoulder seam, being very careful not to clip past the neckline seam and into the body of the garment. (Cut to, but not through. Clipping too aggressively is very easy to do. Think of clipping as if you were to clip only to the intended future stitching line within the seam allowance. If you clip too much you will end up in the body of the garment. If you do clip too far, you can mend a small cut with some masking tape placed on the top and underneath of the area.)
- Place a pin at the shoulder seam/neckline seam intersection.

Shoulder Dart

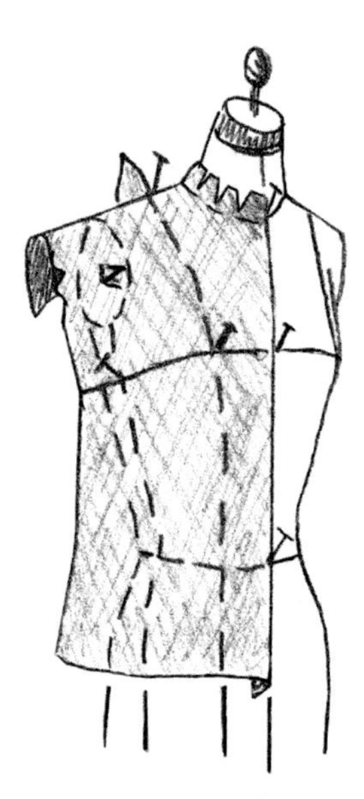

- From the neckline, smooth across the shoulder seam to the princess line. Place a pin at this point.
- From the side seam, smooth the excess fabric up and over the armhole to create a ridge of fabric at the princess line.
- Pinch out about ¼″ (0.6 cm) at the screw level of the arm plate to create ease in the armhole.

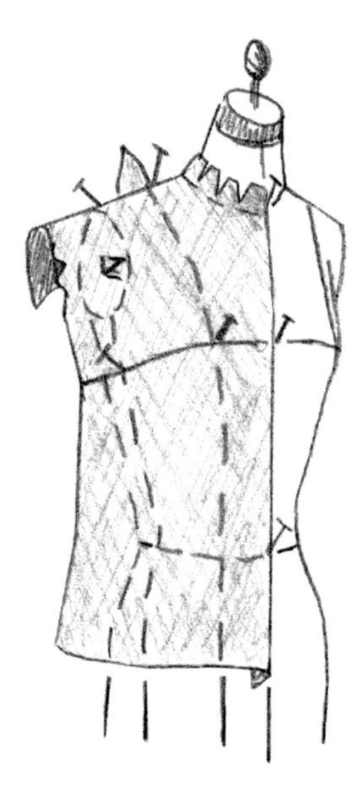

- Place a pin at the shoulder seam on the armhole ridge.

- Arrange the excess fabric that remains on the shoulder seam so that the center of the dart you are creating falls directly over the princess line on the shoulder seam.
- Pinch a ridge on the princess line to create the dart and insert pins along the length of the dart down to a vanishing point 1½" (3.8 cm) above the bust point. Place a pin perpendicularly to indicate the vanishing point. Remember that there needs to be ease so you should not make the dart too tight. The vanishing point might try to go all the way to the bust point or somewhere not on the princess line, but you should mark at 1½" (3.8 cm) above the bust point regardless.

Waist Dart

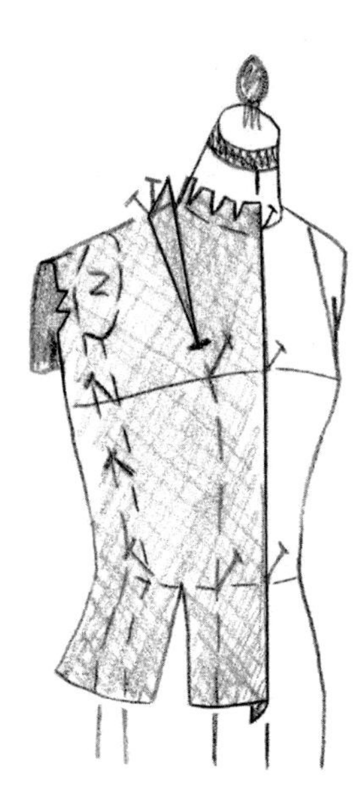

- Smooth down the side seam of the dress form to the waistline, pinning as you smooth.

Bodices

- From the center front, smooth across the waistline until you reach the princess line. Place a pin at this point.
- If the fabric below the waistline begins to pull off grain and you start to see "smile lines", clip to, but not through, the waistline at the princess line. Over-clipping at the waistline will result in a very tight garment with little to no ease.
- Smooth the excess fabric from the side seam over to the princess line so the center of the dart you are creating falls directly over the princess line at the waistline.

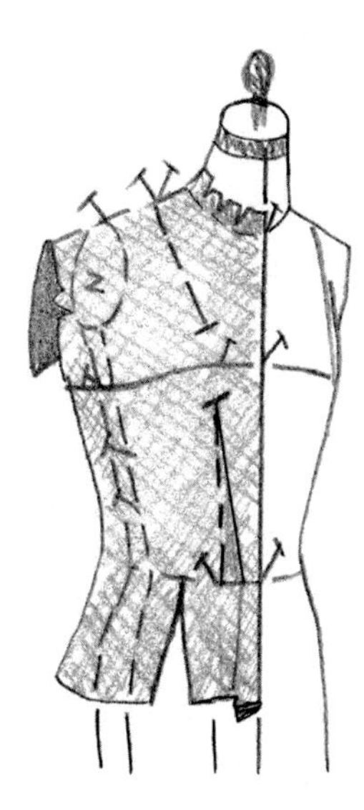

- Pinch a ridge on the princess line to create the dart and insert pins along the length of the dart up toward the bust point up to a vanishing point 1½" (3.8 cm) below the bust point. Place a pin perpendicularly to indicate the vanishing point. Remember that there needs to be ease so you should not make the dart too tight. The vanishing point might try to go to the bust point or somewhere not on the princess line, but you should mark at 1½" (3.8 cm) below the bust point regardless.

Marking the Muslin

- Using a pencil, draw dashed lines on the muslin along the center of the twill tape at waistline, side seam, neckline, and shoulder seam.
- Draw a dashed line on the ridge around the arm plate of the dress form. This may result in a small armscye but it will be adjusted for ease in the trueing.
- Create cross marks on either side of the darts where they intersect the waistline and the shoulder seam, and mark the bust point.
- Mark the vanishing points.

- Create cross marks at the side seam where it intersects the waistline and also the arm ridge.
- Leave the fabric on the dress form, but fold over the excess muslin at the side seam and shoulder seam to allow for draping the Back Bodice.

Bodice Back – With Shoulder and Waist Darts

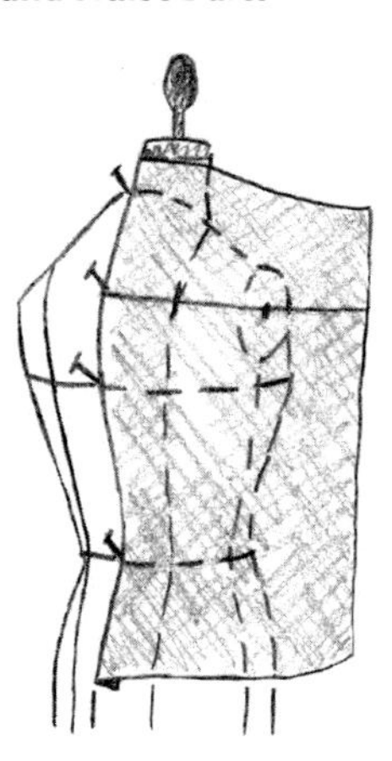

- On your dress form, pin the prepared muslin with the cross-grain line centered over the shoulder blade tape, with about 3–4″ (7.6–10.2 cm) of fabric extending above the neckline seam so that the fabric will drape over the shoulder seam. The CB line of the muslin should line up with the CB of the dress form.
- Place pins along CB at the neckline, at the shoulder line marking, and the waistline.

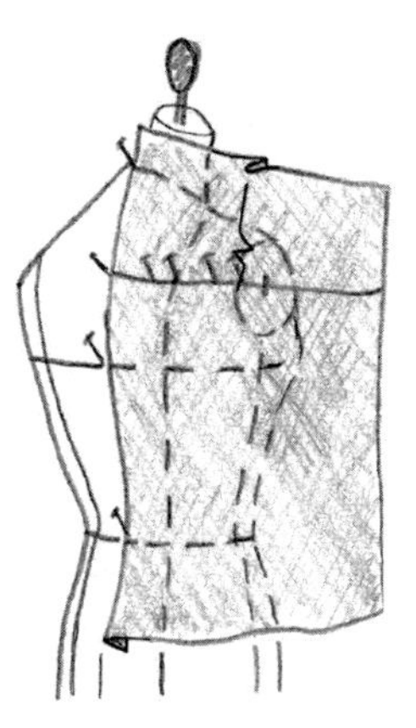

- Smooth the fabric over the shoulder blade line to the arm ridge. At the arm plate, ¼″ (0.6 cm) of ease should be added by creating a ⅛″ (0.3 cm) pinch. Distribute the ease evenly along the shoulder blade line and pin.

Neckline

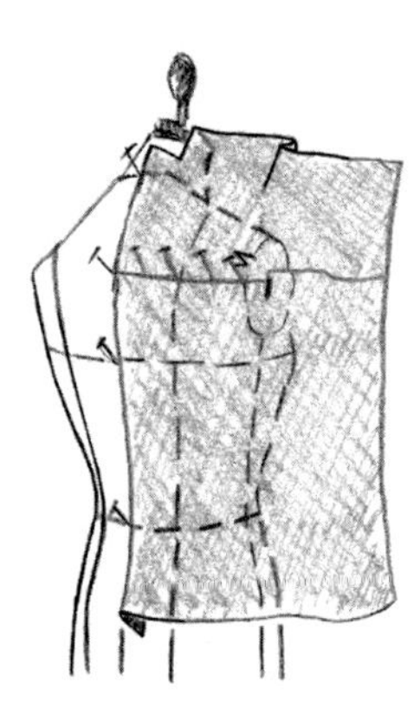

- To smooth around the neckline, make a cut perpendicular to center back line on the muslin about 1" (2.5 cm) above the neck seam on the dress form.

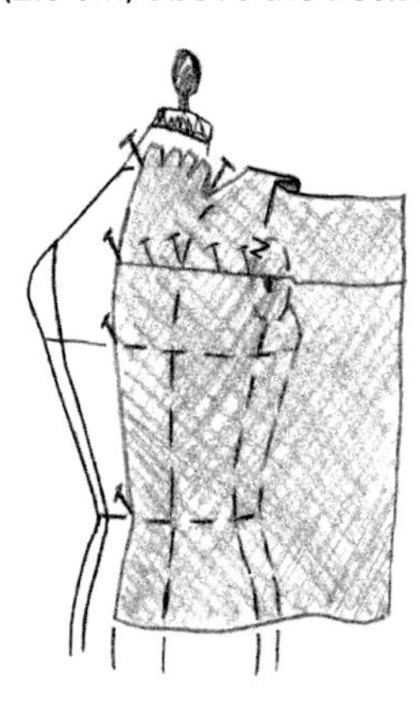

- Cut down to the neckline seam while continuing to smooth around the neck and up to the shoulder seam, being very careful not to clip past the neckline seam and into the body of the garment. (Cut to, but not through. Clipping too aggressively is very easy to do. Think of clipping as if you were to clip only to the intended future stitching line within the seam allowance. If you clip too much you will end up in the body of the garment. If you do clip too far, you can mend a small cut with some masking tape placed on the top and underneath of the area.)
- Place a pin at the shoulder seam/neckline seam intersection.

Shoulder Dart

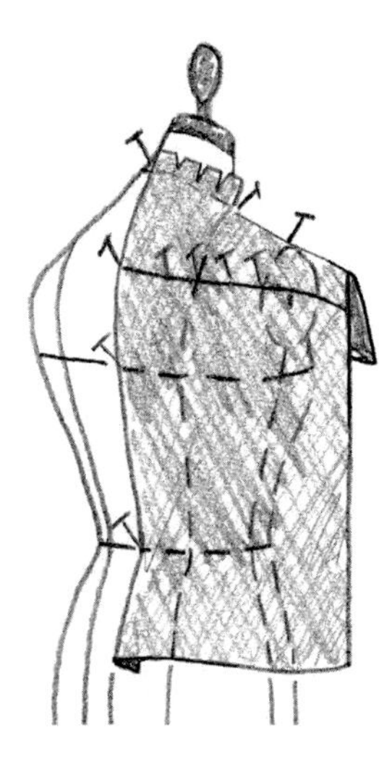

- From the neckline, smooth across the shoulder seam to the princess line. Place a pin at this point.
- From the side seam, smooth the excess fabric up and over the armhole to create a ridge of fabric at the princess line.
- Place a pin at the shoulder seam on the armhole ridge.
- Arrange the excess fabric that remains on the shoulder seam so that the center of the dart you are creating falls directly over the princess line on the shoulder seam.
- Pinch a ridge on the princess line to create the dart and place the pins along the length of the dart down to a vanishing point 3″ (7.6 cm) from the shoulder seam. Place a pin perpendicularly to indicate the vanishing point. The vanishing point might try to go somewhere not on the princess line, but you should still mark at 3″ (7.6 cm) from the shoulder seam.

Waist Dart

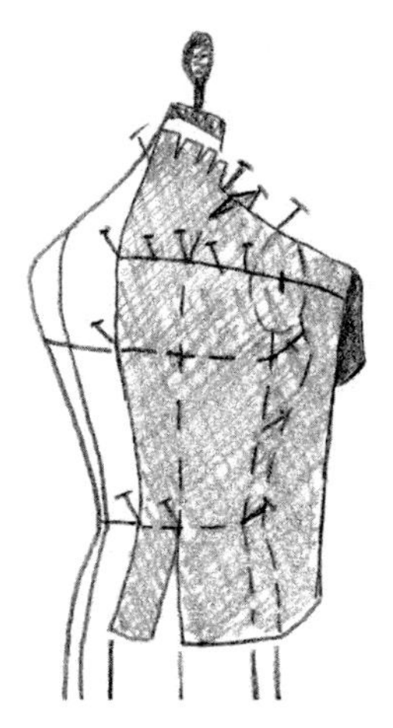

- Smooth down the side seam of the dress form to the waistline, pinning as you smooth.
- From the center back, smooth across the waistline until you reach the princess line. Place a pin at this point.

Bodices

- If the fabric below the waistline begins to pull off grain and you start to see "smile lines", clip to, but not through, the waistline at the princess line. Over-clipping at the waistline will result in a very tight garment with little to no ease.

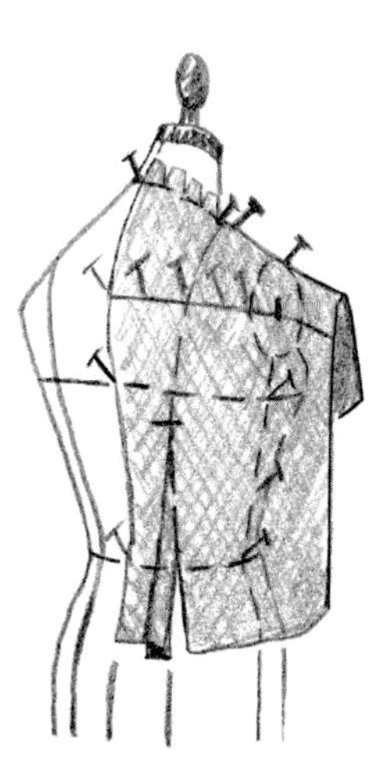

- Smooth the excess fabric from the side seam over to the princess line so the center of the dart you are creating falls directly over the princess line at the waistline.
- Pinch a ridge to create the dart and insert pins along the length of the dart up 7" (17.8 cm).
- Mark the 7" (17.8 cm) point as the vanishing point of the dart. Place a pin perpendicularly to indicate the vanishing point. Remember that there needs to be ease so you should not make the dart too tight. The vanishing point might try to go somewhere not on the princess line, but you should mark at 7" (17.8 cm) regardless.

Marking the Muslin

- Draw dashed lines on the muslin along the center of the twill tape at waistline, side seam, neckline, and shoulder seam.
- Draw a dashed line on the ridge around the arm plate of the dress form. This may result in a small armscye but it will be adjusted for ease in the trueing.
- Create cross marks on either side of the darts where they intersect the waistline and the shoulder seam, and mark the vanishing points.

- Create cross marks at the side seam where it intersects the waistline and the arm plate.
- Add matching notches on the side seam, and shoulder seam. You can carefully use a felt tip type marker to make your matching marks by pulling the fabric away from the dress form and letting the marker create a mark on the front of the garment. Let the marker bleed through to the back of the garment. DO NOT MARK THE DRESS FORM.

(Matching notches should correspond to darts on the other side of the draping: i.e. the shoulder dart on the back should align with the matching notch on the front, and the bust dart on the side seam [if you have one] should align with the matching notch on the back. If you have a bust dart at the shoulder seam and a back dart at the shoulder seam, these should align at the princess line and no additional matching notch is needed there.)

Combining Front and Back Bodice Pieces

- Trim the front and back shoulder seams to 1" (2.5 cm).
- On the front shoulder seam line and the front side seam, fold under and pin to back bodice, matching the shoulder darts at the princess line and the waistlines.
- Check that the shoulder cross mark at the shoulder seam, and the side seam cross marks under the arm plate align.

Trueing the Basic Bodice

(On the actual bodice drape)

Trueing is a term used to describe the process of creating accuracy on a draped or drafted sloper. When the muslin is still on the dress form, it may seem as if the sloper fits well and matches the other sections. It is only when the muslin is removed that the accuracy can be determined. Trueing can be done directly on the draped muslin pieces, or on craft paper. The following instructions will be on the draped muslin pieces. After trueing the muslin, then the pattern can be transferred to paper.

After removing the bodice from the dress form, with front and back panels separate and all pins removed, lay the fabric pieces flat on your table. Do not press the pieces with an iron since the fabric may stretch out of shape.

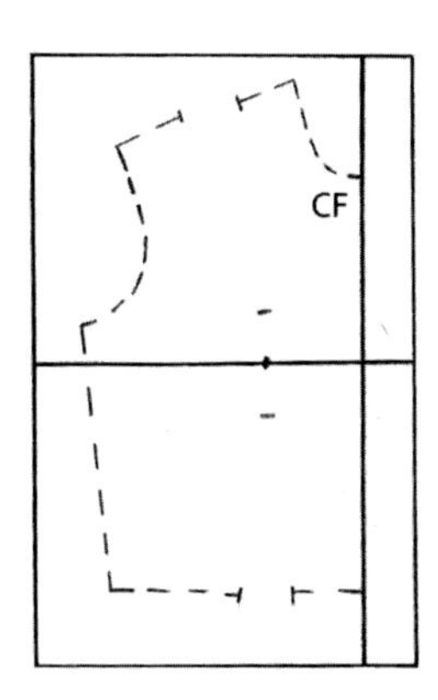

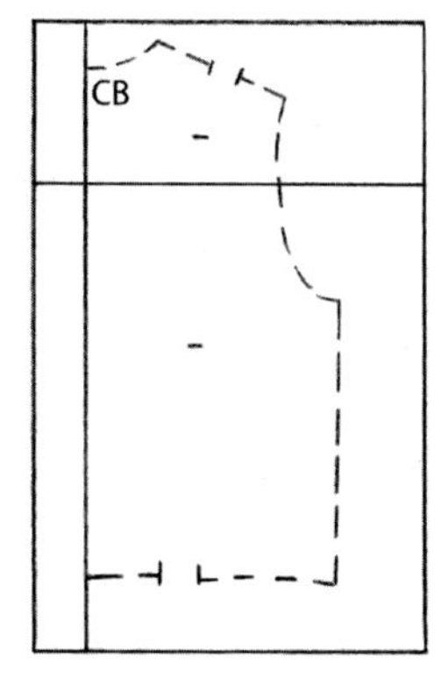

The following locations require a 90-degree angle:

- CF neck for ¼″ (0.6 cm)
- CF waist for ½″ (1.3 cm)
- CB neck for 1″ (2.5 cm)
- CB waist for 1″ (2.5 cm)

(These 90-degree angle lines that are perpendicular to the CF and CB allow for a smooth curve when making a full garment. Otherwise, you will end up with either a V shape or a ^ shape at those locations.)

Trueing the Front Bodice Darts

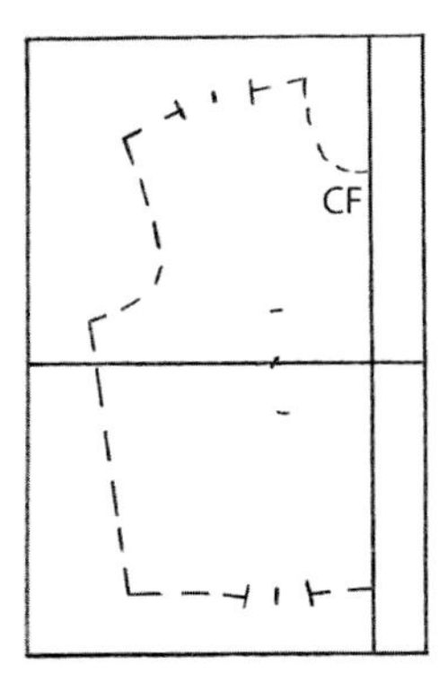

- For the front waist dart, measure the width of the dart opening at the waistline.
- Divide this measurement in half to determine the center point of the dart. Place a mark in the center of the opening on the waistline for the waist dart.
- For the front shoulder dart, measure the width of the dart opening on the shoulder seam.
- Divide this measurement in half to determine the center point of the dart. Place a mark in the center of the opening on the shoulder seam for the shoulder dart.

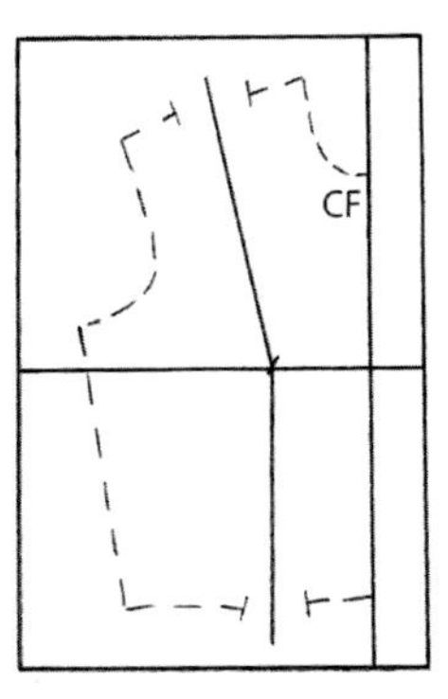

- Using your straight ruler, draw a line from the center point markings for each dart to the bust point.
- It is important that the line from the waistline to the bust point is parallel to the center front line.

Note: You may need to shift the center point so that the line will be parallel to the center front line and go to the bust point.

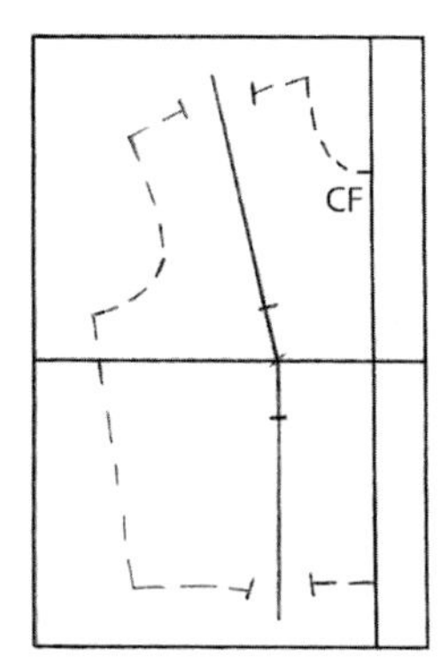

- For the waist dart, measure down 1½" (3.8 cm) from the bust point on the center line and mark this as the vanishing point.
- Mark points on the waistline on either side of the center line that equal half of the dart opening measurement.
- Using your straight ruler, draw in the dart legs from the vanishing point to the new points you marked at the waistline.
- For the shoulder dart, measure up 1½" (3.8 cm) from the bust point on the center line and mark this as the vanishing point.
- Mark points on the shoulder seam on either side of the center line that equal half of the dart opening measurement.

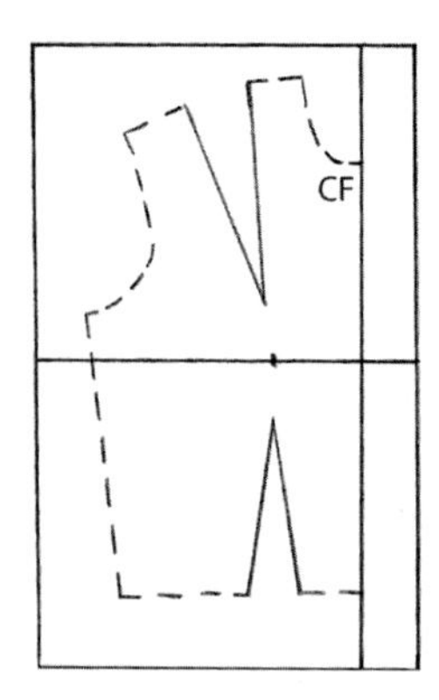

- Using your straight ruler, draw in the dart legs from the vanishing point to the new points you marked at the shoulder seam.
- You should now have a front waist dart and front shoulder dart.

Trueing the Back Bodice Darts

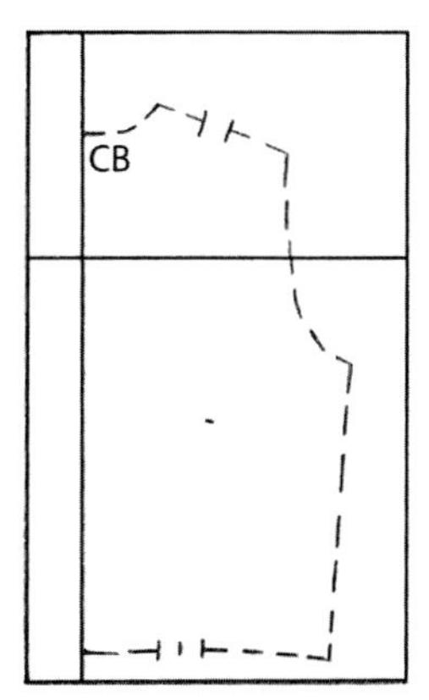

- For the back waist dart, measure the width of the dart opening at the waistline.
- Divide this measurement in half to determine the center point of the dart. Place a mark in the center of the opening on the waistline for the waist dart.

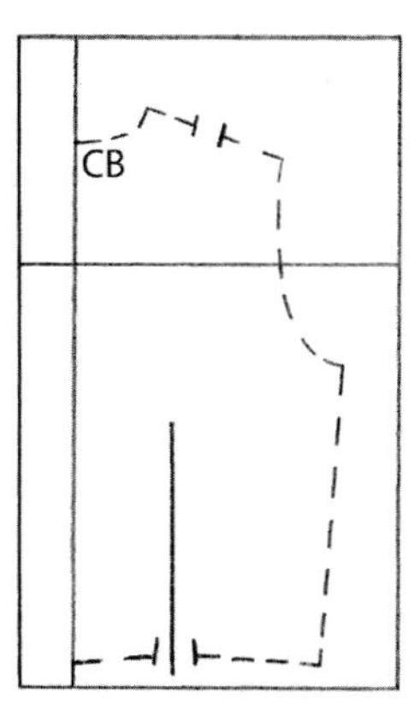

- Using your straight ruler, draw a line from the center point marking at the waistline to a point up 7″ (17.8 cm). (This new point may or may not fall in the same location as the original marking.)
- It is important that this line is parallel to the center back line.
- Mark the point that is 7″ (17.8 cm) up from the waistline on the center line as the vanishing point.

Note: You may need to shift the center point so that the line will be parallel to the center back line.

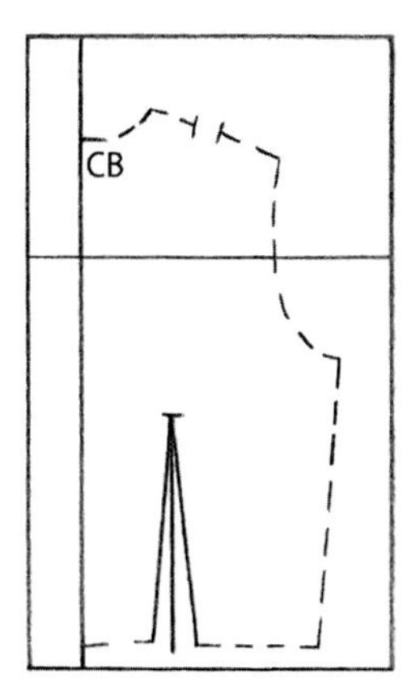

- Mark points on the waistline on either side of the center line that equal half of the dart opening measurement.
- Using your straight ruler, draw in the dart legs from the vanishing point to the new points you marked at the waistline.

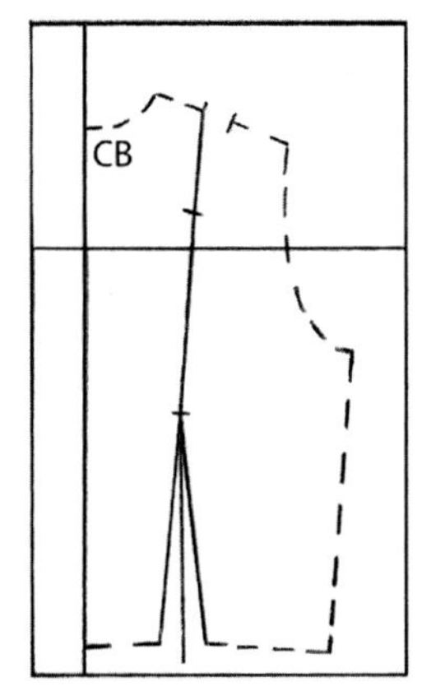

- For the back shoulder dart, extend a line from the back waist dart vanishing point to the shoulder dart marking closest to the neckline. (This line is unlikely to follow the original princess line.)
- Measure down 3″ (7.6 cm) on this line to create a new vanishing point.

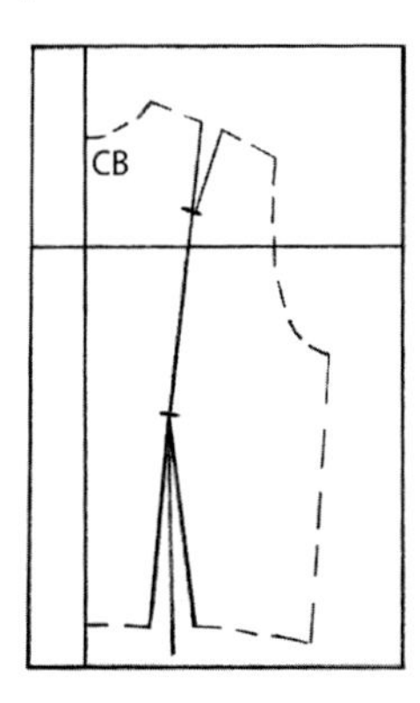

- Connect the other shoulder dart marking to this new vanishing point.
- You should now have a back waist dart and back shoulder dart.

Trueing the Necklines, Shoulder Seams, and Armscyes

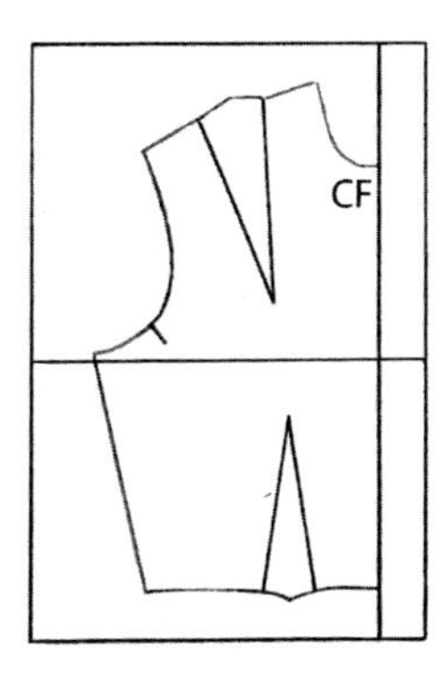

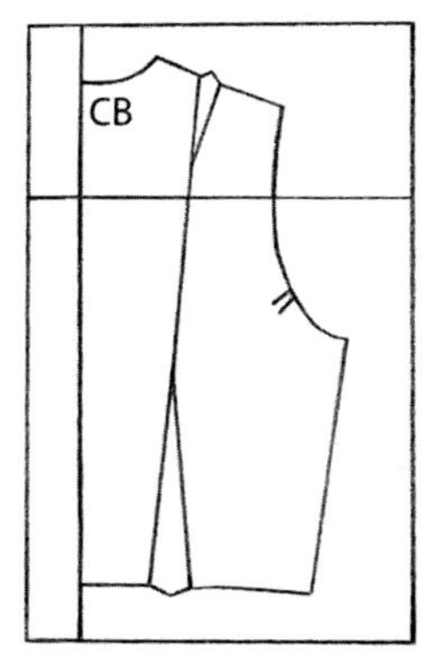

- For the necklines, use your curved ruler and connect your markings, making sure that the 90-degree lines are smoothly blended.

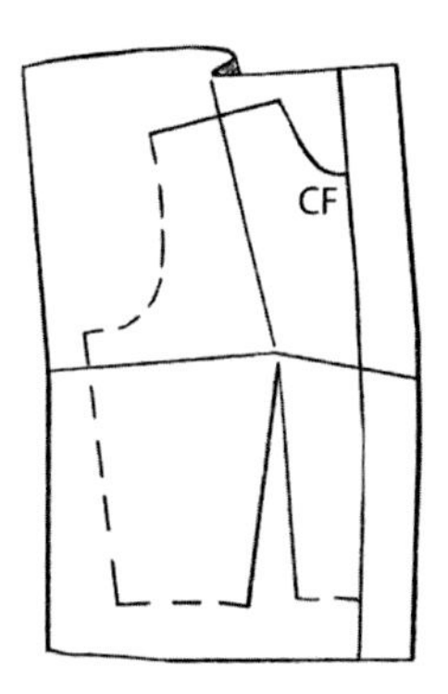

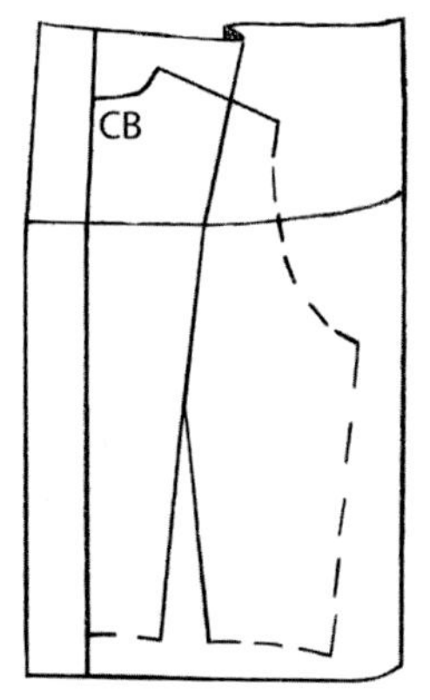

- For the front and back shoulder seams, fold the darts under along the dart legs, and using your straight ruler, draw a line from the neckline/shoulder seam point to the armhole/shoulder seam point of each shoulder seam.

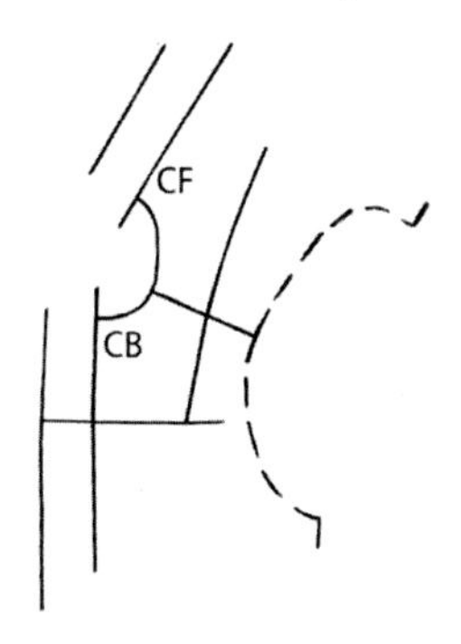

- You will need to check that the front and back shoulder seams are trued to each other by pinning the front shoulder dart and back shoulder dart closed. Then pin the front shoulder seam to the back shoulder seam.

Once pinned make sure that the neckline and the armscye match and are creating smooth transitions. Your darts should also match at the shoulder seam. If any of these are off, take the pinned muslin back to the dress form and check to see which line is correct in its location. Correct the location of the one that is off and draw new lines.

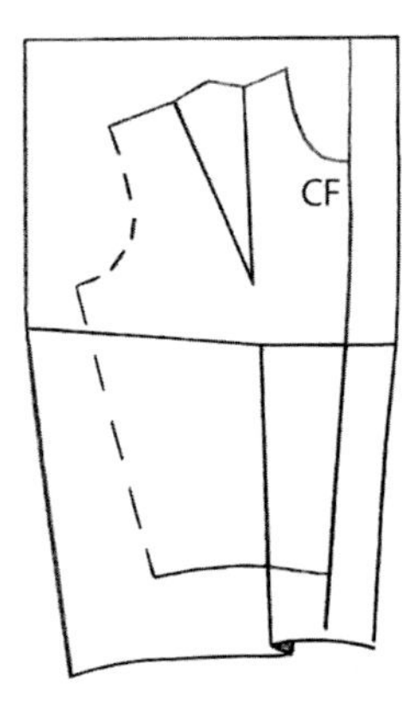

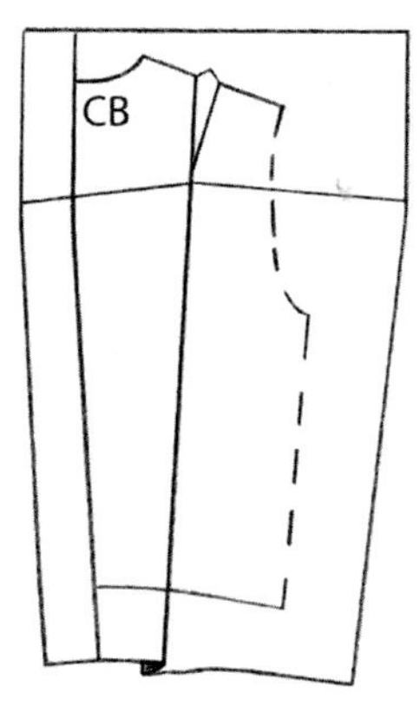

- You will need to true the entire waistline curve by pinning your side seams together.
- Your waistline from CF to CB should be a smooth curve.
- If it is not a smooth curve, you will need to adjust it at the side seam. If one of the side seams is longer than the other, you will need to make adjustments to either one or both of the side seams. Look at the armscye and waistline and judge which to alter based on the general shape of the curves. If it is still not clear which one to adjust, then place the muslin back on the dress form to determine which is more accurate.

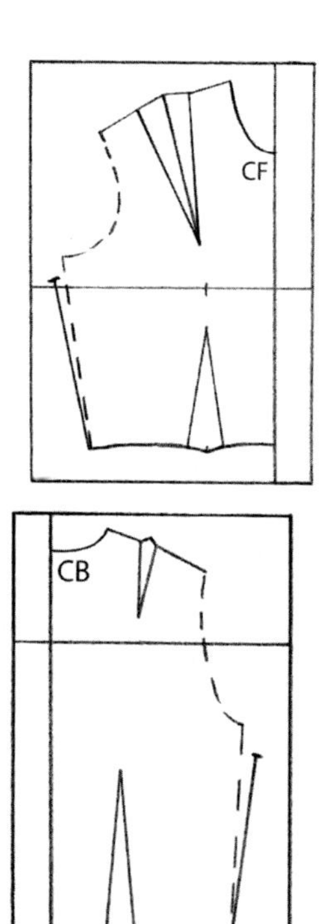

- To add ease at the front and back side seams at the bust line, you will first need to drop the front and back side seams down 1" (2.5 cm) from the armscye, and then bump them out ½" (1.3 cm).
- Using your original total armscye measurement from your person's measurements, check that the total armscye measurement you have created on your draping is about 1–2" (2.5–5.1 cm) larger than the person's measurement This is to allow room in the armscye for the arm to fit through and not inhibit movement. You should measure the front and back pieces of your pattern individually by walking the edge of your 18" grid ruler around the armscye. Then add these numbers together to get your pattern's total armscye measurement. If necessary, expand the armscye by dropping the front and back and bumping it out more than the original ease you added. Keep in mind that you can always mark and cut away the armscye in the fitting of the mock-up if it is too snug.
- From these new points, use your straight ruler and connect the marks from the armhole points down to the original waistline marks.

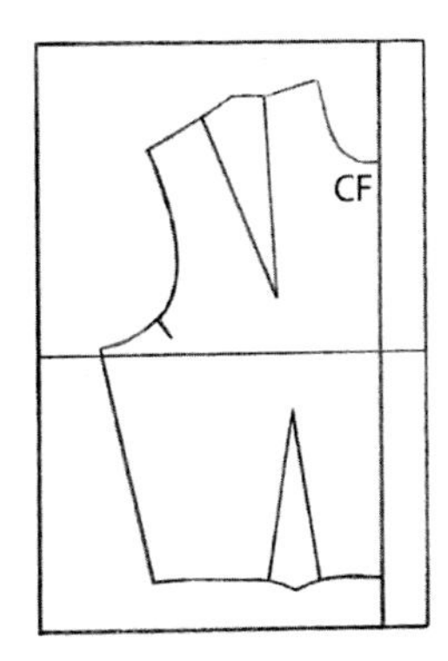

- For the front armscye, use your 12″ curved ruler and connect your shoulder point, your armscye ridge lines, and new side seam/armhole mark.
- Mark the armscye with a single notch at 2.5″ (6.4 cm) from the armscye/side seam intersection.

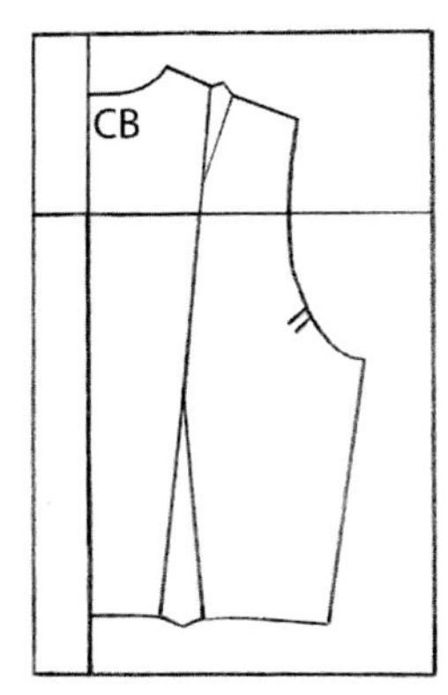

- For the back armscye, use your 12″ curved ruler and connect your shoulder point, your armscye ridge lines, and new side seam/armhole mark.
- Mark the armscye with a double notch at 2.5″ (6.4 cm) from the armscye/side seam intersection.

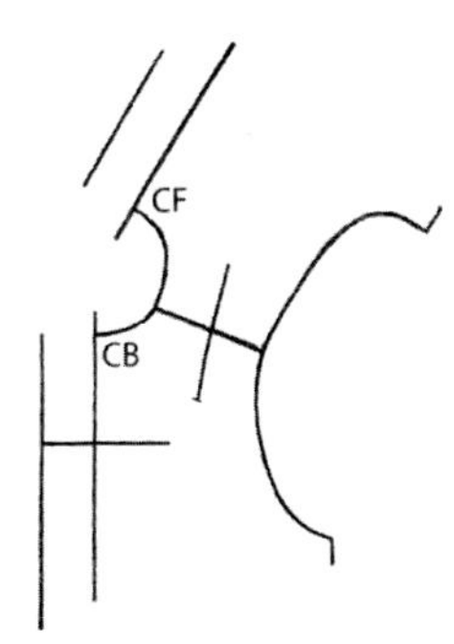

- To true the armscye, pin the front and back shoulder seams together to check that there is a smooth line across the top of the armscye at the shoulder seam and that the armscye does not create a point or "wing" out.

Check List for Fit and Correct Amount of Ease

- Prior to pinning the pieces together to check for fit, trim the excess muslin down to 1″ seam allowance.
- Pin your trued muslin together, including all darts, side seam and shoulder seam and place back on dress form.

Ease Checklist

- At side seam/armhole intersection = ½″ (1.3 cm) per front and back (1″ [2.5 cm] total per side)
- At bust front = ⅛″– ¼″ (0.3–0.6 cm)
- At back shoulder blade = ⅛″– ¼" (0.3–0.6 cm)
- At waist = ¼″ (0.6 cm) per front and back (½″ [1.3 cm] total per side)

After Trueing

- **Fit Check:**
- Pin the bodice to the dress form at neckline, shoulder seam, waistline at center front and center back, and side seam.
- Front and back grainlines should hang straight without twisting or pulling.
- Shoulder seams should align with each other and darts should align.
- Side seams should be the same length.
- The armhole is a smooth fat oval shape.
- Cross-grains should be parallel to the floor.
- Side seam should align with the side seam of the dress form.
- Darts are pinned shut to vanishing points.
- Darts are smooth without twisting.

How to Drape the Princess Bodice

The Princess Bodice is defined as a bodice that follows the lines of the side front seam and side back seam. Commonly known as the "princess lines". The darts that are found on the Basic Bodice do not exist on this sloper due to the seam lines that are created that run along the center of the line that the darts follow.

Later in this chapter you will find the directions for converting darts to seam lines.

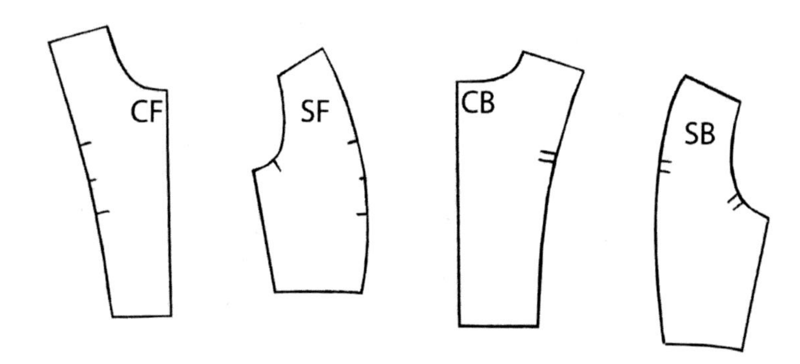

Anatomy of the Princess Bodice

- Prepare the fabric for draping. (See Chapter 4 on Preparing the Muslin for Draping, and Blocking the Muslin.)

Bodice Center Front

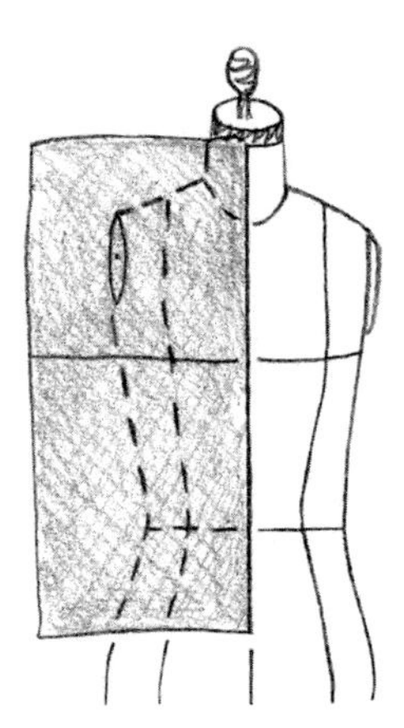

- On your dress form, line up the prepared muslin for the front so that the cross-grain line is centered over the bust tape, with about 3–4" (7.6–10.2 cm) of fabric extending above the neckline seam on the dress form. The fabric should drape over the shoulder seam.
- The center front line of the muslin should line up with the center front of the dress form.

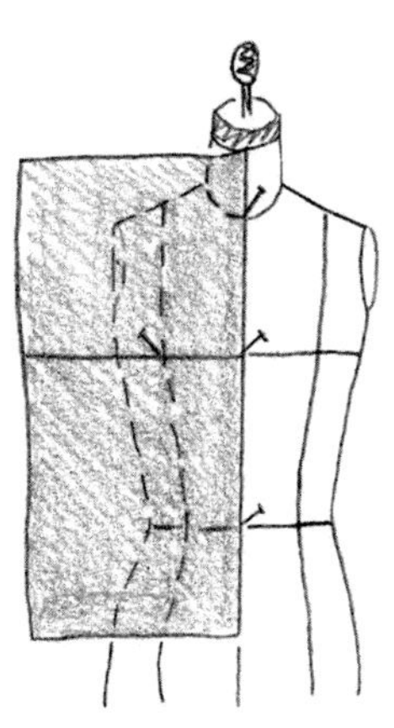

- Place the pins into the dress form at a low angle with the head of the pin facing away from the center of the muslin (this is so that if you pull the fabric to draw it taut, the fabric is anchored and doesn't slide off the dress form).
- Place pins along the center front at the neckline, at the bust line tape, and at the waistline.
- Smooth the fabric over the bust line to the princess line at the bust point. Pin the bust point.

Neckline

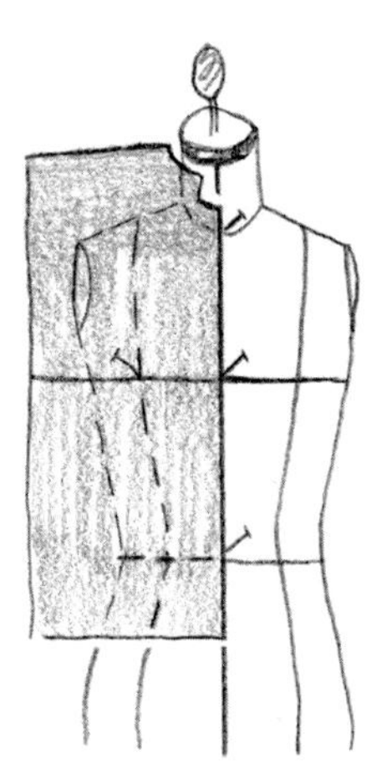

- To smooth around the neckline, make a cut perpendicular to CF line on the muslin about 1″ (2.5 cm) above the neck seam on the dress form.

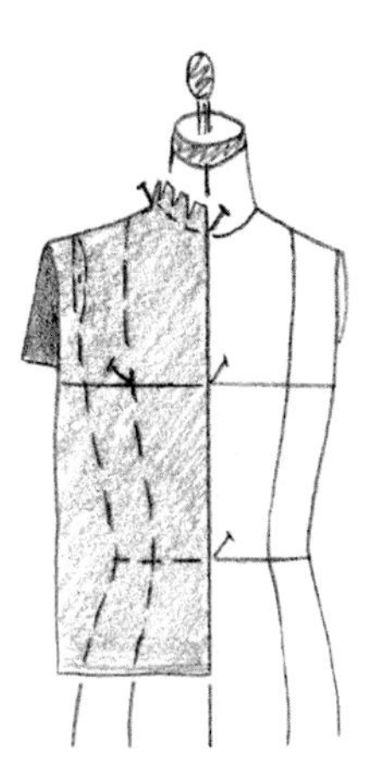

- Cut down to the neckline seam while continuing to smooth around the neck and up to the shoulder seam, being very careful not to clip past the neckline seam and into the body of the garment. (Cut to, but not through. Clipping too aggressively is very easy to do. Think of clipping as if you were to clip only to the intended future stitching line within the seam allowance. If you clip too much you will end up in the body of the garment. If you do clip too far, you can mend a small cut with some masking tape placed on the top and underneath of the area.)
- Place a pin at the shoulder seam/neckline seam intersection.

Draping the Front Panel

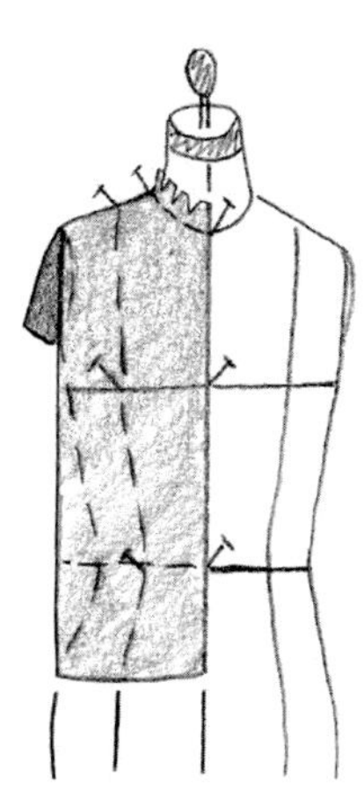

- Smooth the fabric across the upper torso and the shoulder seam to just past the princess seam line on the shoulder seam. Pin at the princess seam line on the shoulder seam.
- Smooth the fabric across the waistline to just past the princess seam line. Pin at the princess seam line on the waistline.
- If necessary, to prevent pull lines at the waistline, clip from the bottom edge of the fabric up to, but not through, the waistline tape on the grainline line. This may not be needed because the distance from the center front to the princess line can be narrow.

Marking the Muslin

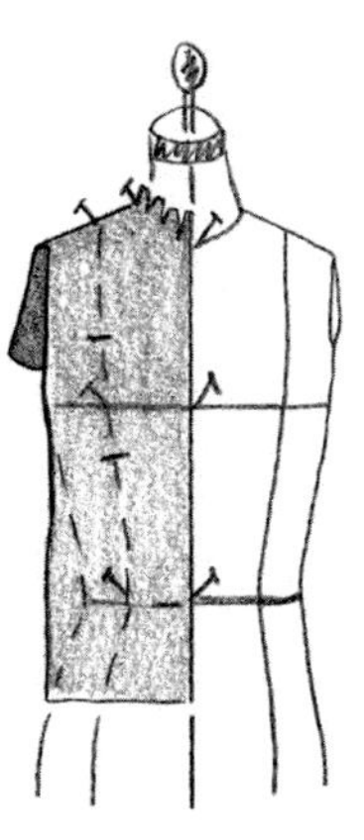

- Draw dashed lines along the center of the twill tape at the waistline, princess line, neckline, and shoulder seam.
- Draw matching notches 2″ (5.1 cm) above and below the bust point making sure that the bust point has been marked.
- Leave the fabric on the dress form, but fold over the excess muslin at the princess line and shoulder seam to allow for draping the side front panel.

Bodice Side Front

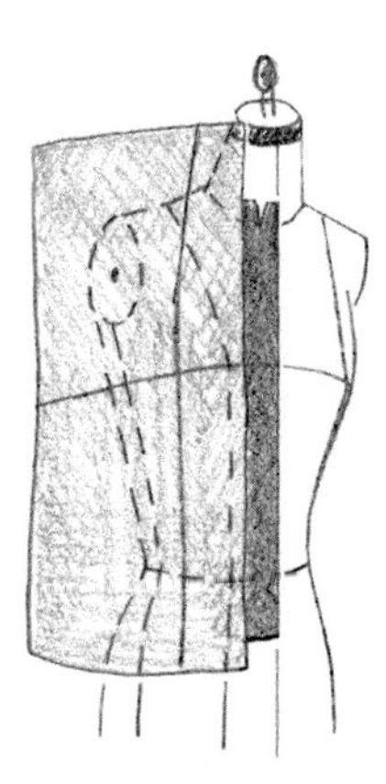

- On your dress form, pin the prepared muslin with the cross-grain line over the bust line tape, and the grainline of the muslin lining up with the center of the side front panel of the dress form. Make sure that there is enough fabric to go up and over the shoulder seam and also have about 3" (7.6 cm) below the waistline tape.
- Place pins at the bust line tape and at the waistline on the straight of grain, making sure that the grainline is vertical and cross-grain is parallel to the floor.

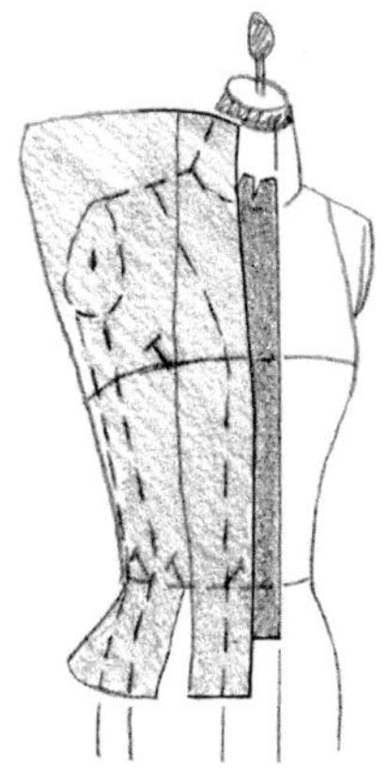

- To prevent pull lines at the waistline, clip from the bottom edge of the fabric up to, but not through, the waistline tape on the grainline line.
- Pin the waistline, smoothing out from the grainline pin toward the side seam, and then from the grainline to the princess line.

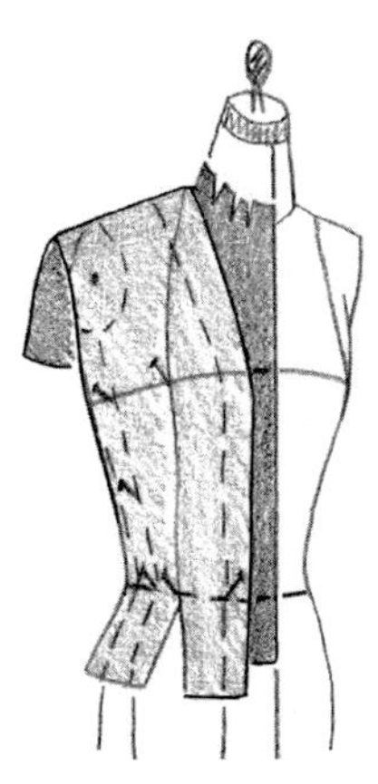

- Pin the side seam smooth from the grainline over, being careful not to alter the straight line of the grainline.

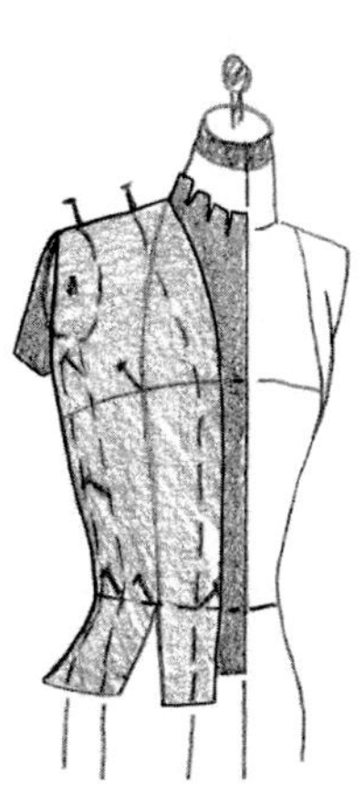

- Pin the armhole area pinching out about ¼" (0.6 cm) at the middle of the arm plate on the ridge to allow for ease placing a pin at the shoulder seam to anchor the ease.
- At the shoulder seam, smooth the excess fabric up, noting that the grainline of the panel will angle toward the neckline.

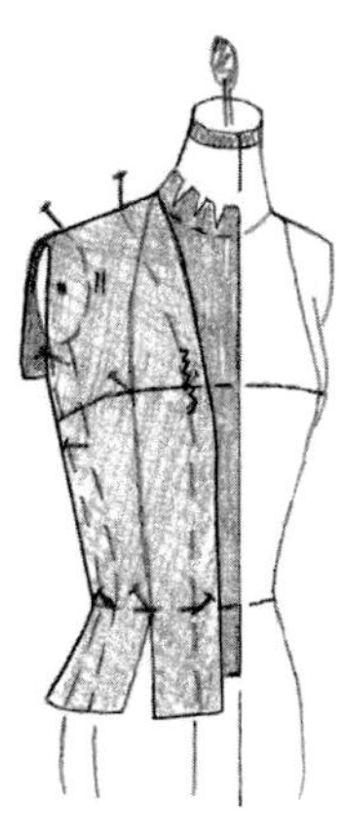

- At the princess seam, smooth the fabric over and pin, noting that there will be some ease at the bust point between the two matching notches.

Bodices

Marking the Muslin

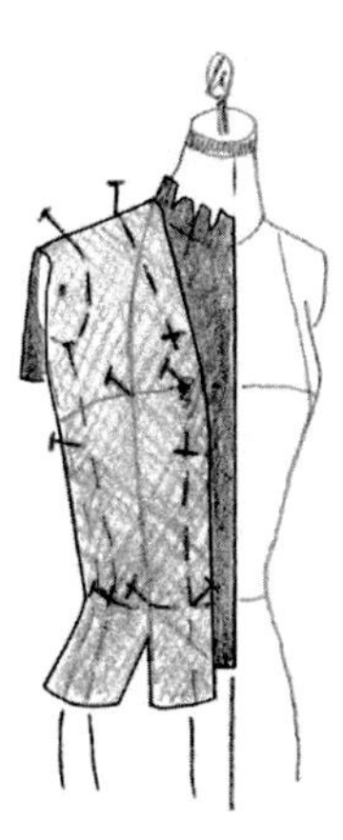

- Draw dashed lines along the center of the twill tape at the waistline, princess line, neckline, and shoulder seam.
- Draw matching notches 2″ (5 cm) above and below the bust point.
- Mark the bust point.
- Draw a dashed line on the ridge around the arm plate of the dress form. This may result in a small armscye but it will be adjusted for ease in the trueing.
- Create cross marks at the side seam where it intersects the waistline and the arm plate.
- Leave the fabric on the dress form, but fold over the excess muslin at the side seam and shoulder seam to allow for draping the side back panel.

Bodice Center Back

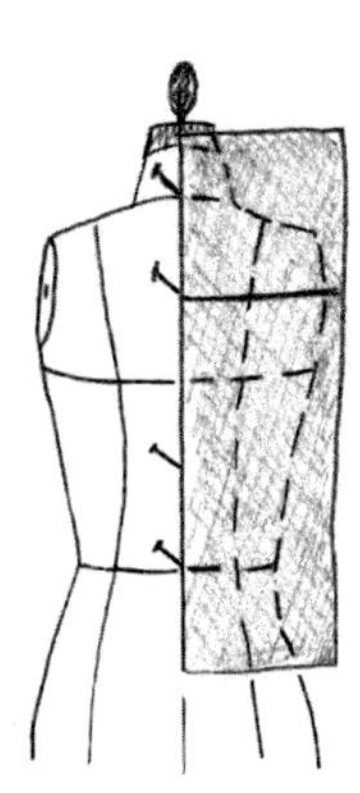

- On your dress form, pin the prepared muslin with the cross-grain line centered over the shoulder blade line, with about 3″–4″ (7.6–10.2 cm) of fabric extending above the neckline seam on the dress form. The fabric should drape over the shoulder seam.
- The center back line of the muslin should line up with the center back of the dress form.
- Place pins along the center back at the neckline, at the shoulder blade level marking, below the bust line tape, and at the waistline.

Neckline

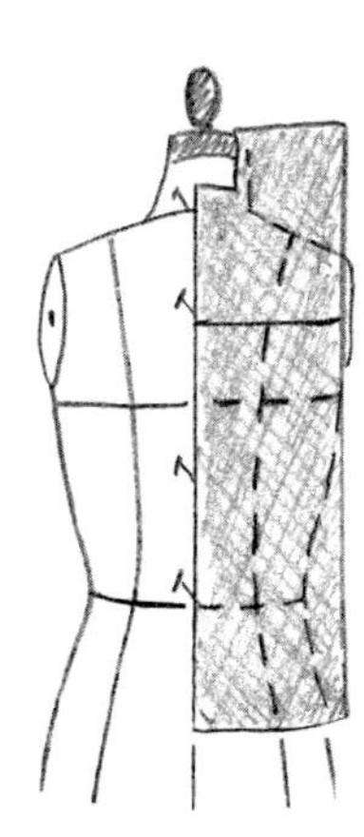

- To smooth around the neckline, make a cut perpendicular to the center back line on the muslin about 1″ (2.5 cm) above the neck seam on the dress form.

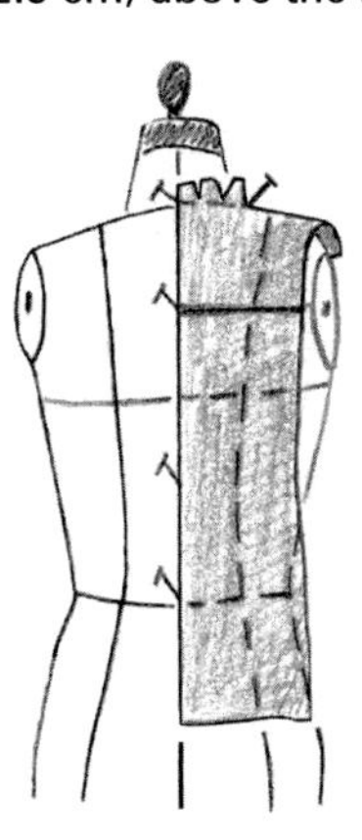

- Cut down to the neckline seam while continuing to smooth around the neck and up to the shoulder seam, being very careful not to clip past the neckline seam and into the body of the garment. (Cut to, but not through. Clipping too aggressively is very easy to do. Think of clipping as if you were to clip only to the intended future stitching line within the seam allowance. If you clip too much you will end up in the body of the garment. If you do clip too far, you can mend a small cut with some masking tape placed on the top and underneath of the area.)
- Place a pin at the shoulder seam/neckline seam intersection.

Draping the Back Panel

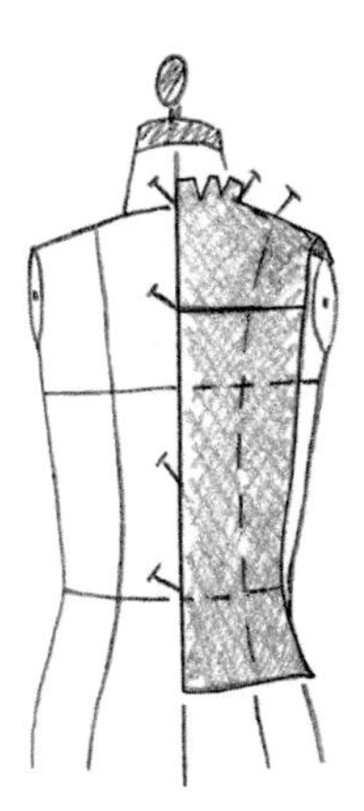

- Smooth the fabric across the upper torso and the shoulder seam to just past the princess seam line on the shoulder seam. Pin at the princess seam line on the shoulder seam.

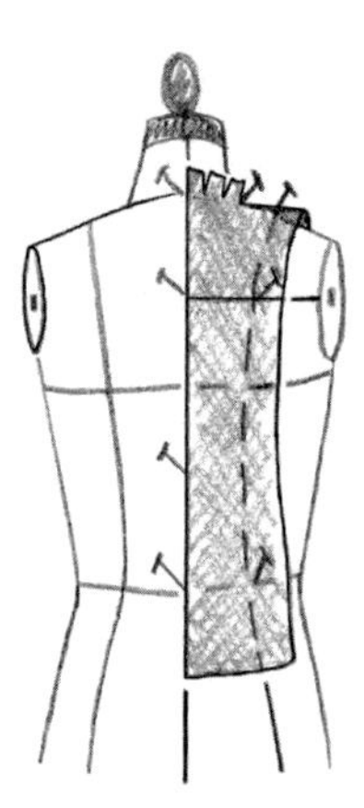

- Smooth the fabric across the waistline to just past the princess seam. Pin at the princess seam line on the waistline.
- If necessary, to prevent pull lines at the waistline, clip from the bottom edge of the fabric up to, but not through, the waistline tape on the grainline line. This may not be needed because the distance from the center back to the princess line can be narrow.
- Smooth the fabric across the dress form toward the princess seam line, pinning at the shoulder blade line.

Marking the Muslin

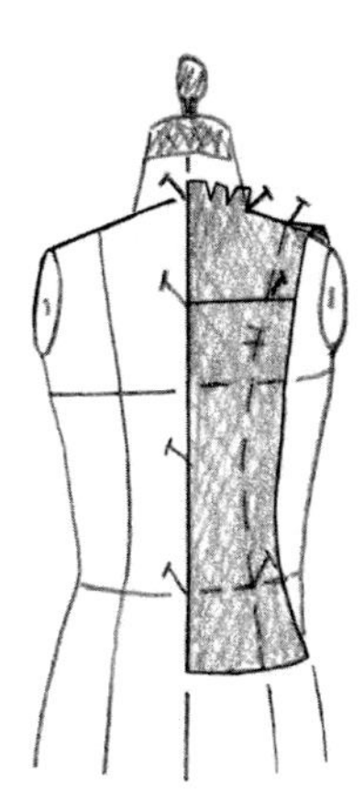

- Draw dashed lines along the center of the twill tape at waistline, princess line, neckline, and shoulder seam.

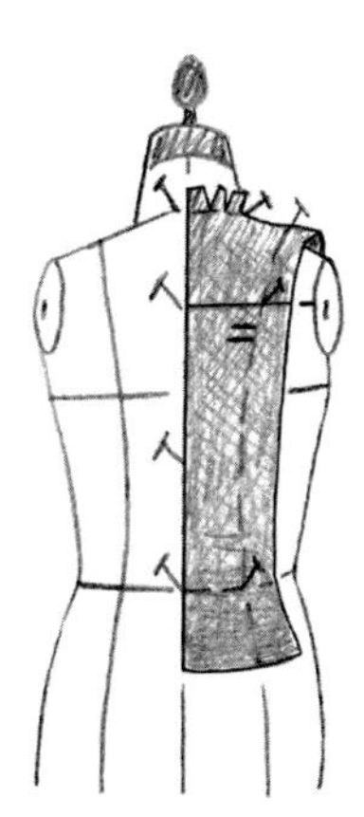

- Draw a double matching notch at 1″ (2.5 cm) below the shoulder blade line on the princess line.
- Leave the fabric on the dress form, but fold over the excess muslin at the princess line and shoulder seam to allow for draping the side back panel.

Bodice Side Back

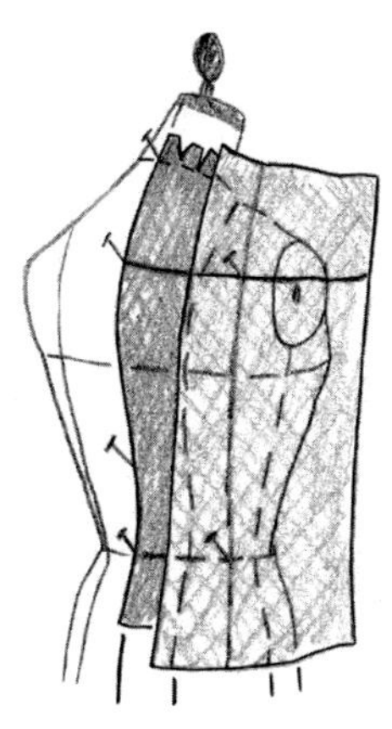

- On your dress form, pin the prepared muslin with the cross-grain line centered over the shoulder blade line and the grainline of the muslin lining up with the center of the side back of the dress form. Make sure that there is enough fabric to go up and over the shoulder seam and also have about 3" (7.6 cm) below the waistline tape.

- Place pins along the shoulder blade line and at the waistline on the straight of grain, making sure that the grainline is vertical and cross-grain is parallel to the floor.

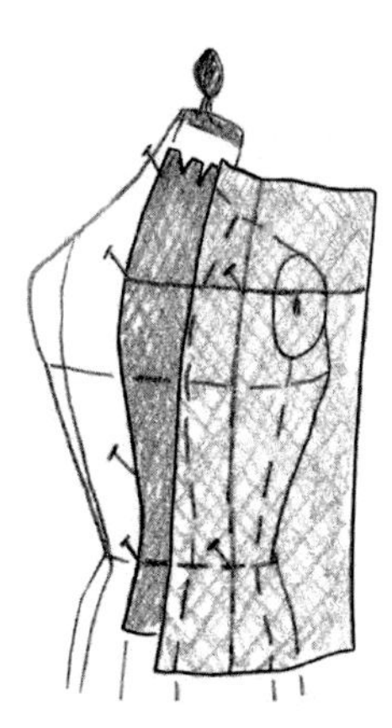

- To prevent pull lines at the waistline, clip from the bottom edge of the fabric up to, but not through, the waistline tape on the grainline line.

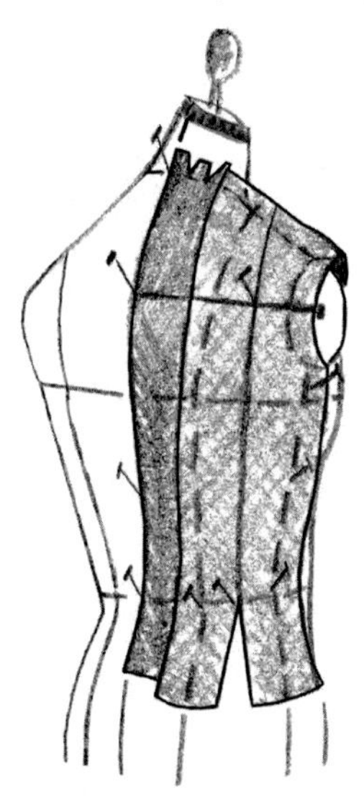

- Pin the waistline, smoothing out from the grainline pin toward the side seam, and then from the grainline to the princess line.
- Pin the side seam smooth from the grainline over, being careful not to alter the straight line of the grainline.
- Pin the armhole area on the ridge.

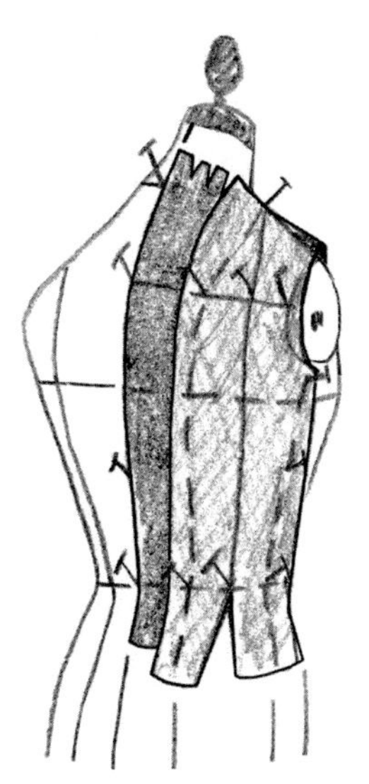

- At the shoulder seam, smooth the excess fabric up, noting that the grainline of the panel will angle toward the neckline.
- At the princess seam, smooth the fabric over and pin.

Marking the Muslin

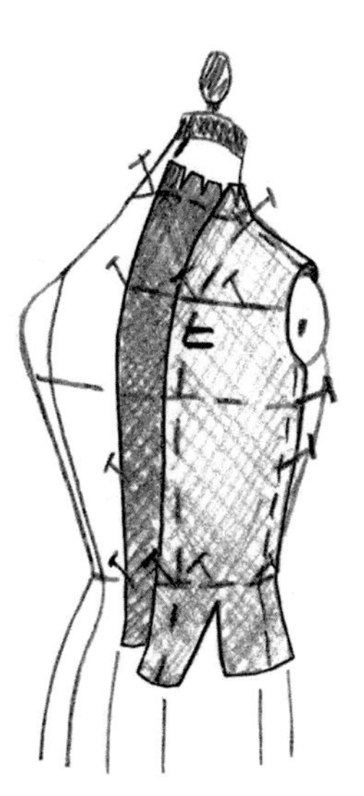

- Draw dashed lines along the center of the twill tape at waistline, princess line, neckline, and shoulder seam.
- Draw a double matching notch at 1″ (2.5 cm) below the shoulder blade line on the princess line.
- Draw a dashed line on the ridge around the arm plate of the dress form. This may result in a small armscye but it will be adjusted for ease in the trueing.
- Create cross marks at the side seam where it intersects the waistline and the arm plate.
- Add matching notches on the side seam, and shoulder seam. You can carefully use a felt tip type marker to make your matching marks by pulling the fabric away from the dress form and letting the marker create a mark on the front

of the garment. Let the marker bleed through to the back of the garment. DO NOT MARK THE DRESS FORM.

– True all panels and check for fit.

Trueing the Princess Bodice

(On the actual bodice drape)

Trueing the Princess Bodice is very similar to trueing the Basic Bodice, but without any darts. As described previously, the darts were removed in favor of creating a seam line.

After removing the bodice from the dress form, with front, side front, side back, and back pieces separate, and all pins removed, lay the fabric flat on your table.

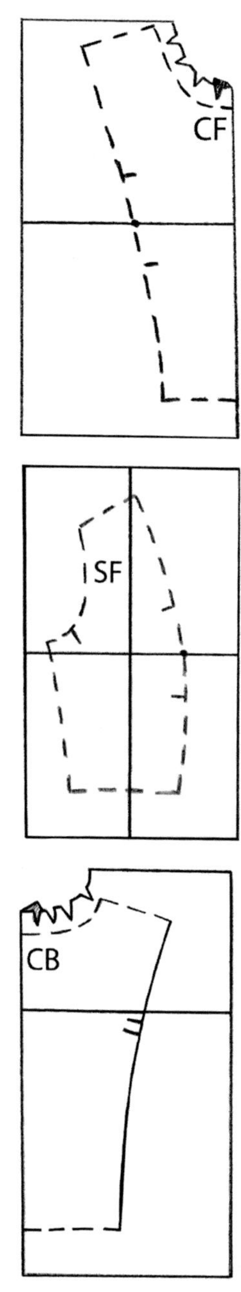

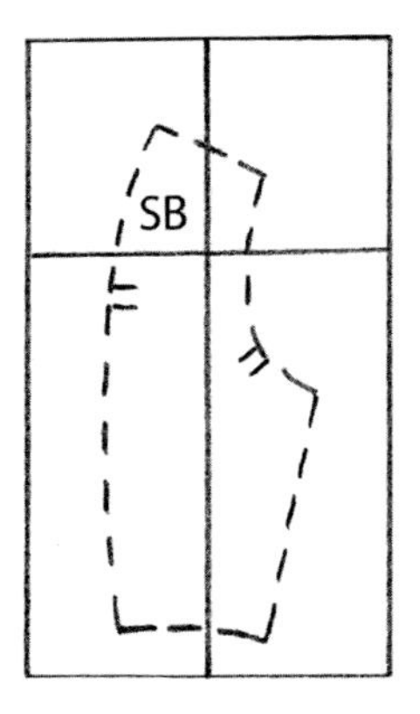

- The following locations require a 90-degree angle:
- CF neck for ¼″ (0.6 cm)
- CF waist for ½″ (1.3 cm)
- CB neck for 1″ (2.5 cm)
- CB waist for 1″ (2.5 cm)

  (These 90-degree angle lines that are perpendicular to the CF and CB allow for a smooth curve when making a full garment. Otherwise you will end up with either a V shape or a ^ shape at those points.)
- Mark the front armhole with a single notch at 2.5″ (6.4 cm) from armscye/side seam intersection.
- Mark the back armhole with a double notch at 2.5″ (6.4 cm) from armscye/side seam intersection.

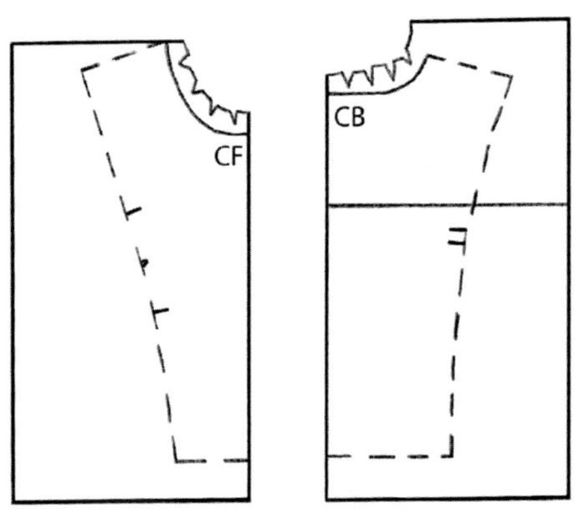

- For the necklines, use your curved ruler and connect your markings making sure that the 90-degree lines at CF and CB are smoothly blended.

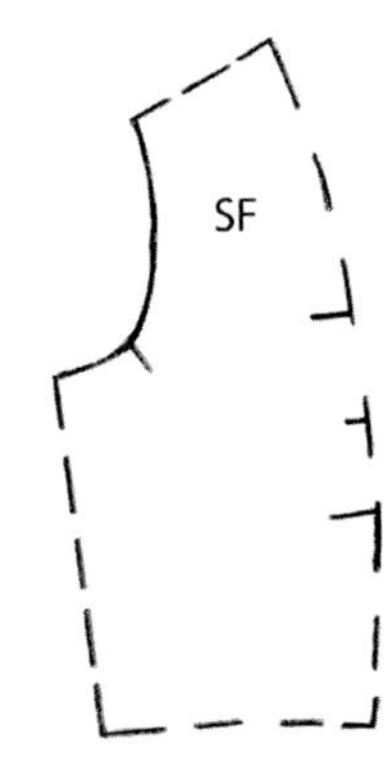

- For the front armscye, use your 12″ curved ruler and connect your shoulder point, your armscye ridge lines, and side seam/armhole mark.
- Mark the armscye with a single notch at 2.5″ (6.4 cm) up from the armscye/side seam intersection.

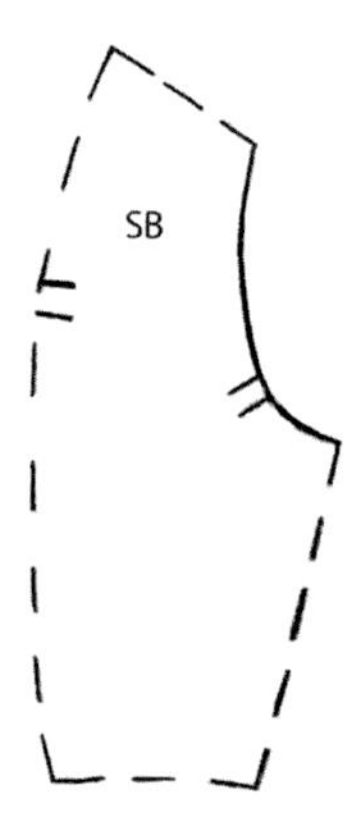

- For the back armscye, use your 12″ curved ruler and connect your shoulder point, your armscye ridge lines, and side seam/armhole mark.
- Mark the armscye with a double notch at 2.5″ (6.4 cm) up from the armscye/side seam intersection.

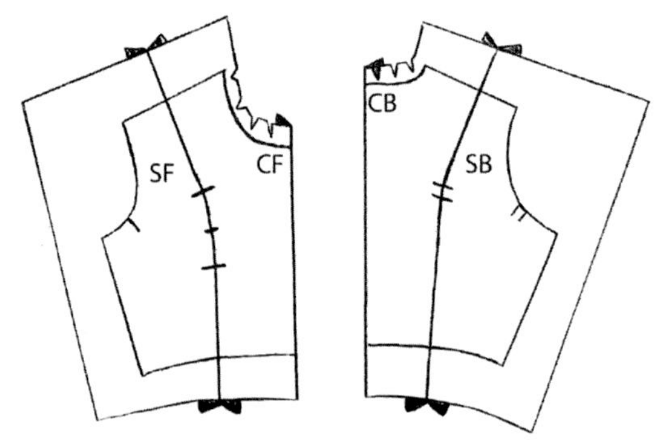

- For the front shoulder seams, pin the front and side front pieces together along the princess line, lining up the matching notches and bust point. Using your straight ruler, draw a line from the neckline/shoulder seam point to the armhole/shoulder seam point.
- For the back shoulder seams, pin the back and side back pieces together along the princess line, lining up the matching notches. Using your straight ruler, draw a line from the neckline/shoulder seam point to the armhole/shoulder seam point and back.
- For the front and back waistlines, and using the pinned draped pieces, draw your waistline using your curved ruler with the straight edge at the center front and center back lines. Draw a line from the center front/waistline to the side seam/waistline, and the center back/waistline to the side seam/waistline marks.

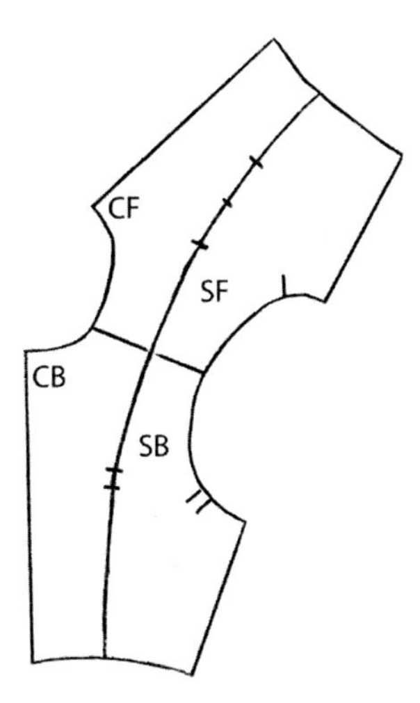

- You will need to check that the front and back shoulder seams are trued by pinning the front/side front pinned pieces to the back/side back pinned pieces. Once pinned make sure that the neckline, the princess line, and the armscye match.
- With the front and back shoulder seams still pinned together, check that there is a smooth line across the top of the armscye at the shoulder seam and that the armscye does not create a point or "wing" out.

Adding Ease

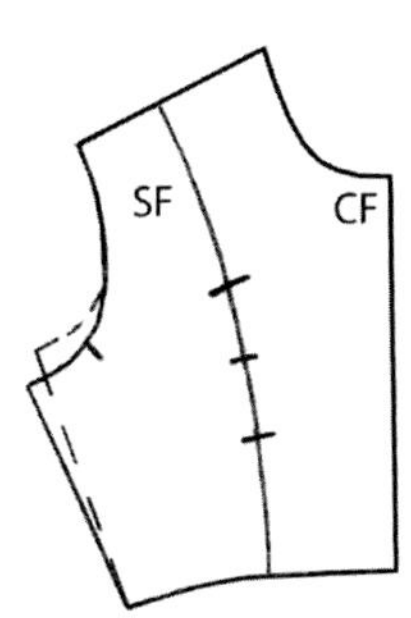

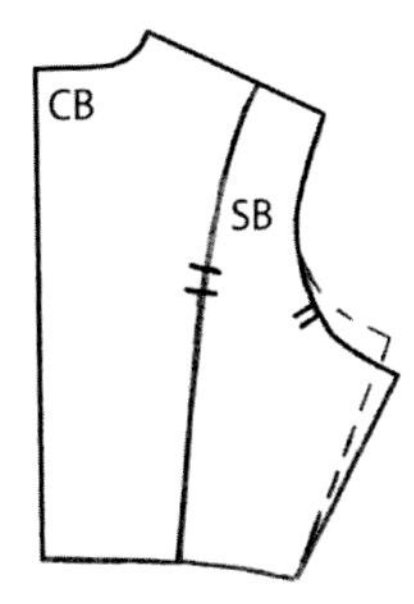

- To add ease to the side seams at the bust line, you will first need to drop the front and back side seams down 1" (2.5 cm) from the armscye, and then bump them out ½" (1.3 cm).
- Using your original total armscye measurement from your person's measurements, check that the total armscye measurement you have created on your draping is about 1–2" (2.5–5.1 cm) larger than the person's measurement. This is to allow room in the armscye for the arm to fit through and not inhibit movement. You should measure the front and back pieces of your pattern individually by walking the edge of your 18" grid ruler around the armscye. Then add these numbers together to get your pattern's total armscye measurement. If necessary, expand the armscye by dropping the front and back and bumping it out more than the original ease you added. Keep in mind that you can always mark and cut away the armscye in the fitting of the mock-up if it is too snug.

- From these new points, draw your new side seams down to the original waistline marks.

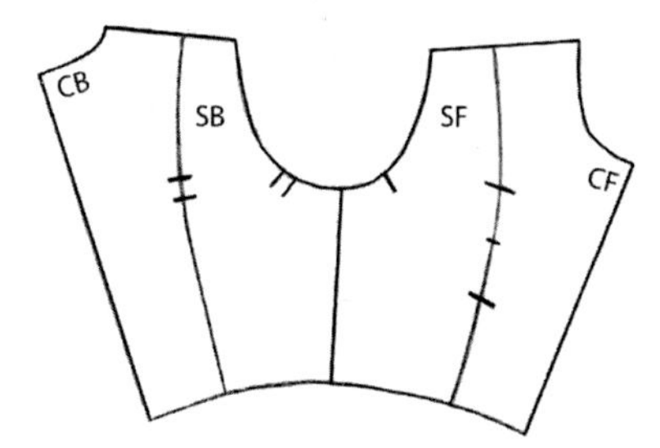

- You will need to true the entire waistline curve by pinning your side seams together.
- Your waistline from CF to CB should be a smooth curve, as should the curve in the armscye.
- If either is not a smooth curve, you will need to adjust the curves at the side seam. If one of the side seams is longer than the other, you will need to make adjustments to either one or both of the side seams. Look at the armscye and waistline and judge which to alter based on the general shape of the curves. If it is still not clear which one to adjust, then place the muslin back on the dress form to determine which is more accurate.

Check List for Fit and Correct Amount of Ease

- Pin your trued muslin together, along princess lines, side seam, and shoulder seam and place back on dress form.

Ease Checklist

- At side seam/armhole intersection = ½″ (1.3 cm) per front and back (1″ (2.5 cm) total per side)
- At bust front = ⅛″– ¼″ (0.3–0.6 cm)
- At back shoulder blade = ⅛″– ¼″ (0.3–0.6 cm)
- At waist = ¼″ (0.6 cm) per front and back (½″ [1.3 cm] total per side)

After Trueing

Fit Check

- Pin the bodice on the dress form at shoulder/neckline, shoulder/armhole, side seam/armhole, center front/neckline and center back/neckline.
- Grainlines should hang straight.
- Shoulder seams should align with each other and darts should align.
- Side seams should be the same length.
- The armhole is a smooth fat oval shape.
- The bodice should hang straight without twisting or pulling.
- Side seam of draped bodice aligns with side seam of dress form without tilting.
- Side seam of draped bodice lays flat and smooth.
- Princess lines of the bodice should fall over the princess lines of the dress form.

How to Draft a Basic Bodice

These instructions were designed to accommodate all figures and bust cup sizes. The accommodations for the Larger Bust Cup sizes remove the gap that often occurs at the armscye.

Measurements Needed:

Neck:	Shoulder to Bust Point:	
Bust:	Shoulder to Waist Front:	Shoulder to Waist Back:
Underbust:	Across Shoulder Front:	Across Shoulder Back:
Waist:	Across Armscye Front:	Across Armscye Back:
Shoulder Seam:	Shoulder Slope Front:	Shoulder Slope Back:
Bust Point to Bust Point:	Neck to Waist Front:	Neck to Waist Back:
	Bust Front:	Bust Back:

*For visual clarity, some lines will be removed from the diagrams after they are no longer needed. These lines will remain on your bodice sloper. It is not necessary to erase the lines on your sloper.

Basic Front Sloper

- Paper size = Height of the paper should allow for Shoulder to Waist Front measurement + 9″ (22.9 cm), and width should allow for ¼ total bust measurement + 6″ (15.2 cm).

To Create the Center Front of the Bodice

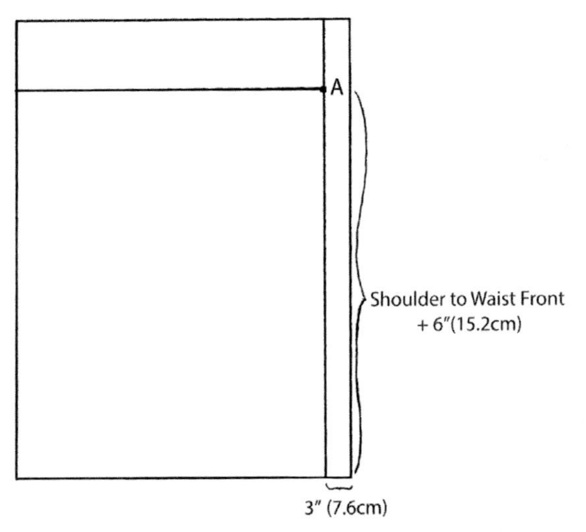

- Using your straight ruler or T-square, draw a line 3″ (7.6 cm) in from the right edge of the paper from the top all the way to the bottom.
- Measure up from the bottom of the page along this line and mark point A at the Shoulder to Waist Front measurement + 6″ (15.2 cm).
- From A, draw a horizontal line across the width of the paper perpendicular to the vertical line.

To Create the Shoulder Seam of the Bodice

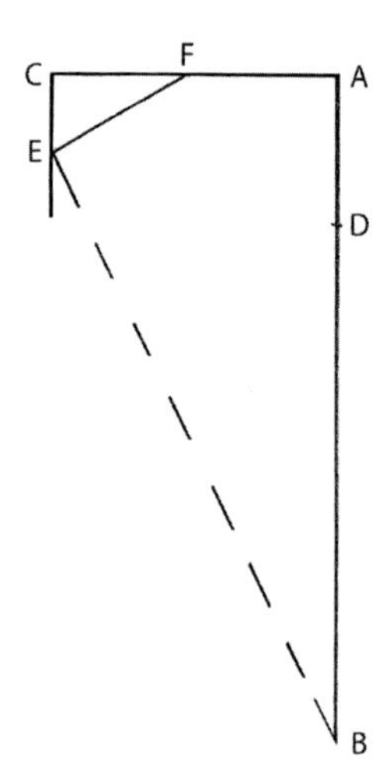

- From A, measure down on the vertical line and mark a new point B at the length of your Shoulder to Waist Front measurement.
- Draw a horizontal line to the left of A, and mark a new point C where C = ½ Across Shoulders Front measurement.
- From C, draw a vertical line down about 6″ (15.2 cm) in length perpendicular to the A-C line.
- From B, mark a new point D on the A-B line, where D = the Neck to Waist Front measurement.
- Using your straight ruler, and starting at point B, angle your ruler diagonally toward the line extending down from C. Mark new point E where your Shoulder Slope Front measurement intersects the line from C.
- From E, angle the ruler diagonally toward the A-C line and measure to new point F, where E-F = the length of the Shoulder Seam.
- Connect E to F with a straight line.

To Create the Neckline of the Bodice

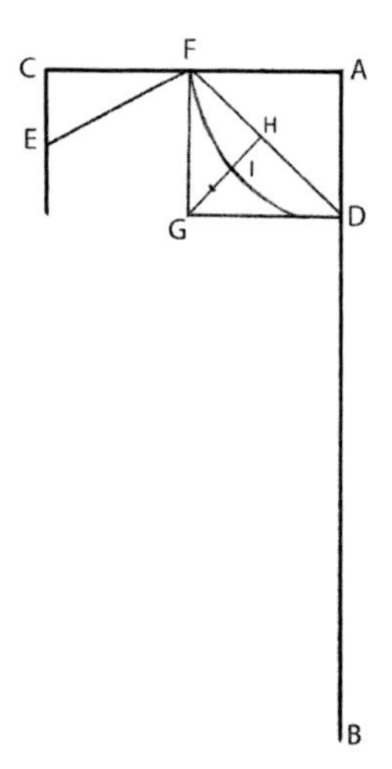

- From F, draw a vertical line down from the top horizontal line A-C. Then from D, draw a perpendicular line from line A-B. Where they connect, mark new point G.
- Connect F to D with a diagonal line.
- Draw a line perpendicular to the F-D line to point G.
- Where the perpendicular line intersects the F-D line, mark a new point H.
- Measure the G-H line and divide it into 3 equal sections. The closest point to H is the new point I.
- Using a curved ruler, connect D-I-F, making sure that at point D there is a ¼″ (0.6 cm) perpendicular line so that the neckline is round and not pointed when matched with the other front half.

To Create the Side Seam of the Bodice

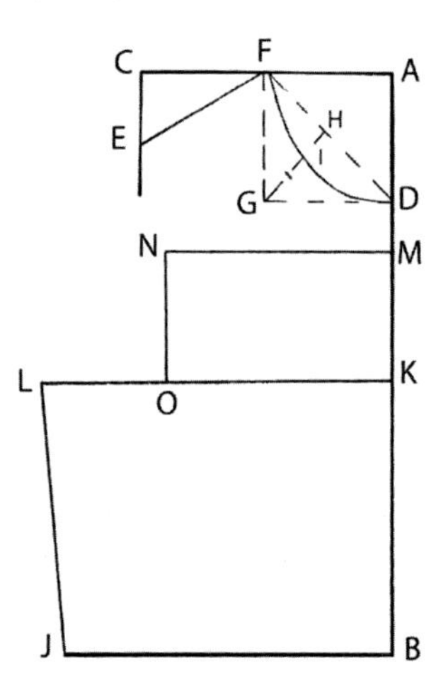

- From B, draw a horizontal line across from the A-B line to new point J, where J = ¼ total bust measurement + ¼″ (0.6 cm) of ease.
- From A, on A-B line, mark new point K where K = ⅙ total bust measurement + 3″ (7.6 cm).

- From K, draw a horizontal line across to new point L, where K-L = ½ Bust Front measurement +¼" (0.6 cm) ease.
- Draw a line to connect points L to J.
- Measure the distance between points A and K, divide this in half, and mark new point M.
- From M, draw a horizontal line across to new point N where N = ½ Across Armscye Front measurement.
- From N, draw a vertical line down to the K-L line. Mark new point O where the line from N connects to the K-L line.

To Create the Armscye of the Bodice

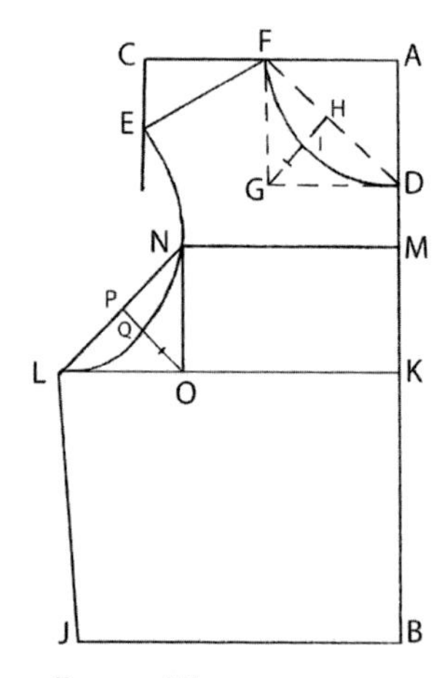

- Connect N and L with a diagonal line.
- Draw a line perpendicular to the N-L line to point O.
- Where the perpendicular line intersects the N-L line, mark a new point P.
- Measure the O-P line and divide it into 3 equal sections. The closest point to P is the new point Q.
- To create your armscye, use your curved ruler and draw a line from point E to point N.
- Still using your curved ruler, draw a line connecting N-Q-L to make a continuous curve for the armscye.

To Create the Bust Point of the Bodice

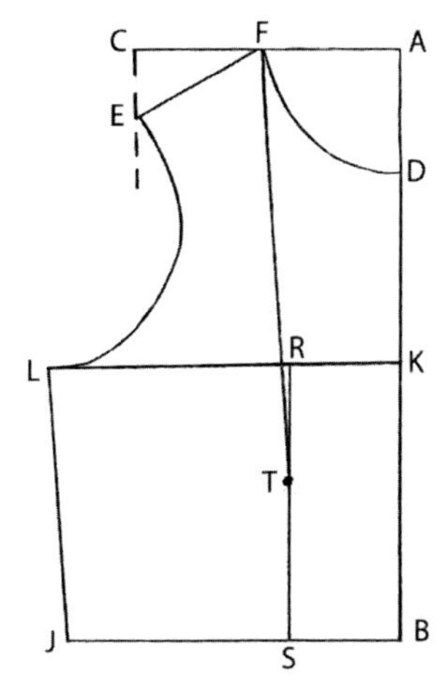

- Measure from K and mark new point R on K-L line where R = ½ Bust Point to Bust Point measurement.
- From R, draw a vertical line to the B-J line and mark the new point S where it intersects the B-J line.

- Using your straight ruler and starting from point F, extend down to the R-S line to new point T, where F-T = Shoulder to Bust Point measurement. T is the bust point of your bodice.

=This is the stopping point for the Bodice Front. We will continue working with it after the Bodice Back has been drafted. There are measurements from the Bodice Back that are necessary to complete the Bodice Front.

Basic Back Sloper

- Paper size = Height of the paper should allow for Shoulder to Waist Back measurement + 9″ (22.9 cm), and width should allow for ¼ total bust measurement + 6″ (15.2 cm).

To Create the Center Back of your Bodice

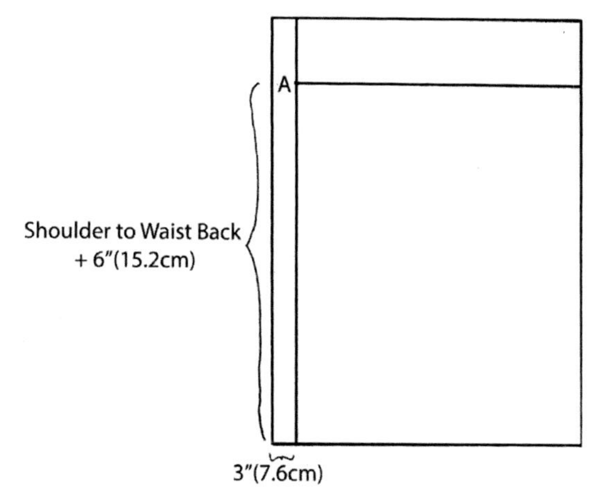

- Using your straight ruler, or T-square, draw a line 3" (7.6 cm) in from the left edge of the paper from the top edge all the way to the bottom edge.
- Measure up from the bottom of the page along this line and mark point A at the Shoulder to Waist Back measurement + 6" (15.2 cm).
- From A, draw a horizontal line across the width of the paper perpendicular to the vertical line.

To Create the Shoulder Seam of the Bodice

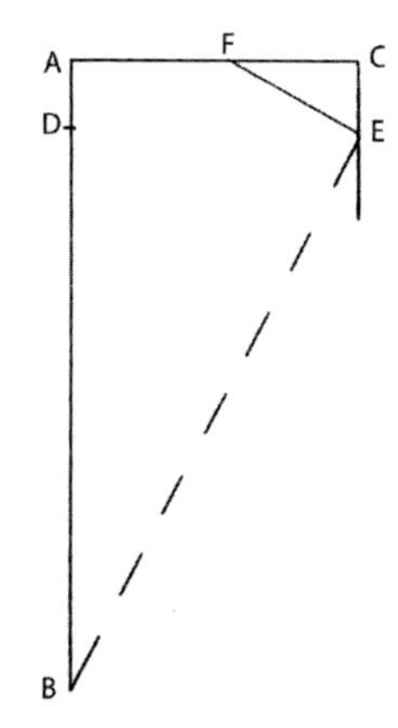

- From A, measure down on the vertical line and mark a new point B, where B = the Shoulder to Waist Back measurement.

- Draw a horizontal line to the right of A, and mark a new point C where C = ½ Across Shoulders Back measurement.
- From C, draw a line straight down about 6" (15.2 cm) in length perpendicular to the A-C line.
- From B, mark a new point D on the A-B line, where D = the Neck to Waist Back measurement.
- Using your straight ruler, and starting at point B, angle your ruler diagonally toward the line extending down from C. Mark new point E where your Shoulder Slope Back measurement intersects the line from C.
- Starting at point E, angle the ruler diagonally toward the A-C line and measure from E to new point F, where E-F = the length of the Shoulder Seam.
- Connect E to F with a straight line.

To Create the Neckline of the Bodice

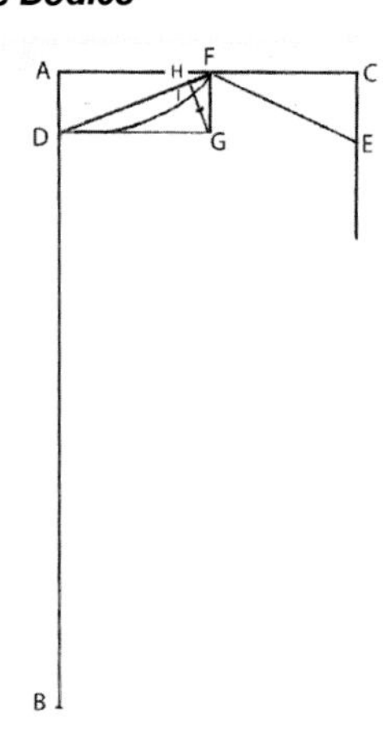

- From F, draw a vertical line down from the top horizontal line A-C, then from D, draw a perpendicular line from line A-B. Where they connect, mark new point G.
- Connect F to D with a diagonal line.
- Draw a line perpendicular to the F-D line to point G.
- Where the perpendicular line intersects the F-D line, mark a new point H.
- Measure the G-H line and divide it into 3 equal sections. The closest point to H is the new point I.
- Using a curved ruler, connect D-I-F, making sure that at point D there is a ½" (1.3 cm) perpendicular line so that the neckline is round and not pointed when matched with the other back half.

To Create the Side Seam of the Bodice

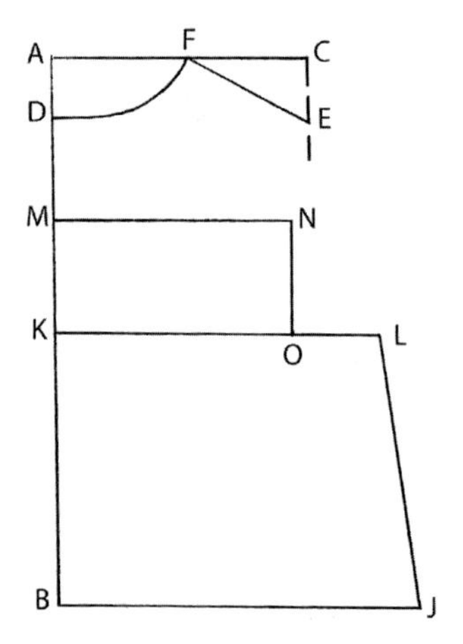

- From B, draw a horizontal line across from the A-B line to new point J, where J = ¼ total bust measurement + ¼″ (0.6 cm) for ease.
- From A, on A-B line, mark new point K, where K = ⅙ total bust measurement + 3″ (7.6 cm).
- From K, draw a horizontal line across to new point L, where K-L = ½ Bust Back measurement + ¼″ (0.6 cm) ease.
- Draw a line to connect points L to J.
- Measure the distance between points A and K, divide this in half, and mark new point M.
- From M, draw a horizontal line across to new point N where N = ½ Across Armscye Back measurement
- From N, draw a vertical line down to the K-L line. Mark new point O where the line from N connects to the K-L line.

To Create the Armscye of the Bodice

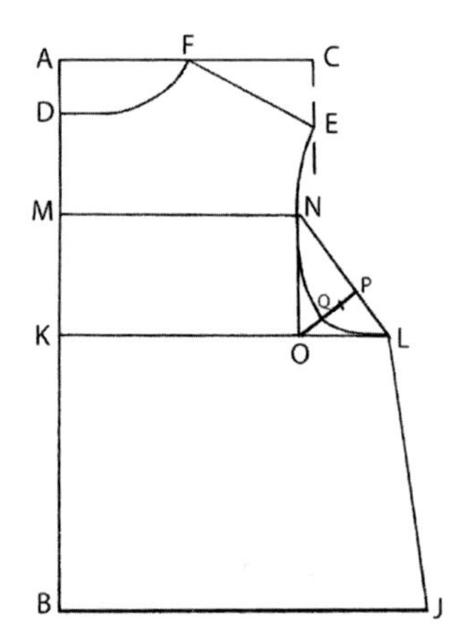

- Connect N and L with a diagonal line.
- Draw a line perpendicular to the N-L line to point O.
- Where the perpendicular line intersects the N-L line, mark a new point P.
- Measure the O-P line and divide it into 3 equal sections. The closest point to O is the new point Q.

- To create your armscye, use your curved ruler and draw a curved line from point E to point N.
- Still using your curved ruler, draw a line connecting N-Q-L to make a continuous curve for the armscye.

=If the Bodice Front needs alterations, then this is the stopping point for the Bodice Back for now. If the Bodice Front does not need alterations, then you will continue ahead with the Bodice Back in the section "ADDING THE WAIST DART TO THE BODICE BACK".

<u>=To determine whether the Bodice Front needs alterations, you must determine the Bust Size Differential.</u>

- Bust Size Differential: if the bust measurement is 6" (15.2 cm) or greater than the underbust measurement, then you will need to continue with the following directions for the Larger Bust Cup size alterations:
- If the bust size differential is less than 6", then skip ahead to: **"ADDING THE WAIST DART TO THE BODICE BACK"**.

<u>*LARGER BUST CUP SIZE ALTERATIONS FOR BODICE FRONT:</u>**

On the Original Bodice Front Sloper:

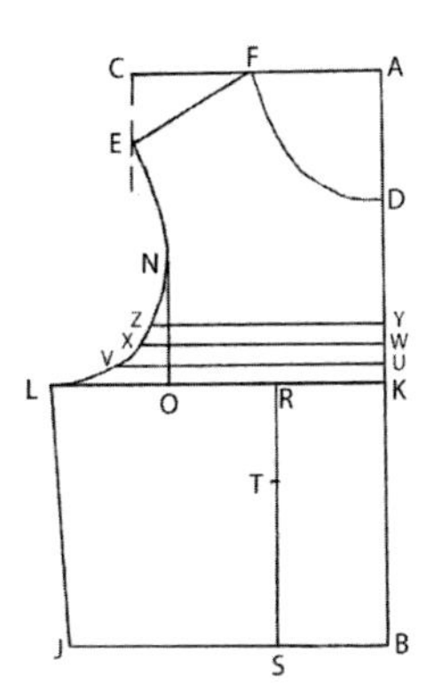

- From A, measure down ⅐ of the total bust measurement + 3" (7.6 cm), and mark a new point U on the A-B line.
- From U, draw a horizontal line going to the armscye, and where the line and armscye intersect, mark a new point V.
- From A, measure down ⅛ of the total bust measurement + 3" (7.6 cm), and mark new point W on the A-B line.
- From W, draw a horizontal line going to the armscye, and where the line and armscye intersect, mark a new point X.
- **If the Total Bust Measurement is larger than 39" (99 cm), then also:**
- From A, measure down ⅑ of the total bust measurement +3" (7.6 cm) and mark new point Y on the A-B line.
- From Y, draw a horizontal line going to the armscye, and where the line and armscye intersect, mark a new point Z.

TO ALTER THE BODICE FOR LARGER CUP SIZES:

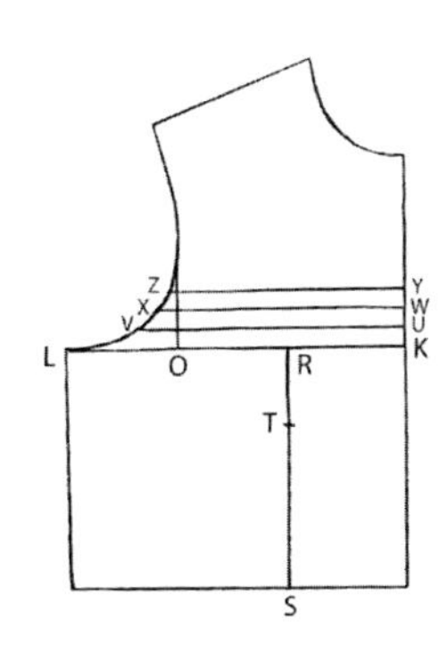

- Make a copy of the sloper and transfer the labels for the following points: Bust Point (point T), and lines N-O, L-K, U-V, W-X, (and Y-Z, if drawn).
- Cut out the Bodice Front.
- Place the sloper pattern on a new sheet of paper, leaving room around the original for waistline and side seam alterations.

- Pin the original down with a pushpin placed through the bust point and additional push pins to anchor the sloper while you trace. Trace the waistline, up the center front, around the neckline, and then across the shoulder seam, stopping at the armscye.

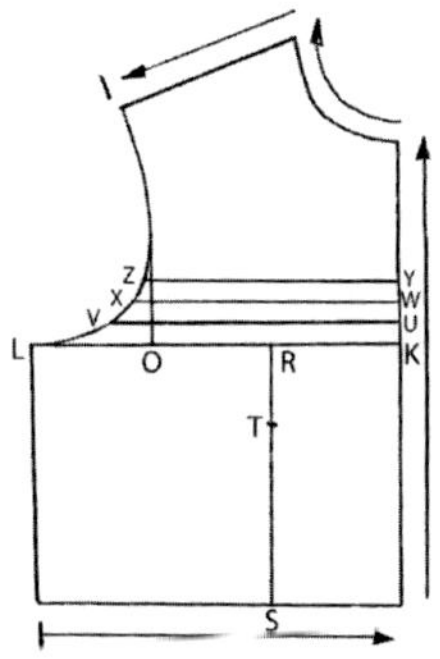

- Trace the armscye from the outer shoulder seam point to point X (if the bust measurement is less than 39" [99 cm]), or to point Z (if the bust measurement is more than 39" [99 cm]) and stop.

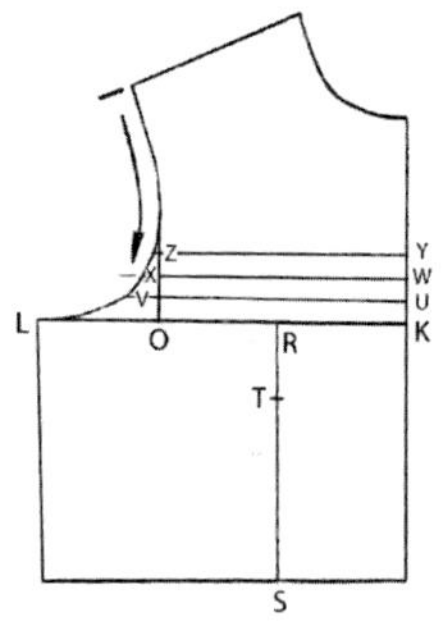

- From X (or Z), draw a line extending out 3" (7.6 cm) from O-X (or O-Z depending on which point you need to use based upon the previous instructions).

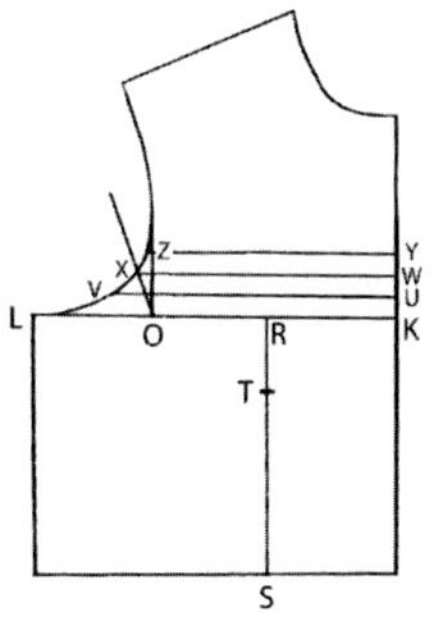

- Keeping your pushpin at the bust point, remove the other push pins and then pivot the bodice *clockwise* so that point V lands on the extended O-X (or O-Z) line.
- Finish tracing the rest of the armscye, but do not trace the side seam.
- Remove the original sloper from the new tracing.

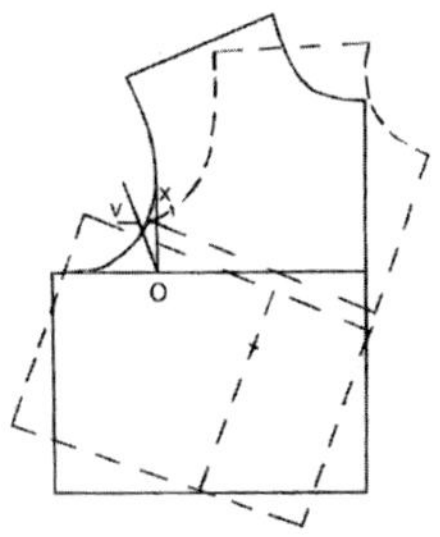

- There is likely to be a gap in the armscye line, which you will need to close with a curved line freehand.

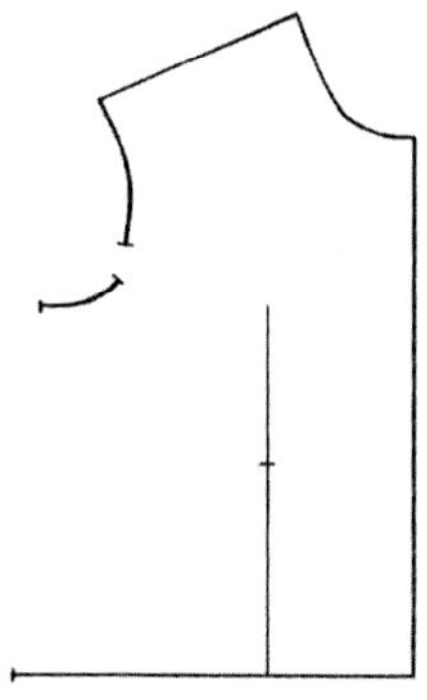

- Draw a line connecting the armscye to the waistline.
- Draw a new bust line starting at the new armscye point connecting to the center front line. This line should be drawn perpendicular to the center front line. (It may go across the bottom of your armscye.)
- From the original sloper, transfer line R-S, and bust point T to the new sloper.

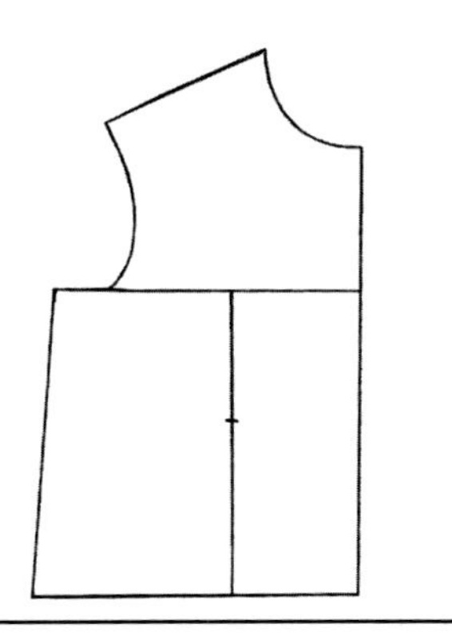

=This is the stopping point for the Bodice Front with Larger Cup Sizes. We will continue working with it after the Bodice Back has had its dart added. There are measurements from the Bodice Back that are necessary to complete the Bodice Front.

Adding the Waist Dart to the Bodice Back

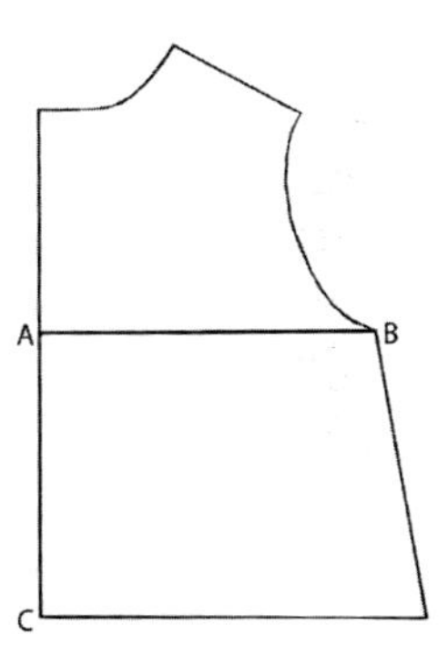

- Cut out the Bodice Back and trace it onto a new piece of paper, but do not transfer the letters (you will be labeling the new sloper differently). Leave at least 3" (7.6 cm) of space around on the new the paper.
- From the original sloper, transfer the bust line to the new sloper (formerly line K-L).
- Mark point A at Center Back Bust line, B at Armscye and Side Seam point, and C at the Center Back and Waistline point.

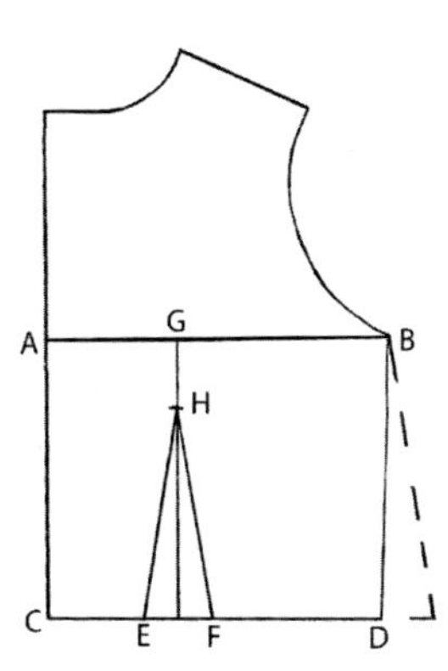

- From C, mark new point D on the waistline where D = ¼ waist measurement + 1″ (2.5 cm) for the dart +¼″ (0.6 cm) for ease.
- Using your straight ruler, draw a line from B to D.
- To the right of C, mark new point E on the waistline at 3″ (7.6 cm).
- To the right of E, measure over 1″ (2.5 cm) to new point F.
- Find the center of the dart on the waistline and draw a vertical line up to the bust line A-B and mark new point G where the lines intersect.
- For the dart tip location, from G, measure down 1″ (2.5 cm) and mark new point H. This is the vanishing point of your dart.
- Connect the dart legs by drawing straight lines from H to E and H to F.

=This is the stopping point for the Bodice Back, but keep it available to take measurements from.

Adding Darts to the Bodice Front

Waist Dart

- Make a copy of the Front Bodice sloper on a new sheet of paper leaving room for waistline and side seam darts. Transfer and label the Bust Point (point T), and transfer the lines for K-L, and R-S but do not label the lines.

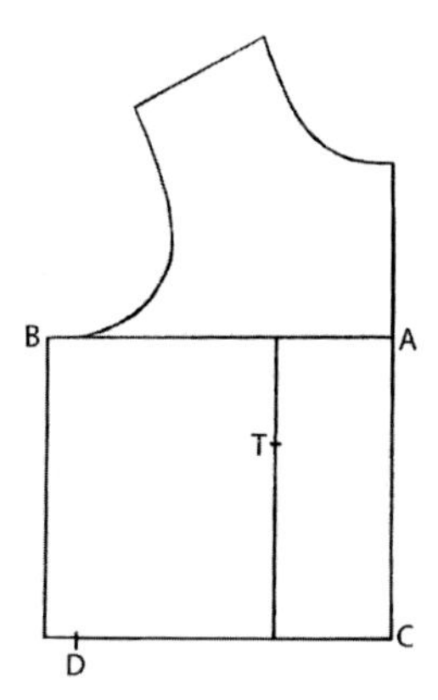

- On your new Front sloper, mark new points: A at Center Front Bust line, B at armscye and side seam point, C at the center front and waistline point, but keep point T as your Bust Point.
- From C, mark new point D on the waistline where D = ¼ waist measurement + 1½″ (3.8 cm) for dart +¼″ (0.6 cm) of ease.

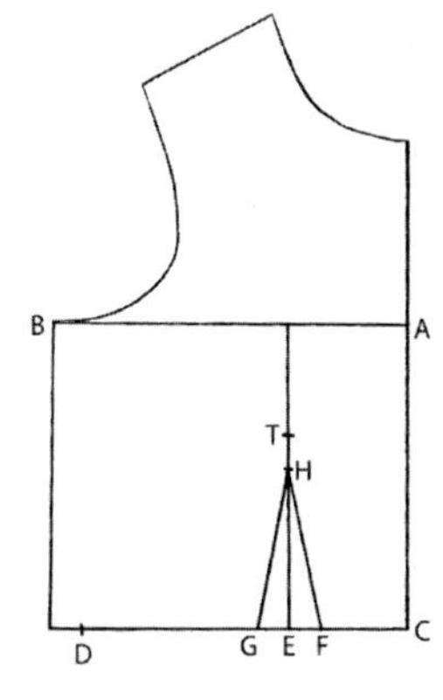

- Mark new point E on the waistline at the intersection of the bust point line, formerly the R-S line.
- To the right of E, measure over ¾" (1.9 cm) and mark new point F, then to the left of E, measure ¾" (1.9 cm) and mark new point G.
- For the dart tip location, from the bust point T, measure down on the bust point line 1½" (3.8 cm), and mark new point H. This is the vanishing point of your dart.
- Connect dart legs by drawing straight lines from H to F and H to G.

Side Seam Dart

- To determine the size of the side dart, measure the Back Side Seam and subtract that number from the Front Side Seam measurement.
- Front Side Seam – Back Side Seam = ______________
- The difference between the measurements is the measurement of the front side seam dart.

*(See note below for Side Seam Adjustment.)

***SIDE SEAM ADJUSTMENT:**

- **If the difference between the front side seam and the back side seam is <u>less than ¾" (1.9 cm)</u>, then the front side seam needs to be extended because you will not be able to create a usable dart for your bodice. Continue with the following instructions.**
- **If the difference between the front side seam and the back side seam is <u>greater than ¾" (1.9 cm)</u>, then the front side seam does not need to be extended and you can skip ahead to the next section, "Placement of the Side Seam Dart".**

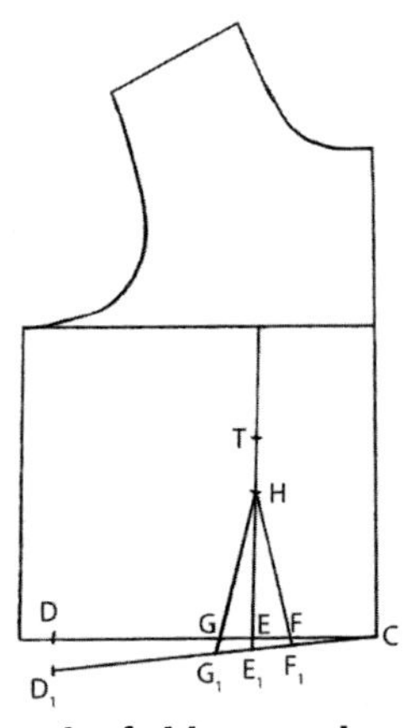

- **In order to create a length of side seam long enough to accommodate an adequate side seam dart, you will need to drop the waistline at the side seam.**
- **To determine the distance that the Front Side Seam should be dropped take the difference between ¾" and the difference between the side seams.**

  ¾" (1.9 cm) – Side Seam Difference = ______________

- **Drop the side seam from point D to a new point D_1 using the measurement you just calculated above. (D_1 should be located perpendicularly below point D.)**
- **Draw a line from point D_1 to point C. This will be the new waistline.**
- **Create your Front Side Seam dart by replacing your previously used Front Side Seam measurement with the measurement B-D_1.**
  Front Side Seam (B-D_1) – Back Side Seam = ____________
- **Extend E, F, and G to the new waistline and label them E_1, F_1, and G_1.**

Placement of the Side Seam Dart

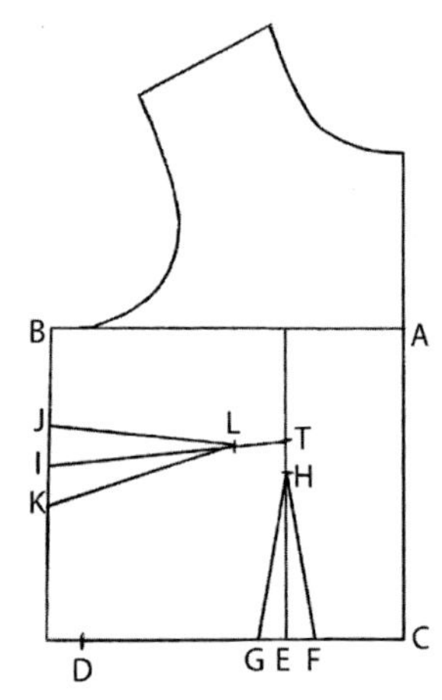

- The side seam dart may be placed anywhere along the side seam depending on the desired look. The dart should be located on the side seam far enough away from the armscye so that your dart does not extend into your armscye. (Make sure that the dart tip is pointed toward the bust point. This is because all bust darts, whether from the waistline, side seam, or shoulder seam, must orient themselves toward the bust point. To do otherwise will make the garment fit irregularly.)
- Mark a point on the side seam where you would like the center of your dart to be located. This is point I.
- Draw a line from new point I extending to the bust point T.
- On the side seam, above point I, mark new point J where J = ½ the total measurement of the side seam dart.
- On the side seam, below point I, mark new point K I where J = ½ the total measurement of the side seam dart.
- From bust point T, measure 1½" (3.8 cm) toward I to mark a new point L. This is the vanishing point of your dart.
- Connect dart legs by drawing straight lines from L to J and L to K.

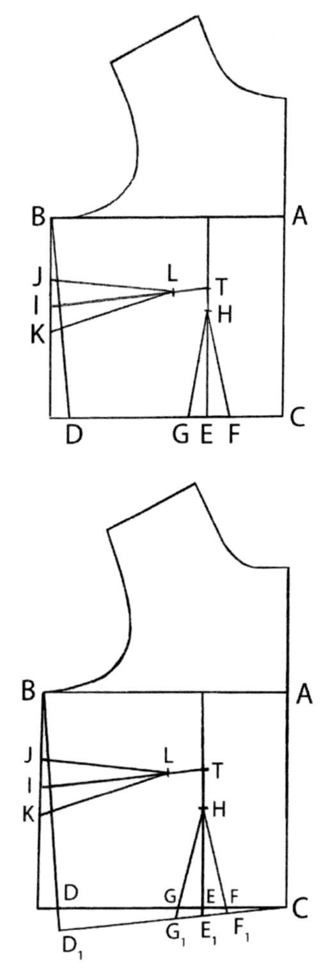

- Connect point B to point D or D_1 to create the new side seam.

*True the darts by following the directions in the Appendix for Trueing Darts.

Chapter 7: Manipulating Darts within the Bodice

Using the Pivot Method to Move Darts

Once you have your basic slopers draped or drafted, you can now modify them based on design choices. This chapter will explore ways to alter the basic slopers and manipulate them to create alternate looks.

Moving darts with the Pivot Method is a faster and easier way to move the darts. By pivoting you can quickly relocate the darts as needed for the design.

For the first few sections, the darts will be relocated. Later sections will convert the darts to gathers or to seam lines. It is important to note that the shaping darts are not eliminated, but instead are converted to another shaping method.

Single Dart Moved: Side Seam Dart to Shoulder Seam

Items Needed:

- Bodice Front Sloper copy with the darts cut out and the bust point marked
- Paper larger than the sloper
- Pencil, pushpin, and ruler

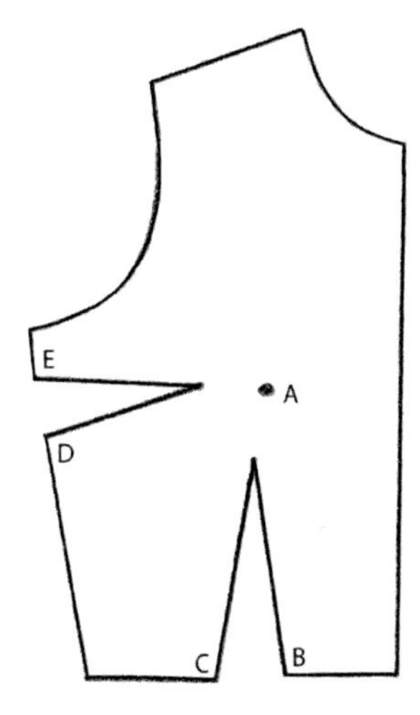

- Using a copy of the bodice front sloper with side seam and waistline darts, relabel points as marked on the diagram above.

DOI: 10.4324/9781003022619-7

*Always use a copy of the original and not the original just in case of any errors. You will want to have the original intact so that you don't have to start from scratch and can go back to it if needed.

Moving a Single Dart

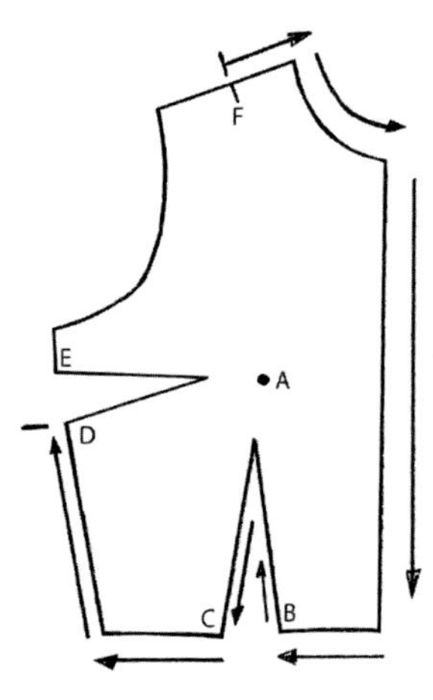

- Using a pushpin placed through the bust point, pin the sloper to the larger piece of paper.
- Mark the placement for the desired location of the new dart on the sloper (for this example, label it point F at the shoulder).
- Begin tracing the sloper at point F and trace up the shoulder seam toward the neckline, around the neckline, down the center front, across the waistline and up and down the dart, across the remainder of the waistline, up the side seam and stop at point D at the base of the bottom leg of the side seam bust dart.

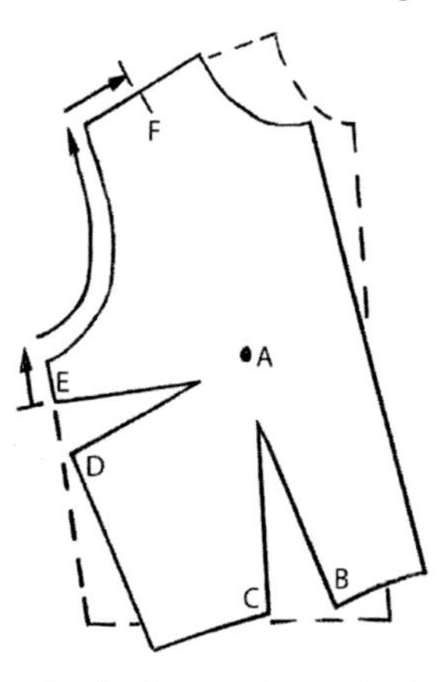

- Pivot the sloper counter-clockwise so that point E meets the point where you stopped tracing at point D.
- Continue tracing the sloper up the side seam, around the armscye, and the section of shoulder seam until you get to the marking for point F again.

Manipulating Darts within the Bodice

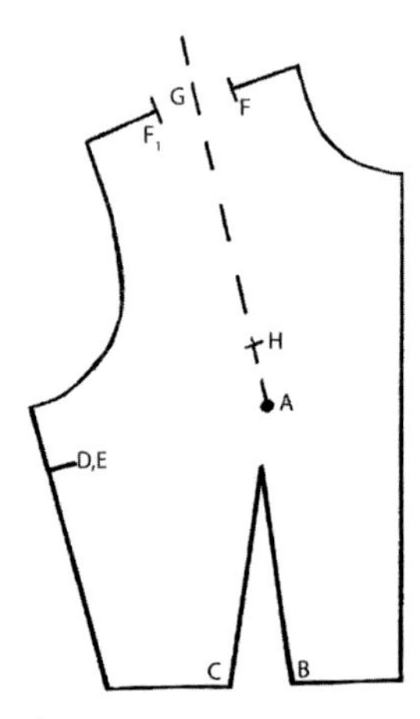

- Remove the original copy of the sloper from your paper.
- The opening at the shoulder on your paper of the new sloper you just traced is the new location of your dart.
- Measure the distance between point F and F_1, and then divide this measurement by two to locate the center line of the dart. Mark this point G.
- Draw the center line from the bust point through the center point and past the shoulder seam.
- Mark the tip of the bust dart at 1½" (3.8 cm) from the bust point and label this point H.

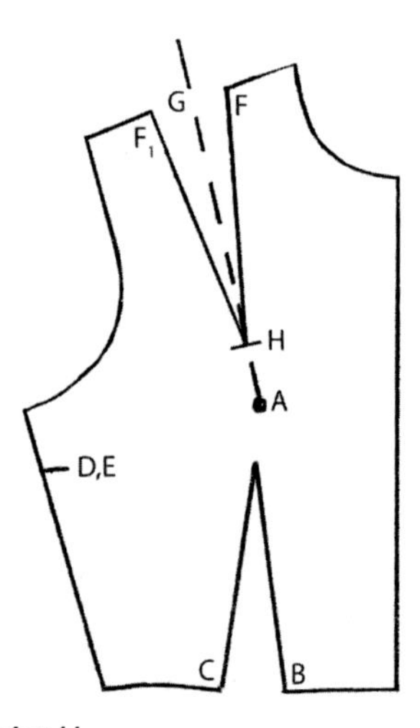

- Connect the legs to point H.

*True the darts by following the directions in the Appendix for Trueing Darts.

Combined Dart at the Shoulder Seam

Moving Both the Side Seam Dart and the Waist Dart to the Shoulder Seam (Combined Dart)

Items Needed:

- Bodice Front Sloper copy with the darts cut out and the bust point marked
- Paper larger than the sloper
- Pencil, pushpin, and ruler

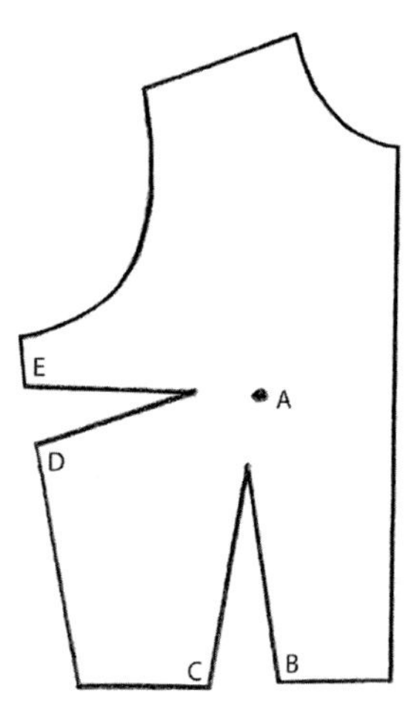

- Using a copy of the bodice front sloper with side seam and waistline darts, relabel points as marked on the diagram above.

*Always use a copy of the original and not the original just in case of any errors. You will want to have the original intact so that you don't have to start from scratch and can go back to it if needed.

Moving the Darts

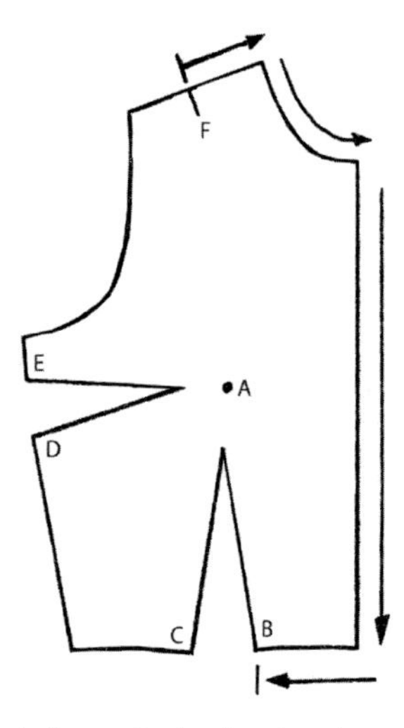

- Using a pushpin placed through the bust point, pin the sloper to the larger piece of paper.

Manipulating Darts within the Bodice

- Mark the placement for the desired location of the new dart on the original sloper. (For this example, label it point F at the shoulder.)
- Begin tracing the sloper at point F and trace up the shoulder seam toward the neckline, around the neckline, down the center front, across to the waistline to point B.

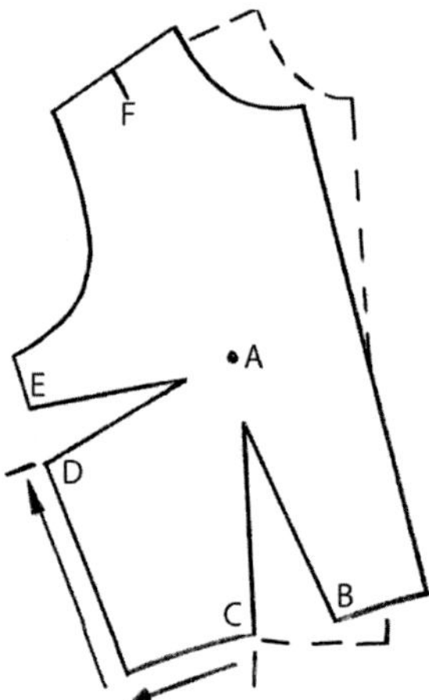

- Pivot the sloper counter-clockwise so that the leg of the waist dart closest to the side seam (C) meets the point where your stopped tracing at point B.
- Continue tracing the sloper across the remainder of the waistline, up the side seam and stop at point D at the base of the bottom leg of the side seam bust dart.

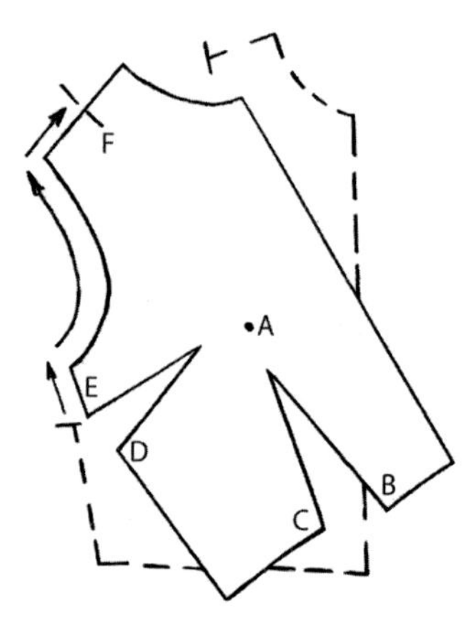

- Pivot the sloper counter-clockwise so that point E meets the point where your stopped tracing at point D.

- Continue tracing the sloper up the side seam, around the armscye, and the section of shoulder seam until you get to the marking for point F again.

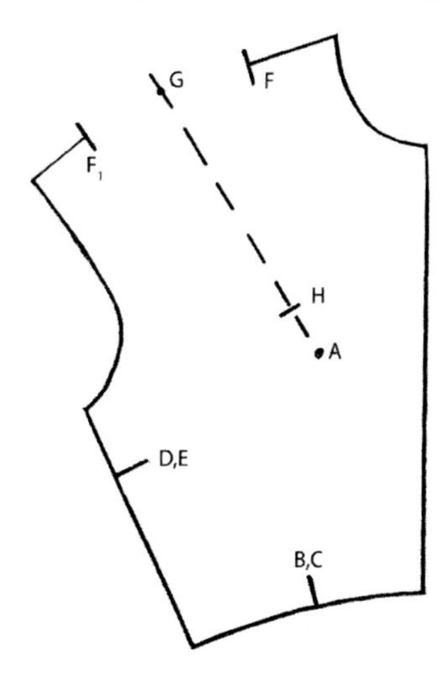

- Remove the original copy of the sloper from your paper.
- The opening at the shoulder is the new location of your dart.
- Measure the distance between point F and F_1. Divide this measurement by two to locate the center line of the dart. Mark this point G.
- Draw the center line from the bust point through the center point G and past the shoulder seam.
- Mark the tip of the bust dart at 1½" (3.8 cm) from the bust point and label it point H.

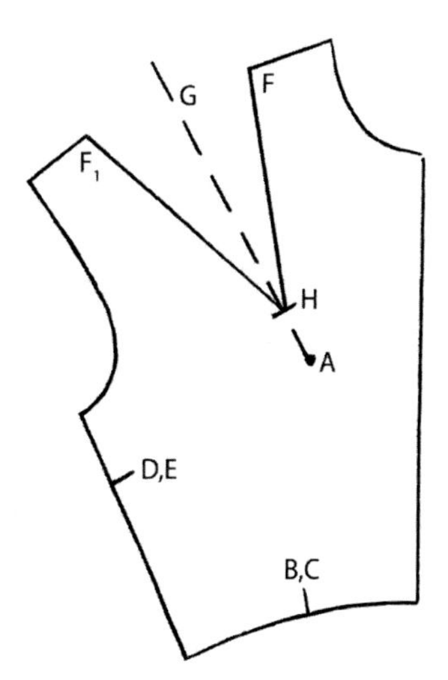

- Connect the legs to this new point H.

*True the darts by following the directions in the Appendix for Trueing Darts.

Manipulating Darts within the Bodice

Combined Dart at the Waistline

Moving the Side Seam Dart to the Waistline (Combined Dart)

This method is used for removing one of the darts and combining it with another already existing dart. For this example, the side seam dart will be moved to combine with the waistline dart.

Items Needed:

- Bodice Front Sloper copy with the darts cut out and the bust point marked
- Paper larger than the sloper
- Pencil, pushpin, and ruler

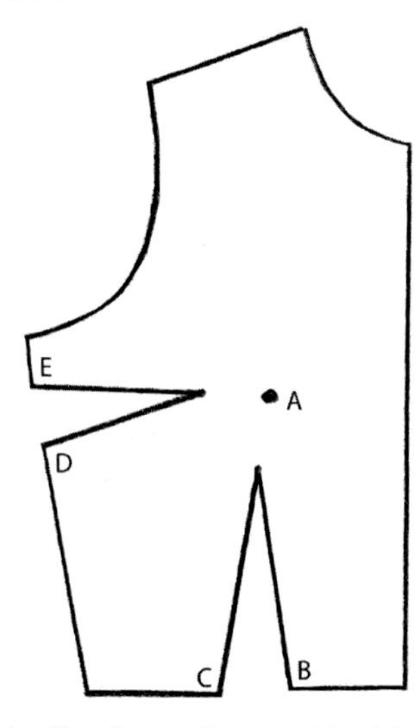

- Using a copy of the bodice front sloper with side seam and waistline darts, relabel points as marked on the diagram above.

*Always use a copy of the original and not the original just in case of any errors. You will want to have the original intact so that you don't have to start from scratch and can go back to it if needed.

Moving the Darts

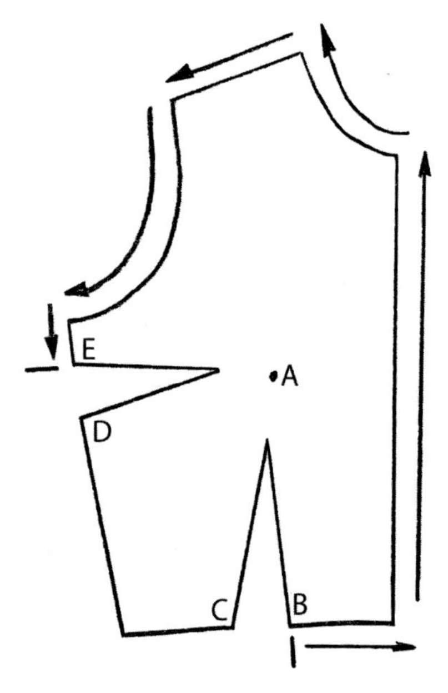

- Using a pushpin placed through the bust point, pin the sloper to the larger piece of paper.
- Begin tracing the sloper at point B and trace across the waistline toward center front, then up the center front, up around the neckline, across the shoulder seam, down the armscye, and down the side seam to point E.

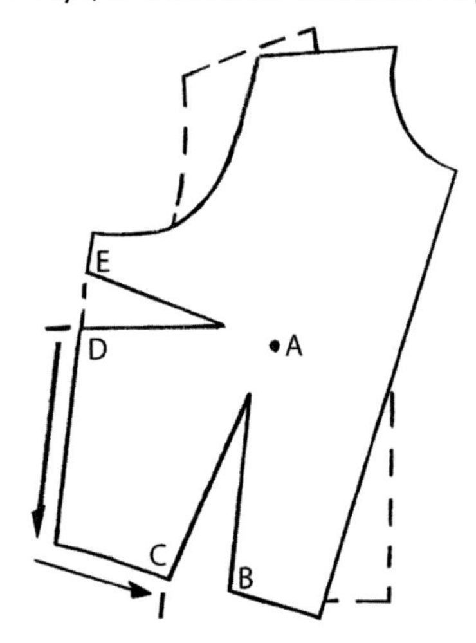

- Pivot the sloper clockwise so that the leg of the side seam dart closest to the waistline (point D) meets the point where you stopped tracing at point E.
- Continue tracing the sloper down the side seam, and across the remainder of the waistline and stop at point C.

Manipulating Darts within the Bodice

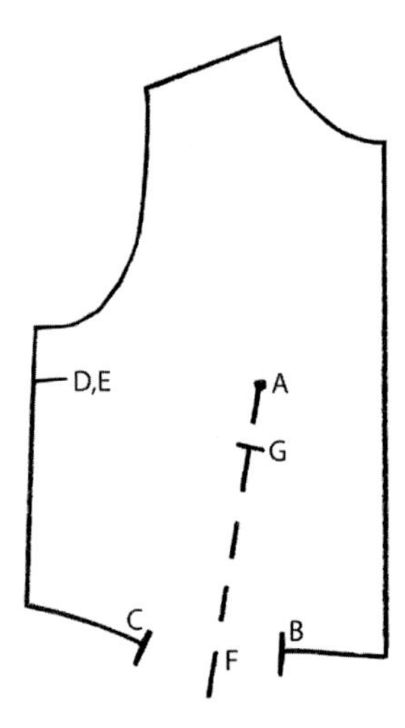

- Remove the original copy of the sloper from your paper.
- The opening at the waistline is the location of your combined dart.
- Measure the distance between B and C. Divide this measurement by two to locate the center line of the dart. Mark this point F.
- Draw the center line from the bust point through the center point of the dart.
- Mark the tip of the bust dart at 1½" (3.8 cm) from the bust point and label it point G.

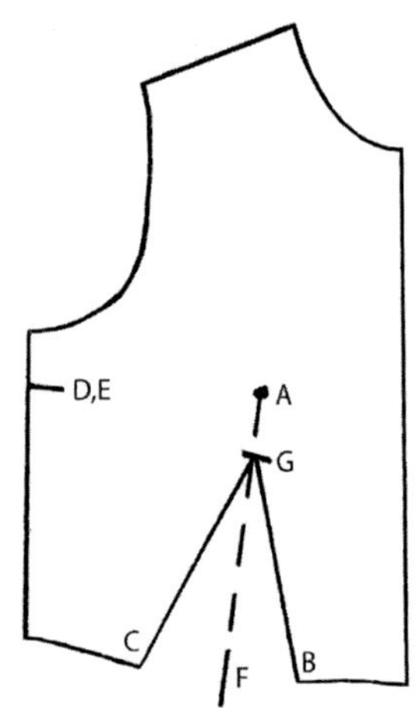

- Connect the legs to this new point G.

*True the darts by following the directions in the Appendix for Trueing Darts.

Using the Slash Method to Move Darts

The method known as "slash and spread" is useful for creating fullness in areas that previously did not have fullness. You can add gathers, pleats, or create new darts, which is what this section covers.

Slash and spread, and alternately, slash and compress, consists of lines drawn on the pattern that are cut to flare out or overlap to change the shape of the garment. If you slash and spread, the pattern will expand in an area creating flare on the finished garment. If you slash and compress, the pattern will shrink in an area creating a narrower look on the finished garment.

Moving the Side Seam Dart to the Shoulder Seam

Items Needed:

- Bodice Front Sloper copy with darts cut out and the bust point marked
- Paper larger than the sloper
- Pencil, pushpin, and ruler
- Tape

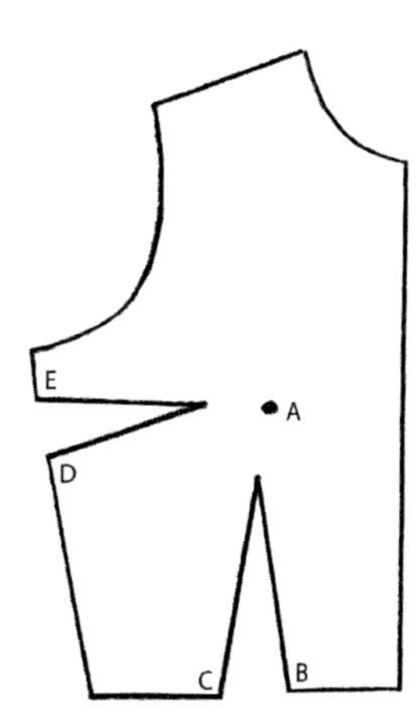

- Using a copy of the bodice front sloper with side seam and waistline darts, relabel points as marked on the diagram above.

*Always use a copy of the original and not the original just in case of any errors. You will want to have the original intact so that you don't have to start from scratch and can go back to it if needed.

Manipulating Darts within the Bodice

Moving the Dart

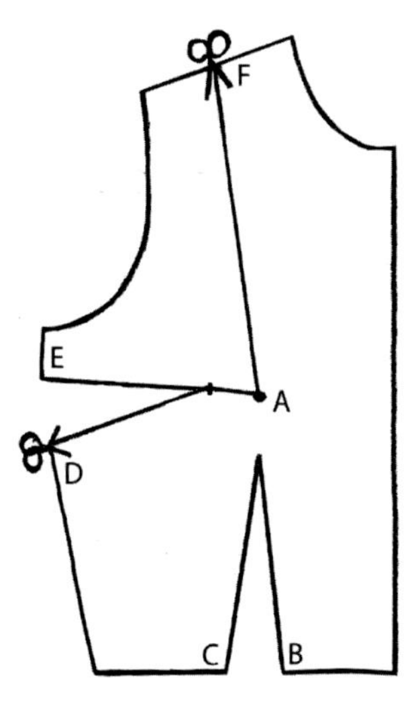

- Mark the placement for the desired location of the new dart on the copy of the sloper. (For this example, label it point F at the shoulder.)
- Draw a line from the new location marking to the bust point.
- Connect the tip of the side seam dart to A with a straight line. (Note: this will not be a straight line from the side seam to A.)
- Cut along the new dart line from F, to but not through point A.
- Cut along the bottom leg of the side seam dart to but not through point A.

*When cutting the legs of the darts, you should cut through the bottom leg for horizontal darts, and the leg closest to center front for vertical darts.

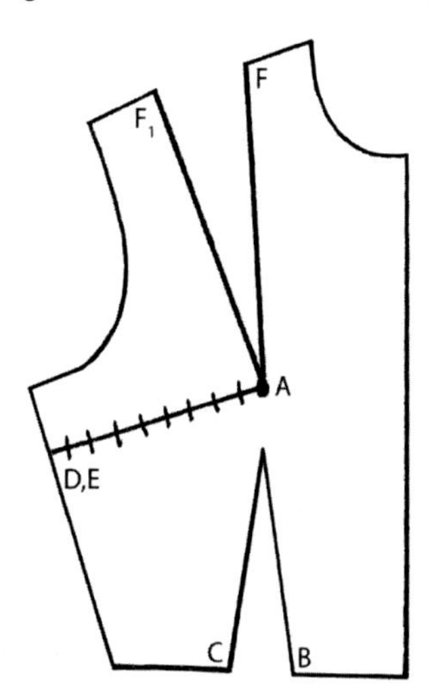

- Close the side seam dart and tape it in place by bringing the lower leg you just cut up to the upper leg line making sure the leg lines are aligned leaving the lengths to be trued later.
- You should now have a new opening for a shoulder seam dart F-A-F_1.

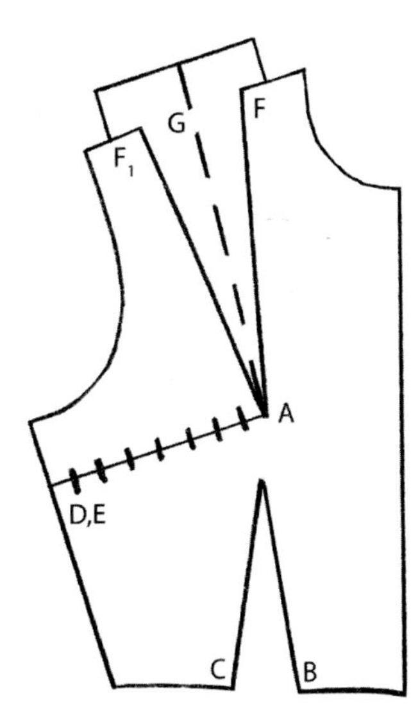

- Place paper under the opening and tape in place.
- Measure the distance between point F and F_1. Divide this measurement by two to locate the center line of the dart. Label this point G.
- Draw the center line from the bust point through point G and past the shoulder seam.

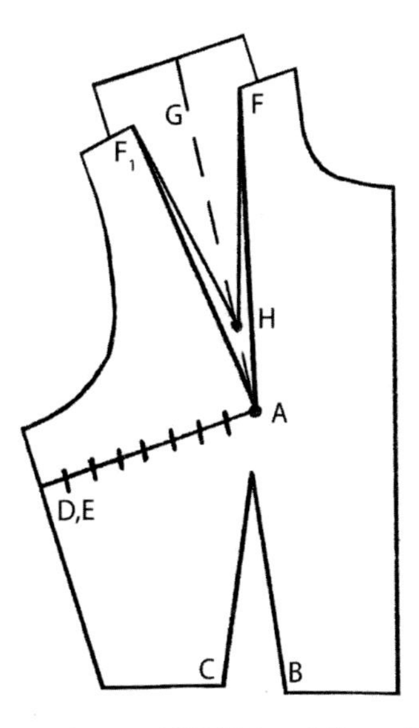

- Mark the tip of the bust dart at 1½" (3.8 cm) from the bust point and label it point H.
- Connect the legs to this new point H.

*True the darts by following the directions in the Appendix for Trueing Darts.

Converting Darts to Gathers

There are three types of gathers: Dart Equivalent, Added Fullness, and the Combination of Dart Equivalent and Added Fullness.

Dart Equivalent Gathers

- Dart Equivalent Gathers follow the rules for darts with the gathers pointing to the bust point.

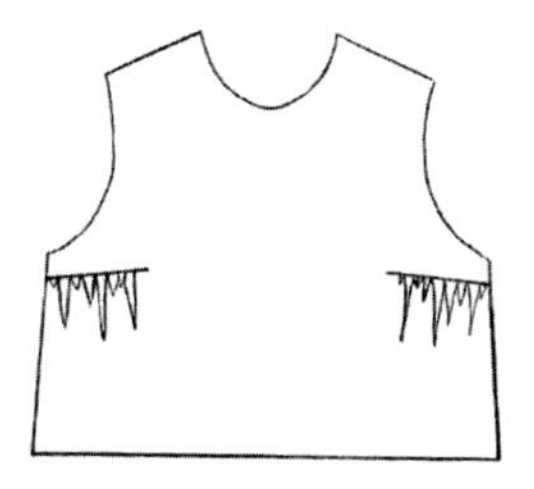

Added Fullness Gathers

- Added Fullness Gathers do not always follow the rules of darts because they can be the result of the slash and spread method. They typically do not point to the bust point but are a decorative feature.

Combination of Dart Equivalent and Added Fullness Gathers

- Combination Gathers are used when Dart Equivalent Gathers do not add enough fullness so Added Fullness Gathers are also used. The slash and spread method is used to increase the fullness in a location that would normally incorporate Dart Equivalent Gathers.

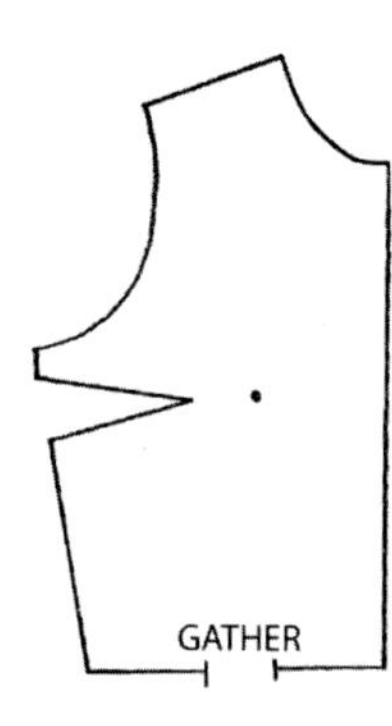

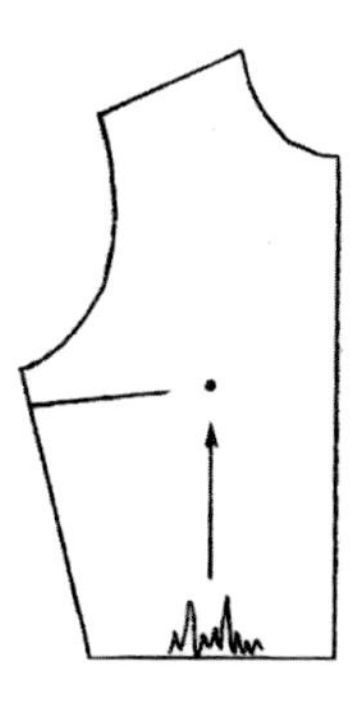

Single Dart Converted to Gathers

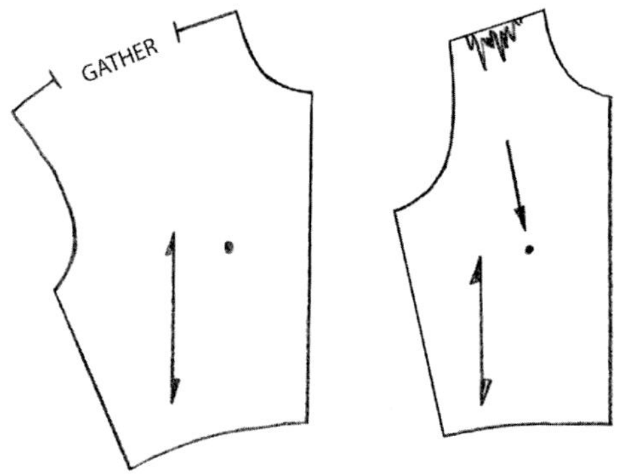

GATHER

Combined Dart at Shoulder Seam Converted to Gathers

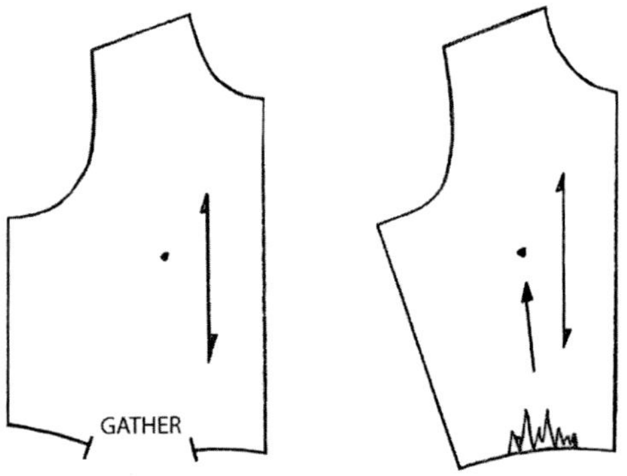

GATHER

Combined Dart at Waistline Converted to Gathers

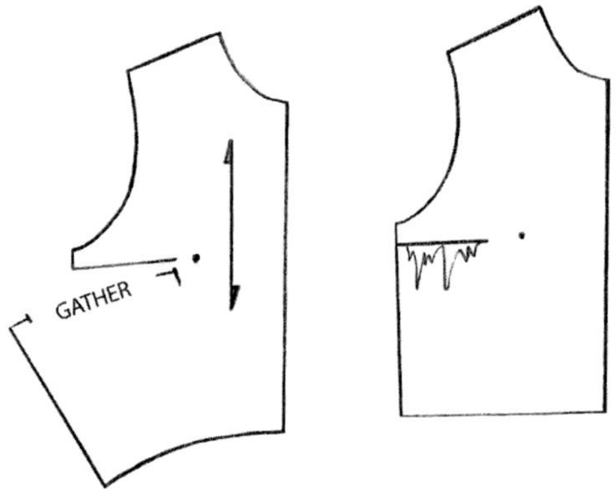

GATHER

Added Fullness Gathers

GATHER

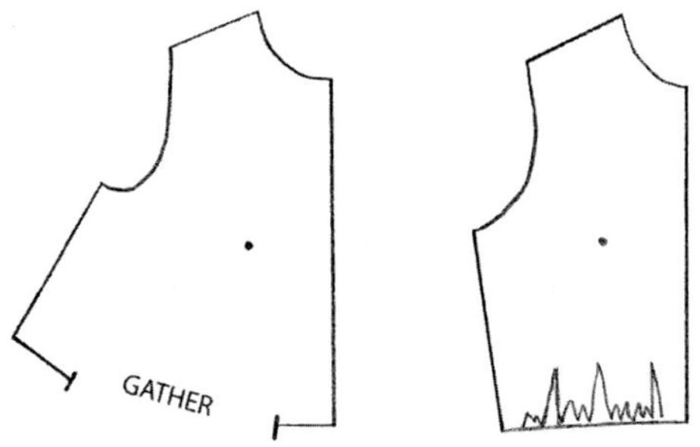

Combined Darts plus Added Fullness Gathers

Princess Seam Lines Made From Darts

Converting Darts to Seam Lines

Note: All princess lines that replace the darts must cross over the bust point.

Princess Line From Shoulder Seam to Waistline

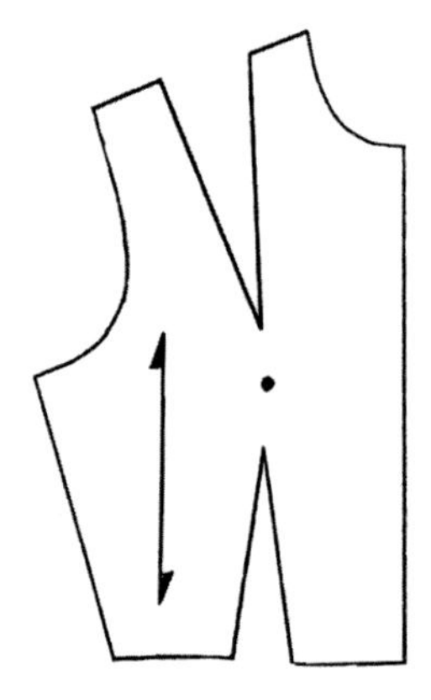

- Start with a copy of the converted sloper with a shoulder seam dart and waistline dart with a bust point marked.
- Draw a grainline in on the side front section. (The side front section is to the left of the bust point and the left legs of the darts.) The grainline is parallel to the center front line.

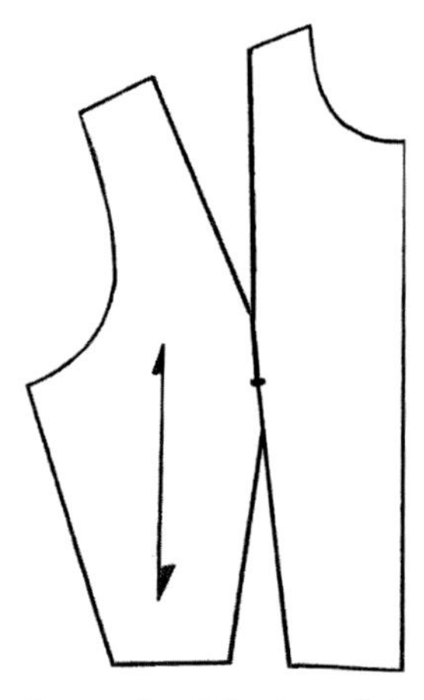

- For the Bodice Front section, extend the leg of the shoulder seam dart closest to the center front line down to the bust point and continue it to the leg of the waistline dart also closest to center front. (This line may be a straight line, but it may not.)

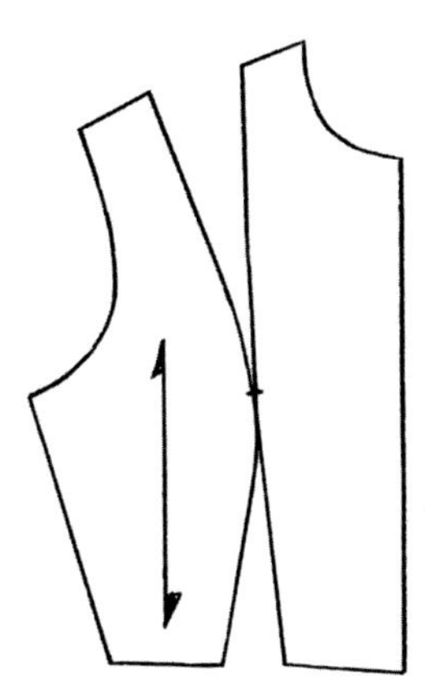

- For the Bodice Side Front section, use your curved ruler to smooth the dart points through the bust point.

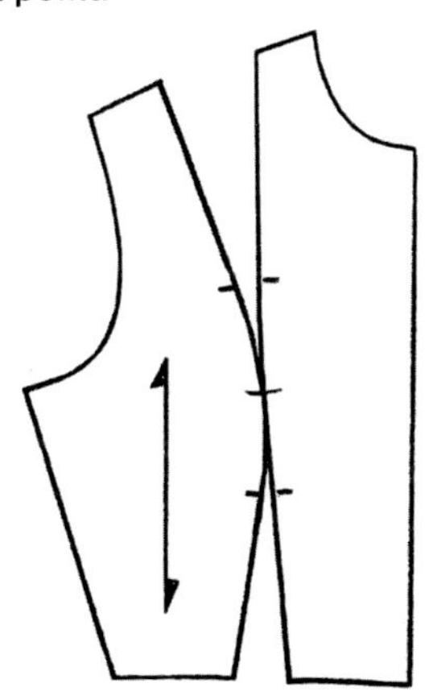

- Due to the new seam line being on the bias, it is encouraged that you add matching notches. One set of matching notches should be at the bust point, one should be above the bust point and one should be below the bust point. You may use a distance of 2″ (5.1 cm) on either side of the bust point for these.

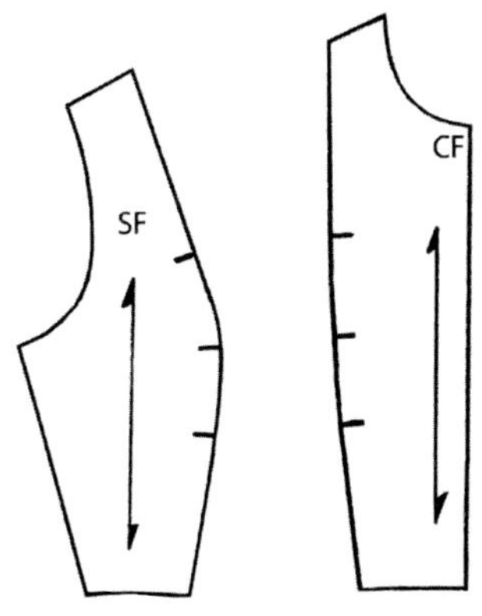

- You should now cut the pattern to create two pieces making sure to label each. You should also make sure that the CF section on the princess line has a smooth curved line by eliminating any angles or points.

Manipulating Darts within the Bodice

Princess Line From Armscye to Waistline

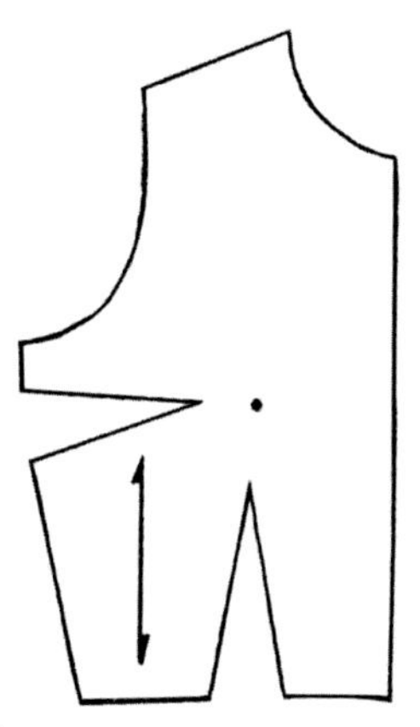

- Use a copy of the converted sloper with a side seam dart and waistline dart, and with the bust point marked.
- Draw a grainline in on the side front section. (The side front section is to the left of the bust point and the left leg of the waistline dart.) The grainline is parallel to the center front line.

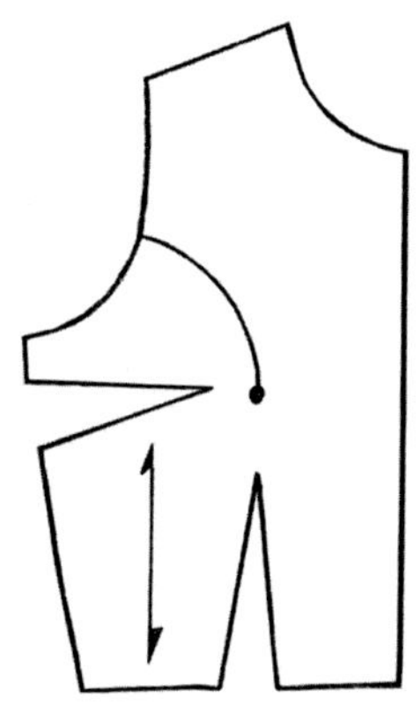

- Draw the desired new seam line from the armscye to the bust point making sure the line is a smooth curve.

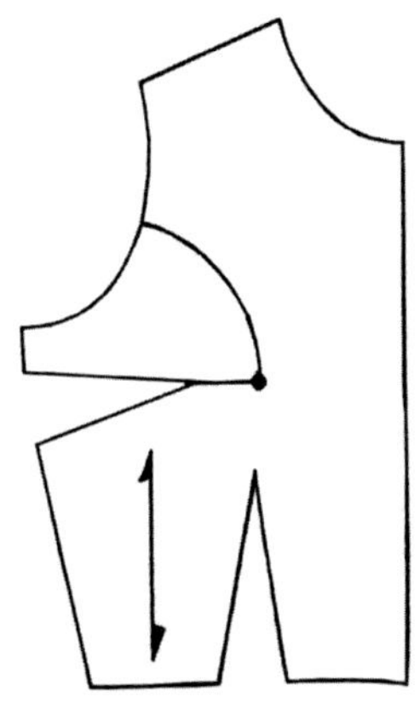

- Using your ruler, draw a line connecting the tip of the side seam dart to the bust point with a straight line.

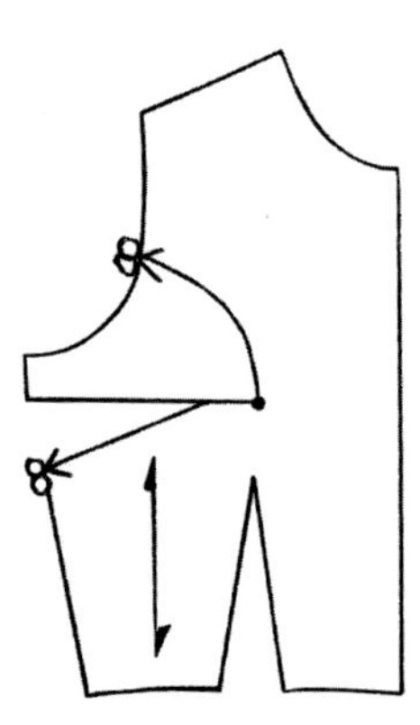

- Cut on this new princess line from the armscye to but not through the bust point. (Note: tape can be added across the bust point to reinforce the point and ensure that it is not cut through.)
- Cut on the lower leg of the side seam dart and the line connecting the dart tip (the vanishing point) to the bust point, to but not through the bust point.

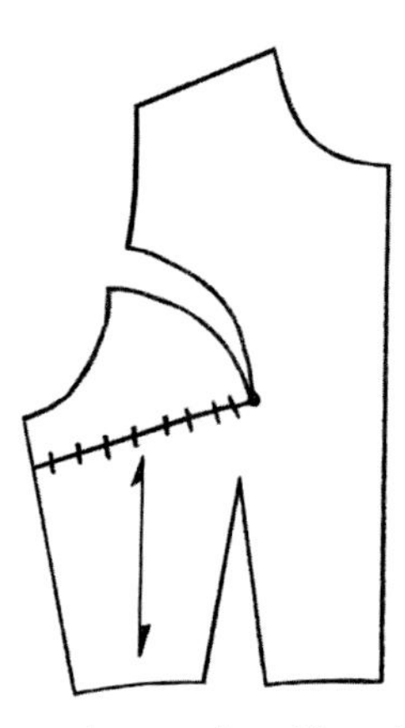

- Close the side seam dart and tape shut. You should now have a gap in the armscye.

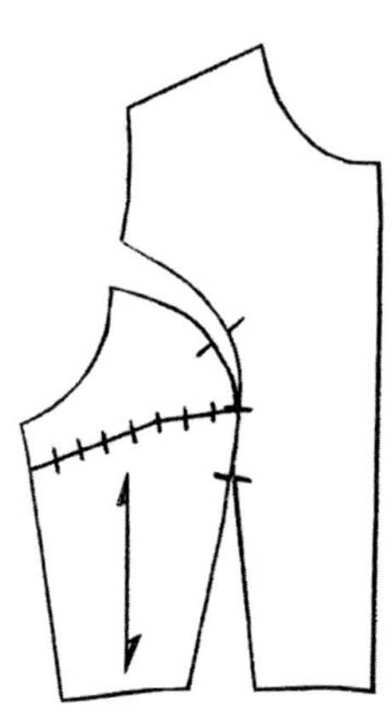

- Using your curved ruler, draw a line connecting the end of the leg closest to the side seam of the waistline dart to the bust point.
- Due to the new seam line being on the bias, it is encouraged that you add matching notches. One set of matching notches should be at the bust point,

one should be above the bust point and one should be below the bust point. You may use a distance of 2″ (5.1 cm) on either side of the bust point for these.

- Using your ruler and a pencil, draw a line straightening the leg of the waist dart from bust point to waistline.

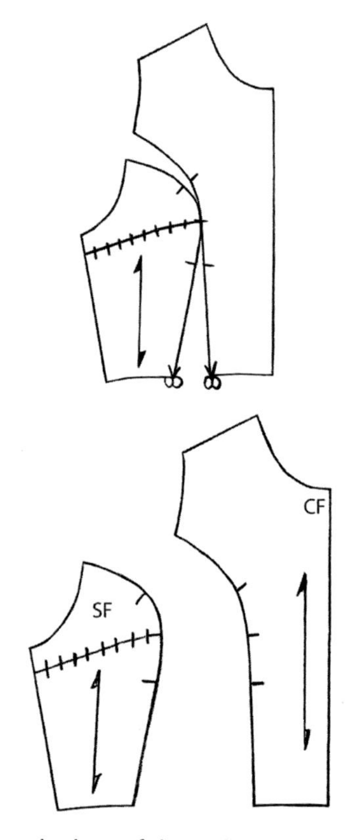

- Cut the pattern along the legs of the waist dart to create two pieces, making sure to label each. You should also make sure that the CF section on the princess line has a smooth curved line by eliminating any angles or points.

Chapter 8: Dresses

How to Drape the Basic Sheath Dress

The Basic Sheath Dress is essentially a combined fitted bodice and fitted skirt. For the draped dress, there are a double-ended darts at the waist. For the drafted pattern, the dress has aligned waist darts from the bodice and skirt, both front and back, that create the double-ended darts.

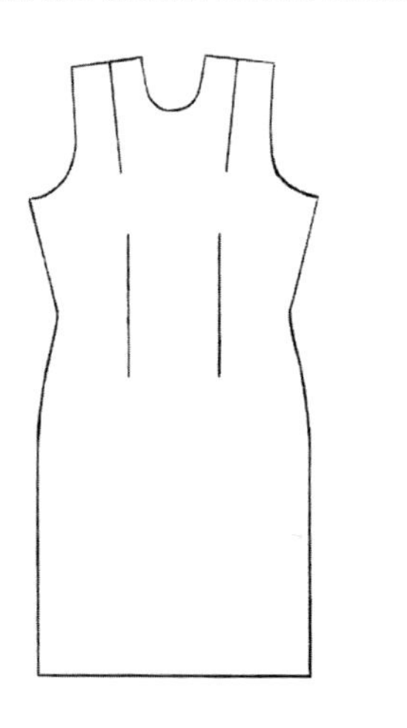

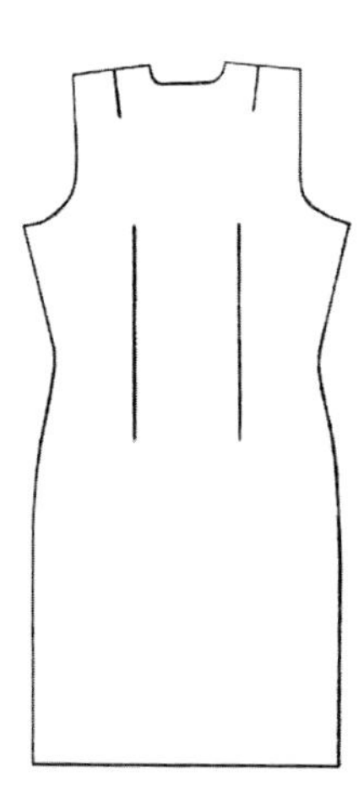

Anatomy of the Basic Sheath Dress

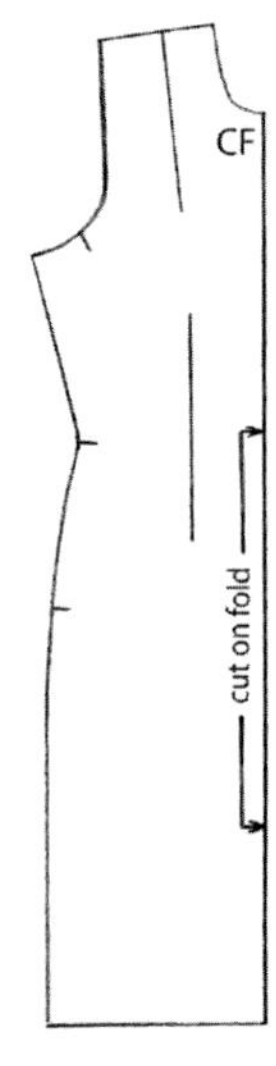

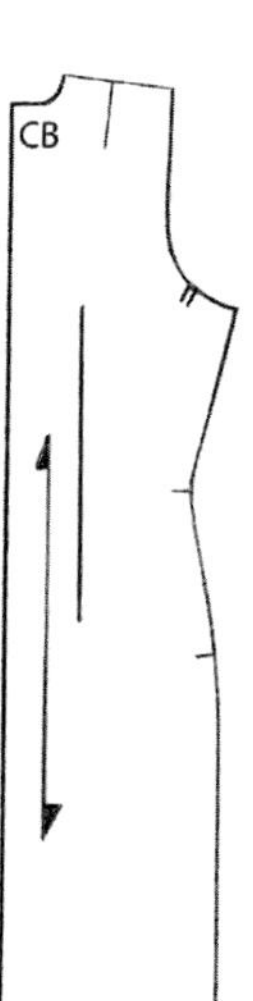

DOI: 10.4324/9781003022619-8

Note: A double-ended dart is also known as a fisheye dart.

- **Prepare the fabric for draping:**

(See Chapter 4 on Preparing the Muslin for Draping, and Blocking the Muslin.)

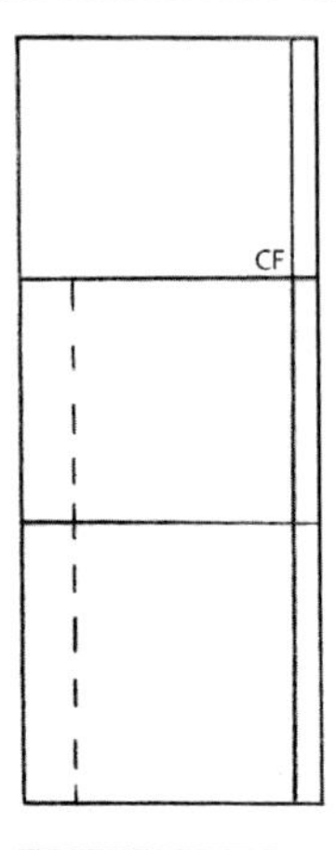

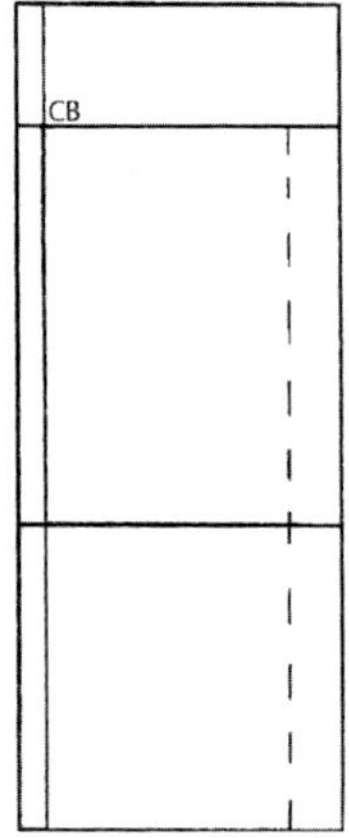

- Measure the length for the front panel from the neckband down CF to the desired length of the hem and add 4″ (10.2 cm).

Note: The length of the fabric must be on the straight of grain.

- Measure the width of the front panel from CF, across the bust line, to the side seam, and add 6″ (15.2 cm). (Use the hip level measurement if it is wider to ensure enough fabric.)
- Repeat these steps for the back panel.
- Mark the 1″ (2.5 cm) guidelines for the CF and CB panels along the grainline edge. Press under along this 1″ line. (CF will be on the right side of the fabric, and CB will be on the left side of the fabric.)
- Draw a cross-grain line on the front panel at 14″ (35.6 cm) down from the top edge.
- This will line up with the Bust line.
- Draw a second cross-grain line on the front panel 14″ (35.6 cm) down from the bust line cross-grain.

- This will line up with the Hip level line.
- To draw the cross-grain lines on the back panel, place the panels next to each other and draw the cross-grain line on the back panel to match the Hip level line on the front panel.
- From the back Hip level line, measure up to the shoulder blade line and draw the cross-grain.
- On the dress form, measure the width of the hip level from CF to side seam + ½" (1.3 cm) for ease.
- Place a cross-mark at this measurement on the front panel on the hip level line.
- Repeat these steps for the back panel.
- On the front panel, draw a line parallel to the grainline through this point from bust line to hem.
- On the back panel, draw a line parallel to the grainline through this point from shoulder blade to hem.

Directions for Draping

Front

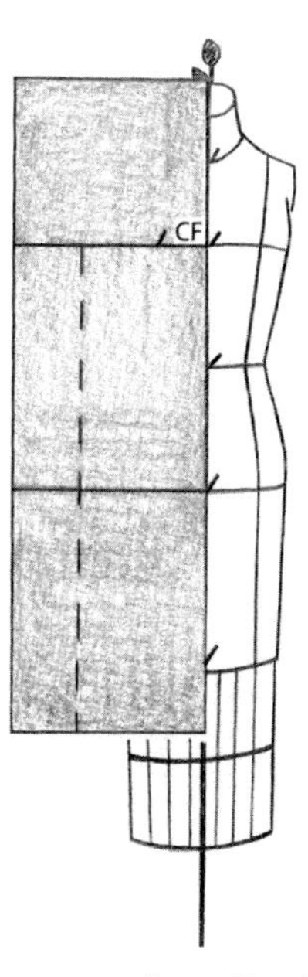

- On your dress form, pin the prepared muslin with the cross-grain line centered over the bust tape and the CF line of the muslin lining up with the CF of the dress form.
- Place pins along CF at neckline, bust line tape, waistline, hip level tape, and bottom edge above cage.
- Place a pin at the bust point.

Side Seam

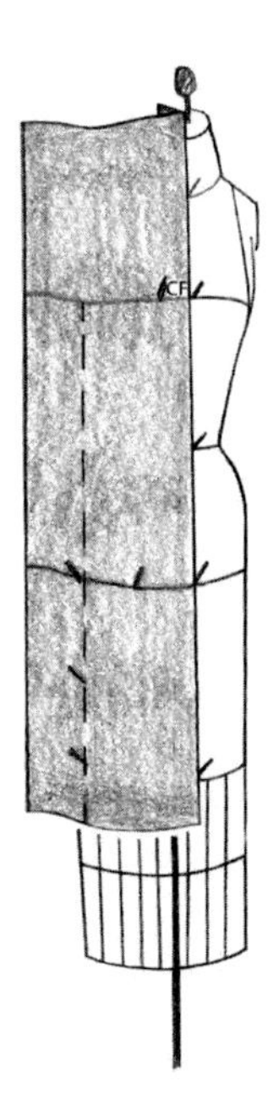

- Smooth across the hipline, matching the long side seam line to the dress form's side seam, and pin at the hip level line at the side seam.
- Distribute the ease evenly along the front hip level line and pin making sure the cross-grain stays parallel to the floor.
- Pin the side seam to the dress form below the hip level line.

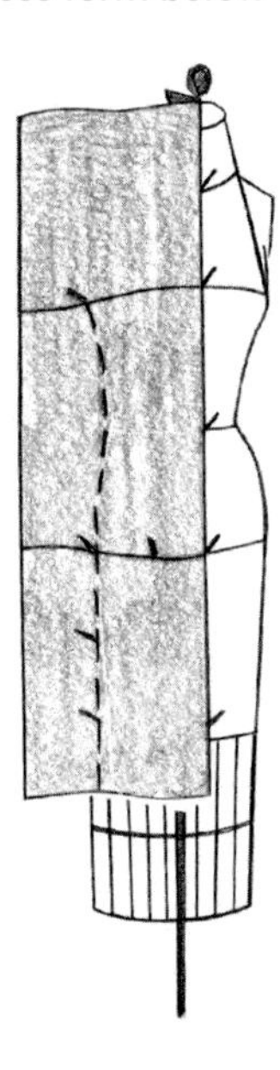

- Smooth the side seam up toward the arm plate and shoulder.
- Pin the side seam of the panel to the side seam of the dress form at the bust line tape.

Neckline

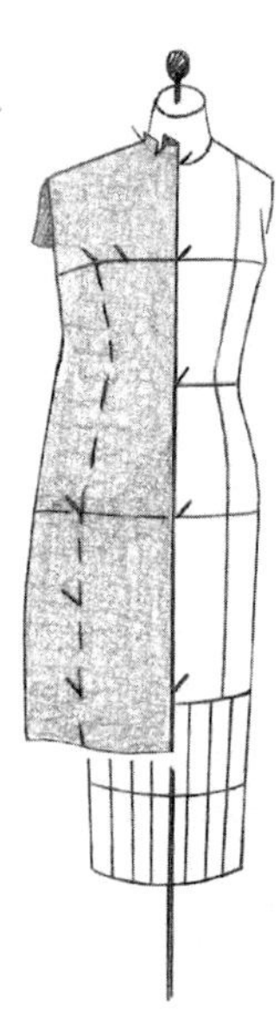

- To smooth around the neckline, make a cut perpendicular to CF line about 1" (2.5 cm) above the neck seam.
- Cut down to the neckline seam while continuing to smooth around the neck and up to the shoulder seam, being very careful not to clip past the neckline seam and into the body of the garment. (Cut to, but not through. Clipping too aggressively is very easy to do. Think of clipping as if you were to clip only to the intended future stitching line within the seam allowance. If you clip too much you will end up in the body of the garment. If you do clip too far, you can mend a small cut with some masking tape placed on the top and underneath of the area.)
- Place a pin at the shoulder seam/neckline seam point.

Shoulder Dart

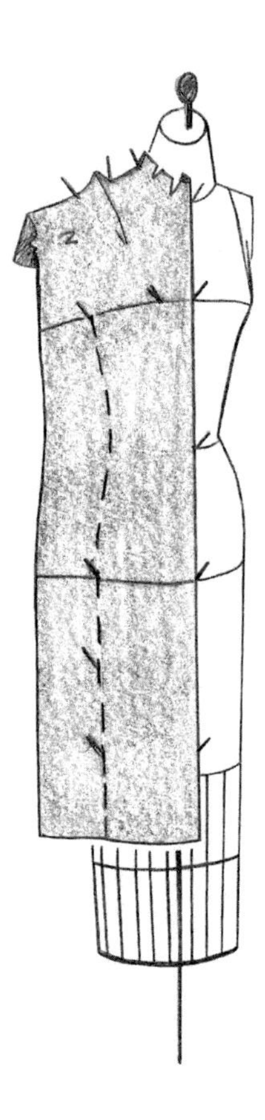

- From the neckline, smooth across the shoulder seam to the princess line. Place a pin at this point.
- From the side seam, smooth the excess fabric up and over the armhole to create the shoulder dart at the princess line.
- Pinch out about ¼″ (0.6 cm) at the screw level of the arm plate to create ease in the armhole.
- Place a pin at the shoulder seam on the armhole ridge.

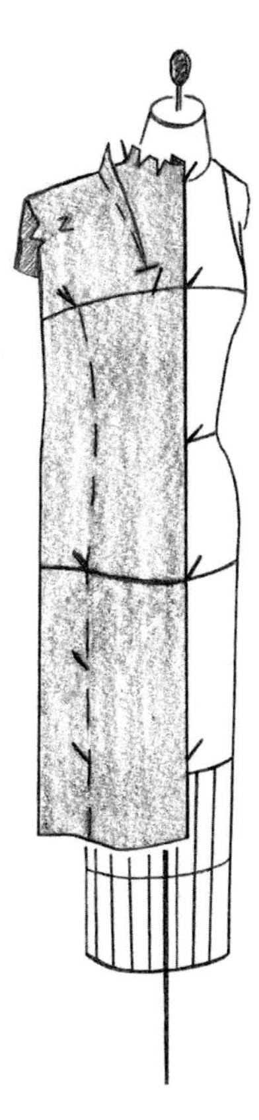

- Remove the pin at the shoulder seam/princess line point and pinch the excess fabric so the center of the dart falls directly over the princess line on the shoulder seam.
- Pinch a ridge to create the dart and place the pins along the length of the dart down to a vanishing point 1″ (2.5 cm) above the bust point.
- Mark the vanishing point with a horizontal pin.

(The dart may be too long or off grain, but this will be fixed in the trueing.)

Double-Ended Waist Dart

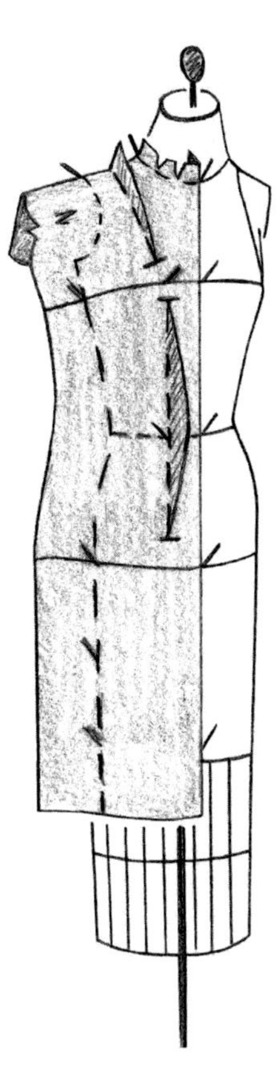

- Along the princess line, with a vanishing point starting 1½″ (3.8 cm) below the bust point, pinch out a vertical double-ended dart.
- Pin both sides of the dart at the princess line at the waistline.
- Taper the dart down toward the hipline to a vanishing point that ends about 6″ (15.2 cm) below the waistline and pin the dart with the pins running the length of the dart.
- Mark the vanishing points with horizontal pins.

(The dart may be too long or off grain but this will be fixed in the trueing.)

Marking the Muslin

- Draw dashed lines along the center of the twill tape at the waistline, side seam, neckline, armhole, darts, and shoulder seam.
- Draw a dashed line on the ridge around the arm plate of the dress form. This may result in a small armscye but it will be adjusted for ease in the trueing.
- Create cross marks on either side of the darts where they intersect the waistline and the shoulder seam, and mark the bust point.
- Create cross marks at the side seam where it intersects the waistline and the arm plate.
- Add matching notches on the side seam, and shoulder seam. You can carefully use a felt tip type marker to make your matching marks by pulling the fabric

away from the dress form and letting the marker create a mark on the front of the garment. Let the marker bleed through to the back of the garment. DO NOT MARK THE DRESS FORM.

(Matching notches should correspond to darts on the other side of the draping: i.e. the shoulder dart on the back should align with the matching notch on the front, and the bust dart on the side seam [if you have one] should align with the matching notch on the back. If you have a bust dart at the shoulder seam and a back dart at the shoulder seam, these should align at the princess line and no additional matching notch is needed there.)

- Leave the fabric on the dress form, but fold over the excess muslin at the side seam and shoulder seam to allow for draping the Back Sheath Dress. (You may want to pin it out of the way.)

Back

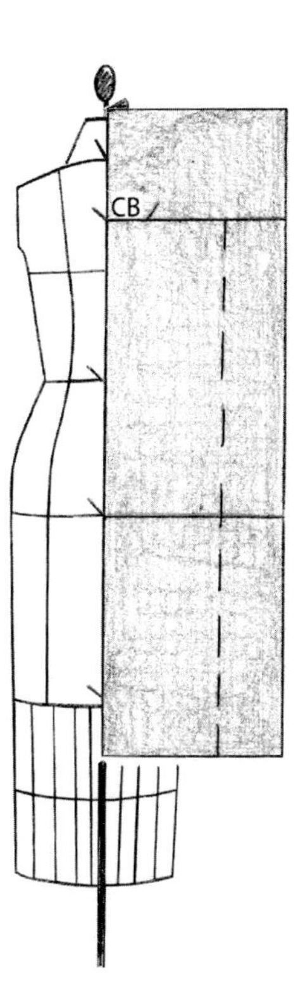

- On your dress form, pin the prepared muslin with the cross-grain line centered over the shoulder level tape and the CB line of the muslin lining up with the CB of the dress form.
- Place pins along CB at neckline, shoulder level tape, waistline, hip level tape, and bottom edge above cage.
- Place a pin at the shoulder level on the princess seam making sure the cross-grain is parallel to the floor.

Side Seam

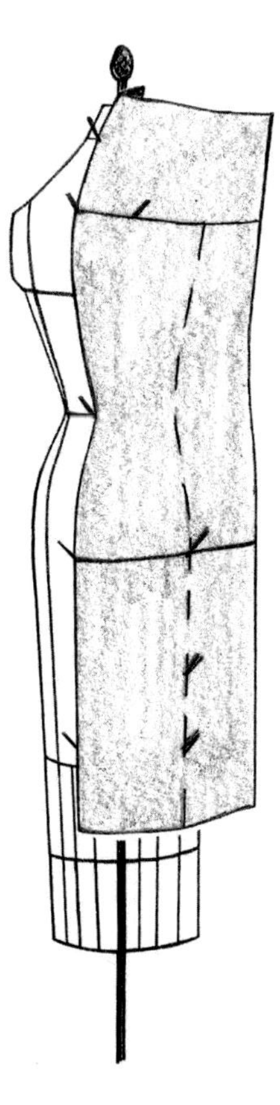

- Smooth across the hipline, matching the long side seam line to the dress form's side seam, and pin at the hip level line at the side seam.
- Distribute the ease evenly along the back hip level line and pin making sure the cross-grain stays parallel to the floor.
- Pin the side seam to the dress form below the hip level line.

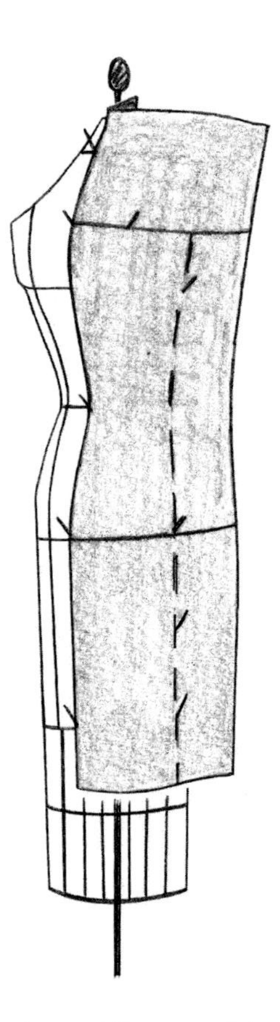

- Smooth the side seam up toward the arm plate and shoulder.
- Pin the side seam of the panel to the side seam of the dress form at the bust line tape.

Neckline

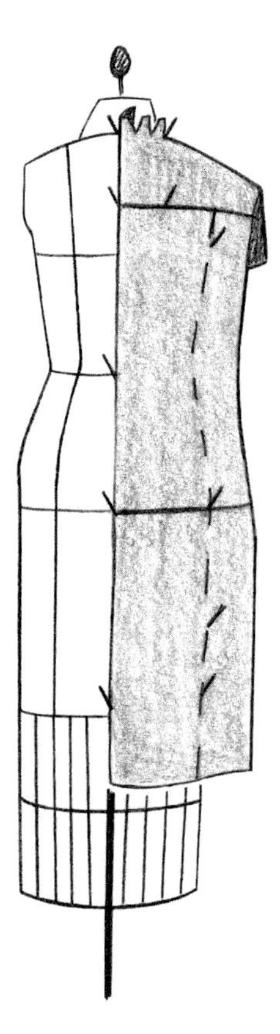

- To smooth around the neckline, make a cut perpendicular to CB line about 1″ (2.5 cm) above the neck seam.
- Cut down to the neckline seam while continuing to smooth around the neck and up to the shoulder seam, being very careful not to clip past the neckline seam and into the body of the garment. (Cut to, but not through. Clipping too aggressively is very easy to do. Think of clipping as if you were to clip only to the intended future stitching line within the seam allowance. If you clip too much you will end up in the body of the garment. If you do clip too far, you can mend a small cut with some masking tape placed on the top and underneath of the area.)
- Place a pin at the shoulder seam/neckline seam point.

Shoulder Dart

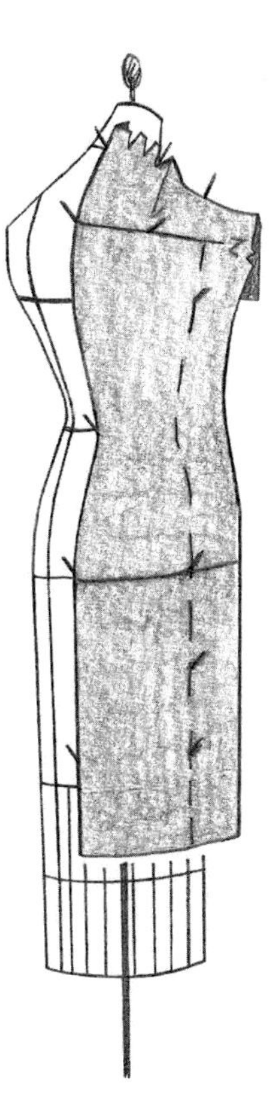

- From the neckline, smooth the fabric across the shoulder seam to the princess line. Place a pin at this point.
- From the side seam, smooth the excess fabric up and over the armhole to create the shoulder dart at the princess line.
- Pinch out about ¼″ (0.6 cm) at the screw level of the arm plate to create ease in the armhole.
- Place a pin at the shoulder seam on the armhole ridge.

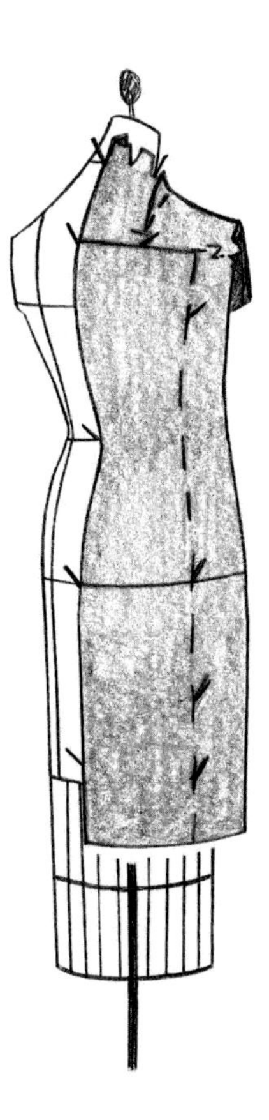

- Remove the pin at the shoulder seam/princess line point and pinch the excess fabric so the center of the dart falls directly over the princess line on the shoulder seam.
- Pinch a ridge to create the dart and place the pins along the length of the dart down 3" (7.6 cm).
- Mark the 3" (7.6 cm) point as the vanishing point of the dart with a horizontal pin.

Waist Dart

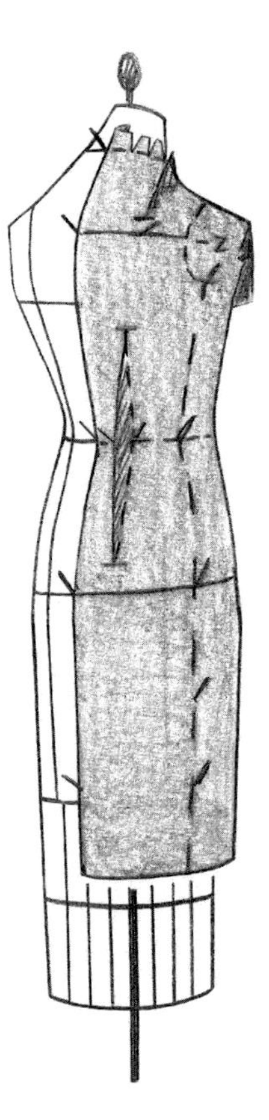

- On the princess line, with a vanishing point starting 7″ (17.8 cm) above the waistline tape, pinch out a vertical double-ended dart.
- Pin both sides of the dart at the princess line at the waistline.
- Taper the dart down toward the hipline to a vanishing point and pin the dart with the pins running the length of the dart.
- Mark the vanishing points with horizontal pins.

Marking the Muslin

- Draw dashed lines along the center of the twill tape at waistline, neckline, shoulder seam, and side seam.
- Draw a dashed line on the ridge around the arm plate of the dress form. This may result in a small armscye but it will be adjusted for ease in the trueing.
- Create cross marks on either side of the darts where they intersect at the waistline, and mark the vanishing points.
- Create cross marks at the side seam where it intersects the waistline and the arm plate.
- Add matching notches on the side seam, and shoulder seam. You can carefully use a felt tip type marker to make your matching marks by pulling the fabric away from the dress form and letting the marker create a mark on the front of the garment. Let the marker bleed through to the back of the garment. DO NOT MARK THE DRESS FORM.

(Matching notches should correspond to darts on the other side of the draping: i.e. the shoulder dart on the back should align with the matching notch on the front, and the bust dart on the side seam [if you have one] should align with the matching notch on the back. If you have a bust dart at the shoulder seam and a back dart at the shoulder seam, these should align at the princess line and no additional matching notch is needed there.)

Combining Front and Back Dress Pieces

- Trim the front and back shoulder seams to 1" (2.5 cm)
- Trim the front and back side seams to 1" (2.5 cm)
- With the dress pinned together at the side seams below the hip level line, mark on the CB line the desired length.
- Draw a hem from this mark parallel to the hipline.

Fit Check

- On the front shoulder seam line and the front side seam, fold under and pin to back panel, matching the shoulder darts at the princess line and also the hip level lines.
- Check that the shoulder cross mark at the shoulder seam, and the side seam cross marks under the arm plate align.
- Pin the skirt to the dress form at waistline CF, CB, and side seam.
- Front and back grainlines should be straight without twisting or pulling.
- Cross-grains should be parallel to the floor.
- Side seam should align with the side seam of the dress form.
- Darts are pinned shut to vanishing points.
- Darts are smooth without twisting. (Twisting happens in the pinched-out area of the dart. If twisted, it will not be a smooth flat dart, but will exhibit a contorted "twist" which means that the grainline is off within the dart. The grainline of the dart should be parallel to the grainline of the center front of the skirt. The center line of the dart should follow the grainline.)

Trueing the Basic Sheath Dress

(On the actual dress drape)

Trueing is a term used to describe the process of creating accuracy on a draped or drafted sloper. When the muslin is still on the dress form, it may seem as if the sloper fits well and matches the other sections. It is only when the muslin is removed that the accuracy can be determined. Trueing can be done directly on the draped muslin pieces, or on craft paper. The following instructions will be on the draped muslin pieces. After trueing the muslin, then the pattern can be transferred to paper.

After removing the sheath dress from the dress form, with front and back panels separate and all pins removed, lay the fabric pieces flat on your table. Do not press the pieces with an iron since the fabric may stretch out of shape.

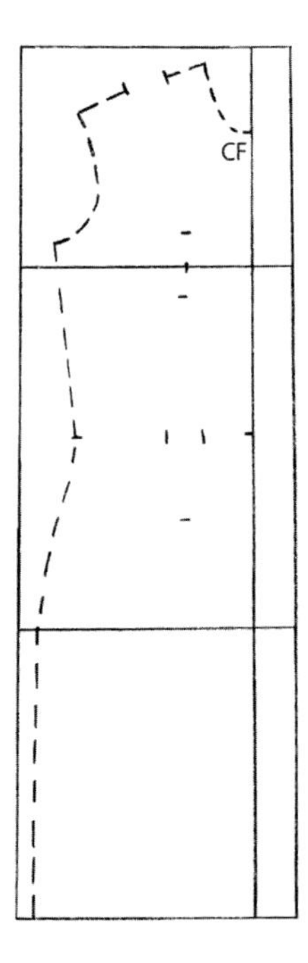

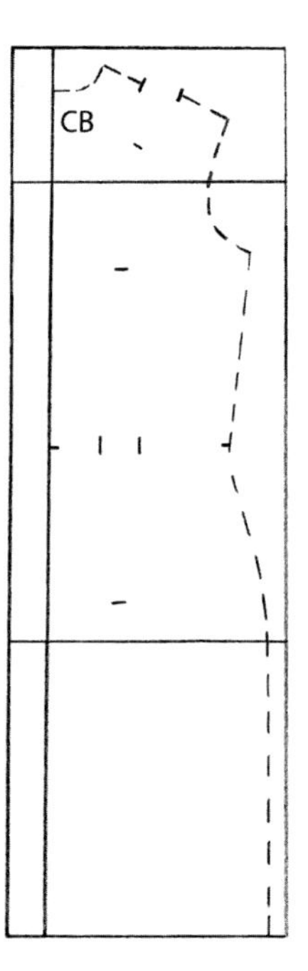

The following locations require a 90-degree angle:

- CF neck for ¼″ (0.6 cm)
- CB neck for 1″ (2.5 cm)

(These 90-degree angle lines that are perpendicular to the CF and CB allow for a smooth curve when making a full garment. Otherwise you will end up with either a V shape or a ^ shape at those locations.)

Trueing the Front Sheath Dress Shoulder Dart

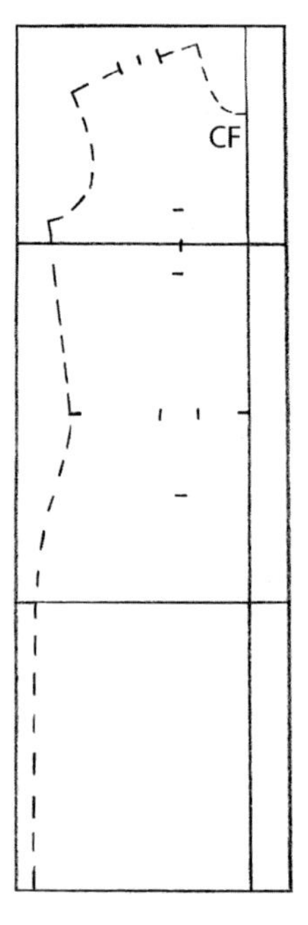

- For the front shoulder dart, measure the width of the dart opening. Divide the measurement in half to determine the center point of the dart. Place a mark in the center of the opening on the shoulder seam.

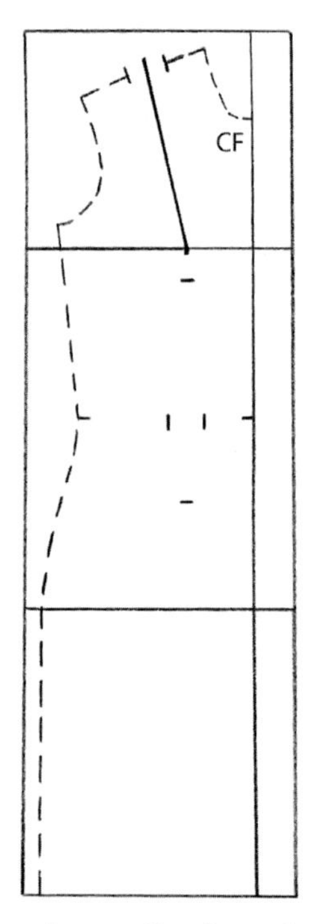

- Using your straight ruler, draw a line from the center point marking at the shoulder seam to the bust point.

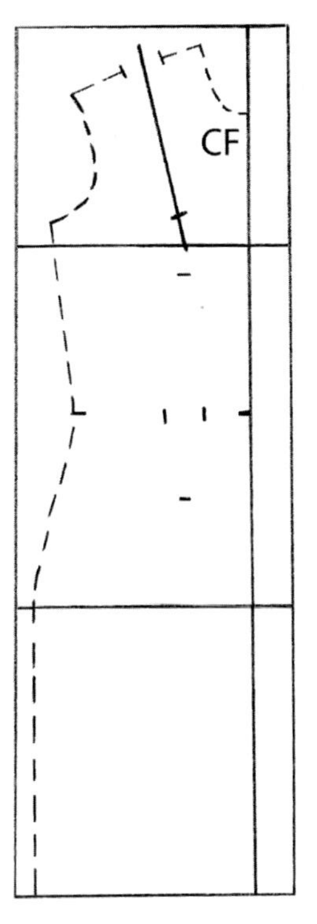

- For the shoulder dart, measure up 1½" (3.8 cm) from the bust point on the center line and mark the vanishing point.

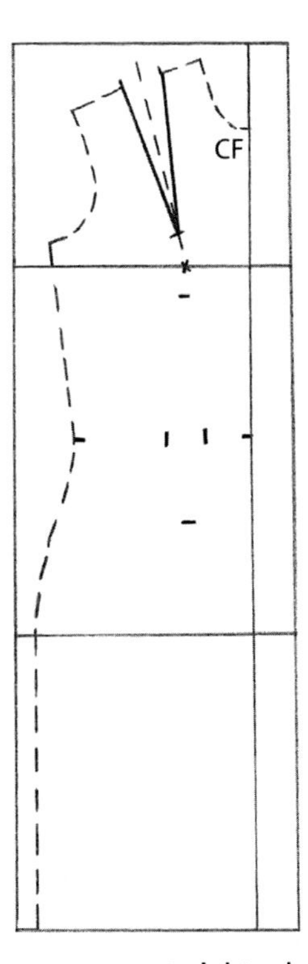

- From the vanishing point, use your straight ruler to connect the dart opening markings on the shoulder seam to create the legs of the dart.
- You should now have a front shoulder dart.

Trueing the Front Sheath Dress Double-Ended Waist Dart

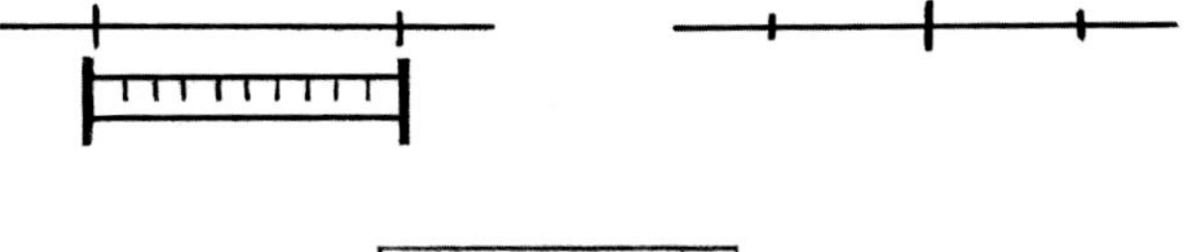

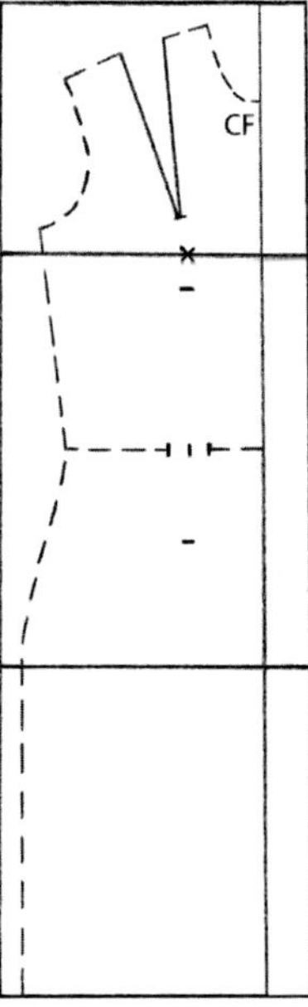

- For the front double-ended waist dart, measure the width of the dart at the widest part at the waistline.
- Divide this measurement in half to determine the center line of the dart. Place a mark in the center of the opening on the waistline.

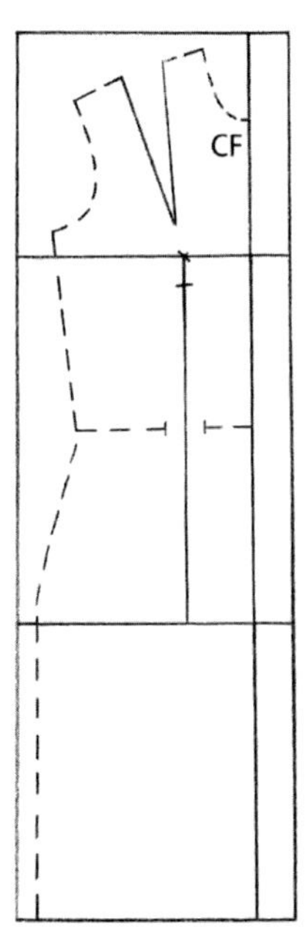

- Using your straight ruler, draw a line from the center point marking at the waistline to the bust point, and then from the waistline down to the hipline. It is important that this line is parallel to the center front line.

- Working with the double-ended dart above the waistline, measure down 1½" (3.8 cm) from the bust point on the center line and mark the vanishing point.

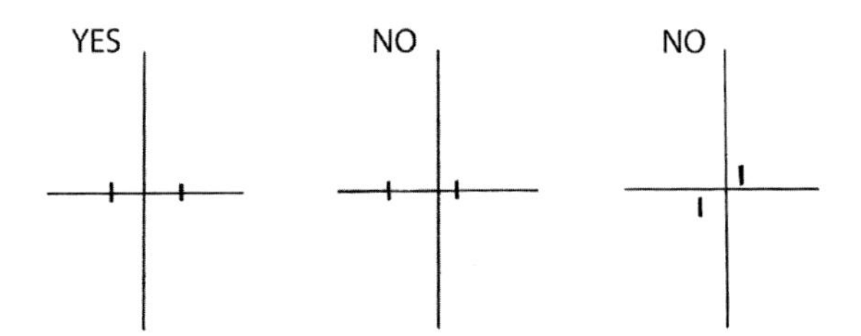

Note: Measure out from the center line perpendicularly along the waistline to points that equal half the total waist opening measurement. It is important that the points at the waistline are perpendicular to the center line of the dart and are not unevenly aligned.

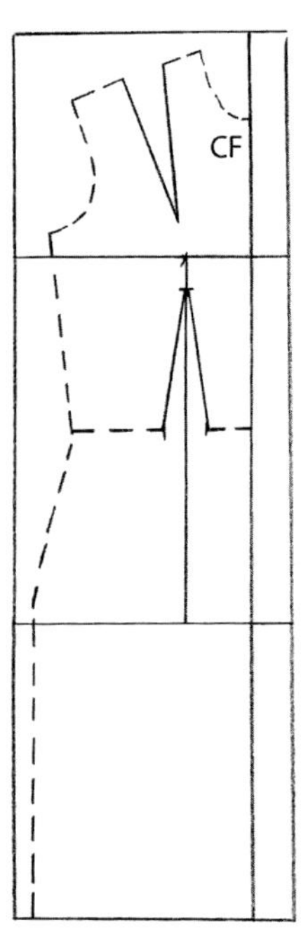

- From the vanishing point under the bust point, use your straight ruler to connect to the dart opening markings on the waistline to create the legs of the top of the dart.

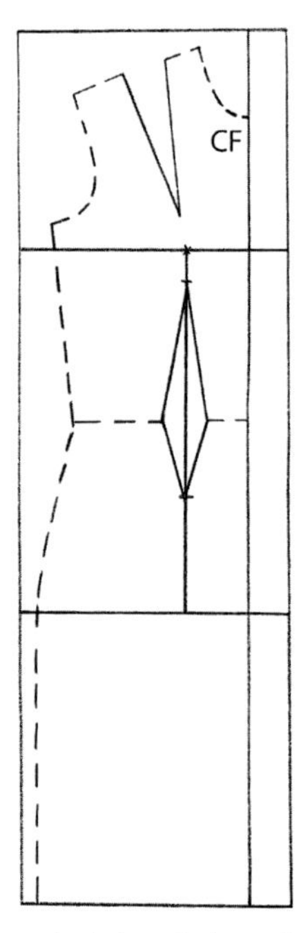

- Working with the double-ended dart below the waistline, measure down 3″ (7.6 cm) from the waistline on the center line and mark the vanishing point.

Note: Dart lengths: Front darts below the waistline are about 3″ (7.6 cm) long depending on the size and shape of the figure.

- From the vanishing point, connect the dart opening markings on the waistline to create the legs of the dart.
- You should now have a front double-ended waist dart.

Trueing the Back Sheath Dress Double-Ended Waist Dart and Shoulder Dart

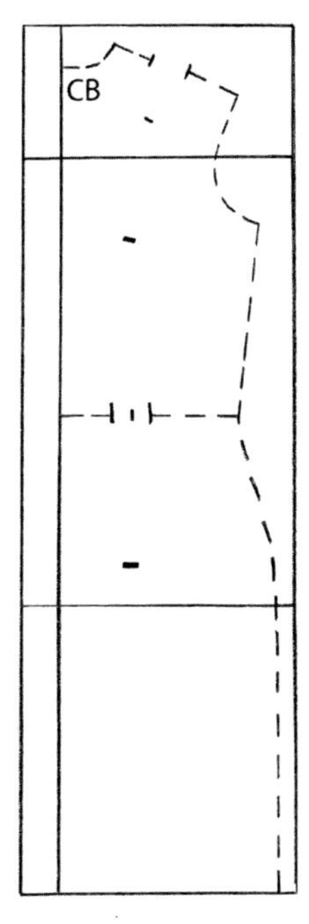

- For the back double-ended waist dart, measure the width of the dart opening. Divide this measurement in half to determine the center point of the dart. Place a mark in the center of the opening on the waistline.
- Using your straight ruler, draw a line to extend the center point marking from the waistline to a point up 7″ (17.8 cm). (This new point may or may not fall in the same location as the original marking.) Then from the waistline continue the line down to the hipline. It is important that this complete line is parallel to the center back line.
- Working with the double-ended dart above the waistline, mark the point that is 7″ (17.8 cm) up on the center line as the vanishing point.

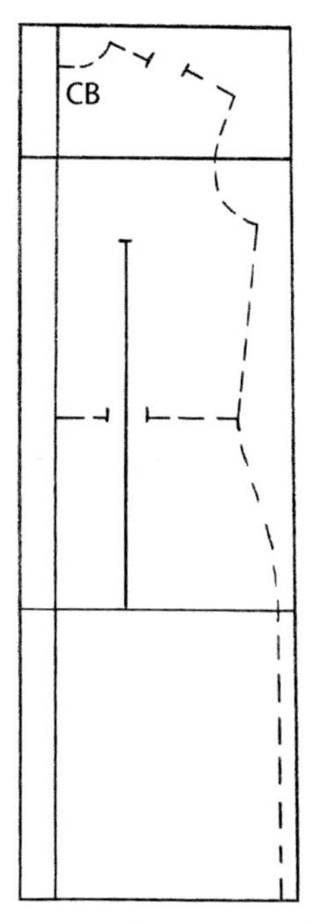

Note: Measure out from the center line perpendicularly along the waistline to points that equal half the total waist opening measurement. It is important that the points at the waistline are perpendicular to the center line of the dart and are not unevenly aligned.

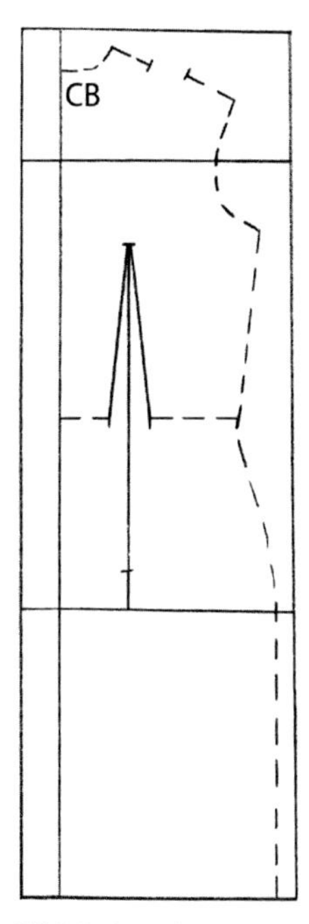

- From the vanishing point 7″ (17.8 cm) up on the center line, use your straight ruler to connect to the dart opening markings on the waistline to create the legs of the top of the dart.

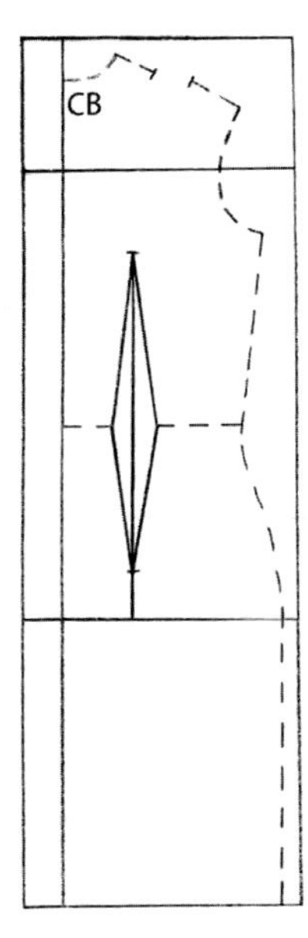

- Working with the double-ended dart below the waistline, measure down 6" (15.2 cm) from the waistline on the center line and mark the vanishing point.

Note: Dart lengths: Back darts below the waistline are longer than front darts. They are usually about 6" (15.2 cm) long, but you do not want to extend them beyond 2" (5.1 cm) above the hipline.

- From the vanishing point, draw lines to the dart opening markings on the waistline to create the legs of the dart.
- You should now have a back double-ended waist dart.

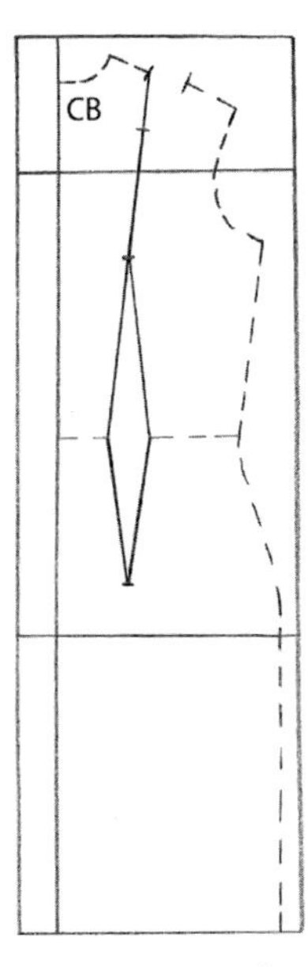

- For the back shoulder dart, extend a line from the back double-ended waist dart vanishing point to the shoulder dart marking closest to the neckline. (This line is unlikely to follow the original princess line.)

- Measure down 3" (7.6 cm) on this line to create a new vanishing point.

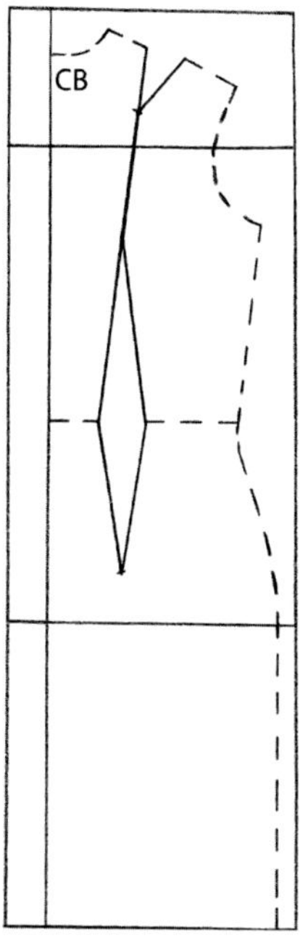

- Connect the other shoulder dart marking to this new vanishing point.
- You should now have a back double-ended waist dart and back shoulder dart.

Trueing the Necklines, Shoulder Seams, and Armscyes

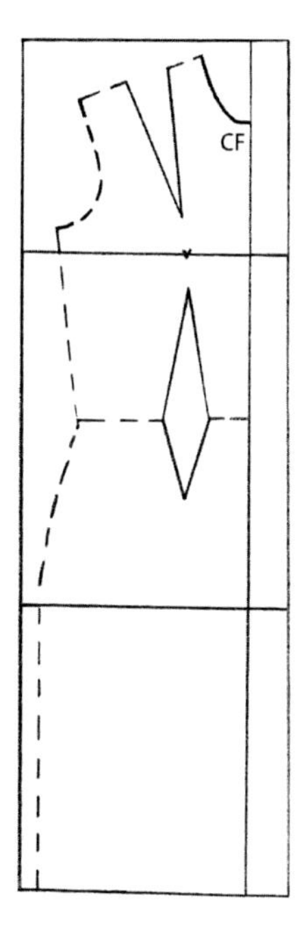

Front

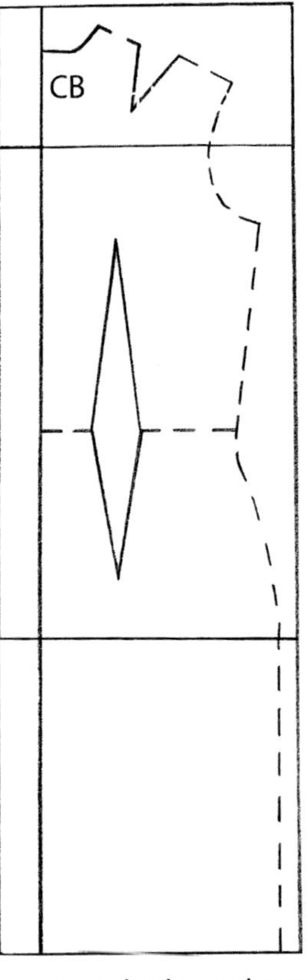

Back

- For the necklines, use your curved ruler and connect your markings, making sure that the 90-degree lines are smoothly blended.

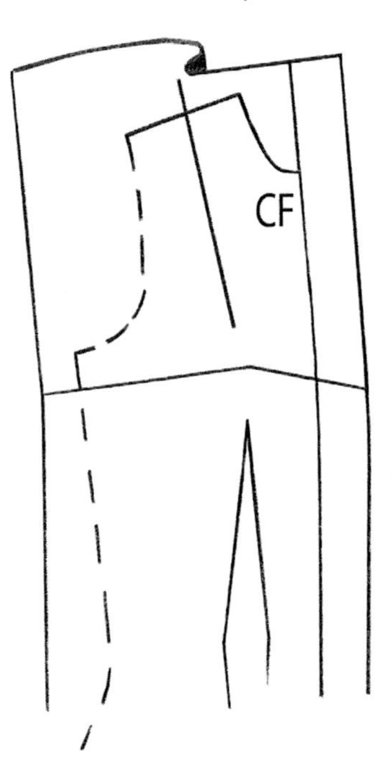

Front

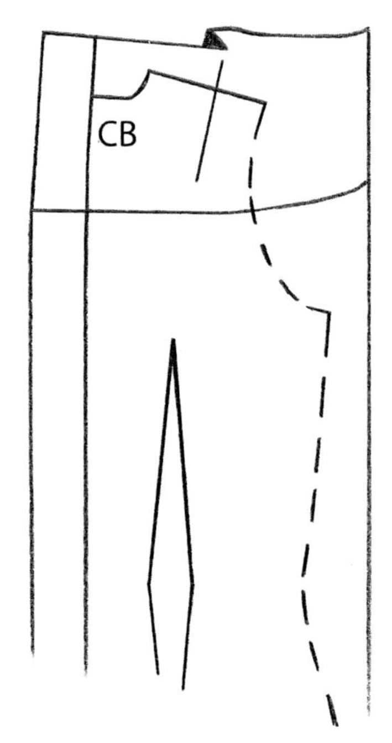

Back

- For the front and back shoulder seams, fold the darts under and using your straight ruler, draw a line from the neckline/shoulder seam point to the armhole/shoulder seam point.

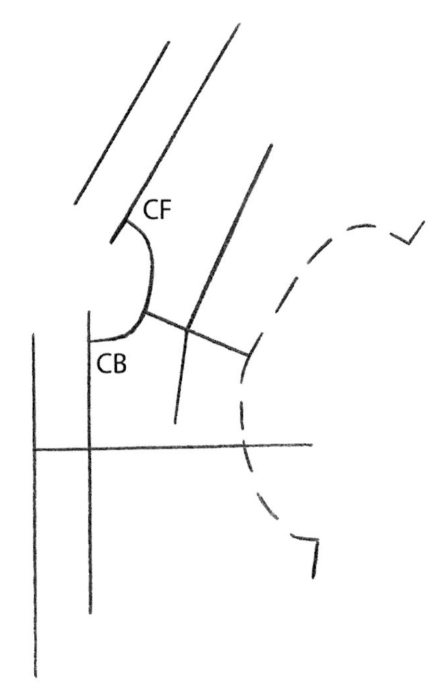

- You will need to check that the front and back shoulder seams are trued to each other by pinning the front shoulder seam to the back shoulder seam. Once pinned, make sure that the neckline, shoulder seams, and the armscye match and are creating smooth transitions.

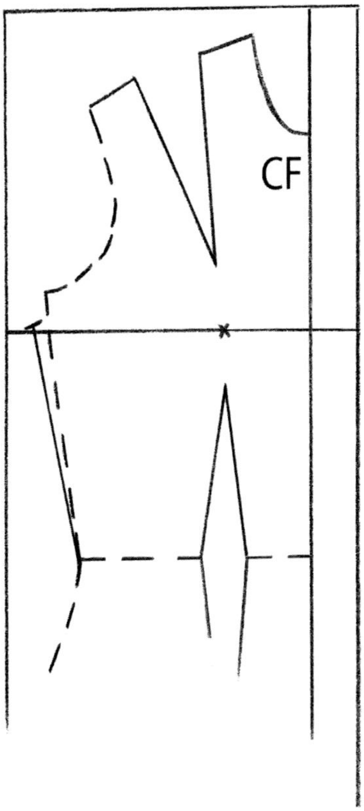

CF

Front

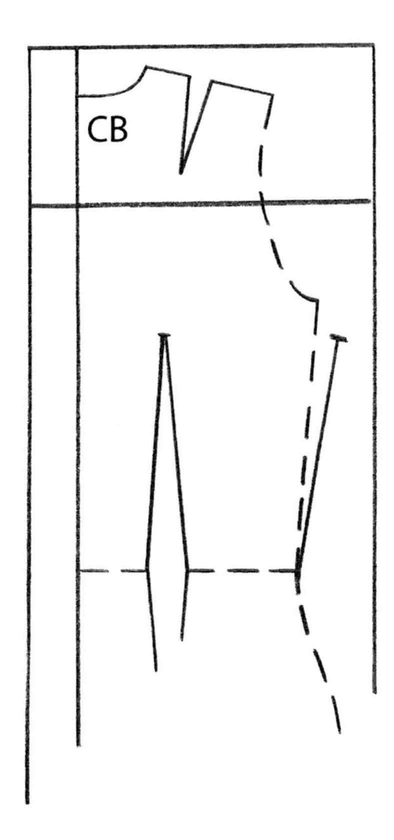

Back

- To add ease at the front and back side seams at the bust line, you will first need to drop the front and back side seams down 1″ (2.5 cm) from the armscye, and then bump them out ½″ (1.3 cm).
- Using your original armscye measurement from your person's measurements, check that the armscye you have created on your draping is about 1–2″ (2.5–5.1 cm) larger than that measurement. If necessary, expand the armscye by dropping it and bumping it out more than the original ease you added. Keep in mind that you can always mark and cut away the armscye in the fitting of the mock-up if it is too snug, but the higher the side seam under the armscye, the more movement is allowed after attaching the sleeve.
- From these new points, use your straight ruler and connect the marks from the armhole points down to the original waistline marks.

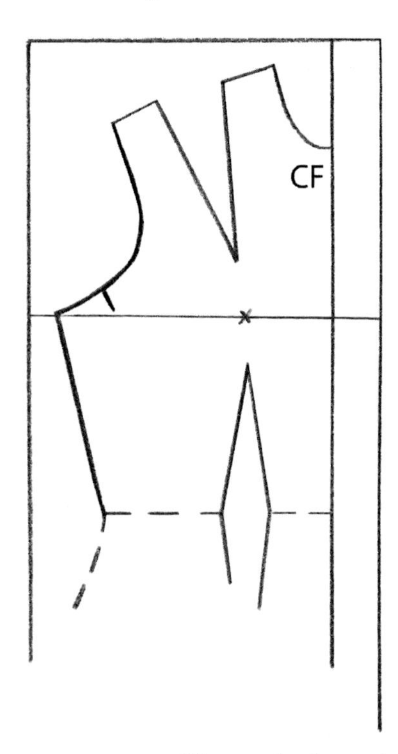

- For the front armscye, use your 12″ curved ruler and connect your shoulder point, your armscye ridge lines, and new side seam/armhole mark.
- Mark the armscye with a single notch at 2.5″ (6.4 cm) from the armscye/side seam intersection.

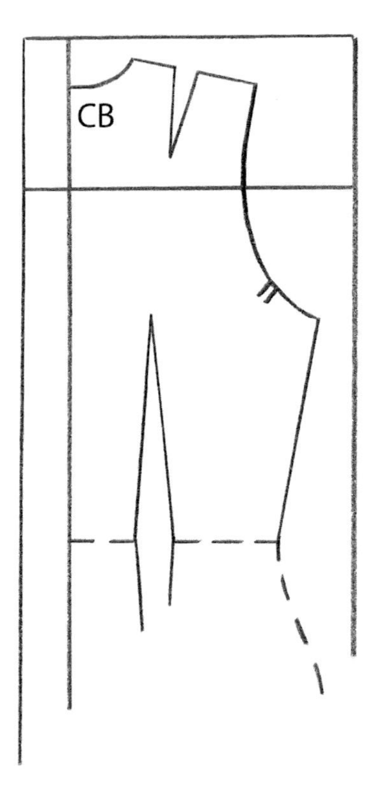

- For the back armscye, use your curved ruler and connect your shoulder point, your armscye ridge lines, and new side seam/armhole mark.
- Mark the armscye with a double notch at 2.5″ (6.4 cm) from the armscye/side seam intersection.

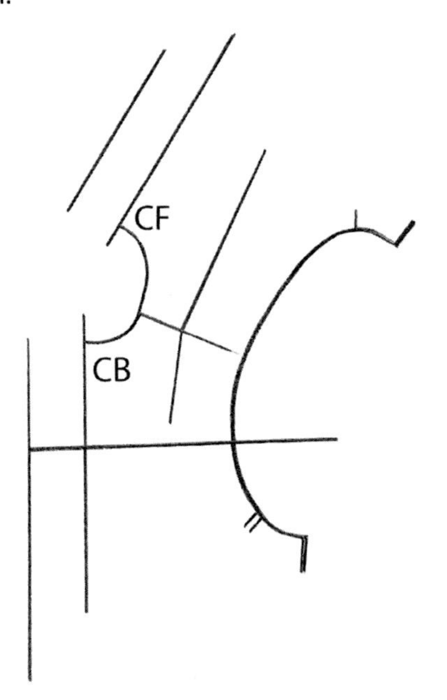

- To true the armscye, pin the front and back shoulder seams together to check that there is a smooth line across the top of the armscye at the shoulder seam and that the armscye does not create a point or "wing" out.

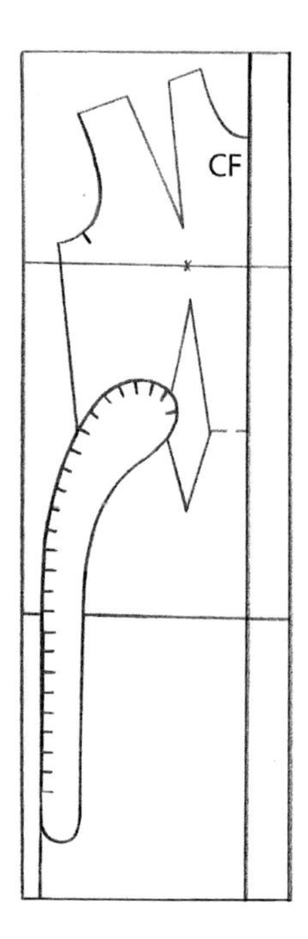

- For the front side seam below the waistline, use your curved ruler with the curved end up at the waistline and the straight end down toward the hem to finesse your side seam line.

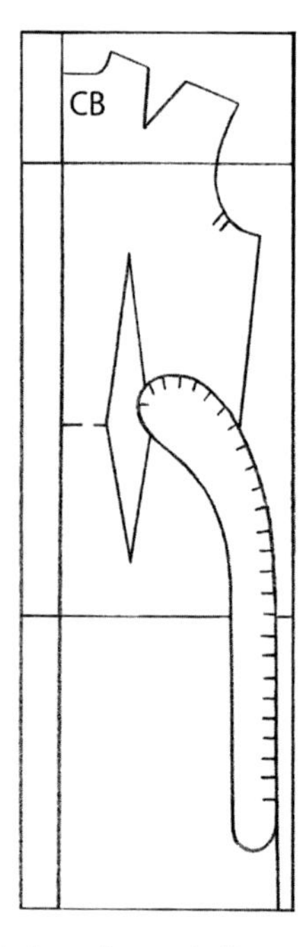

- For the back side seam below the waistline, use your curved ruler with the curved end up at the waistline and the straight end down toward the hem to finesse your side seam line.

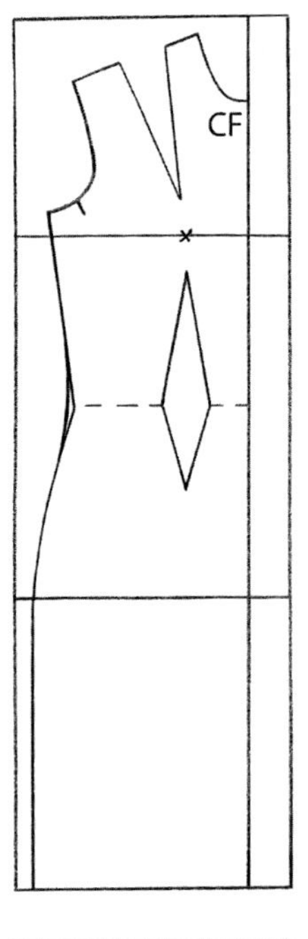

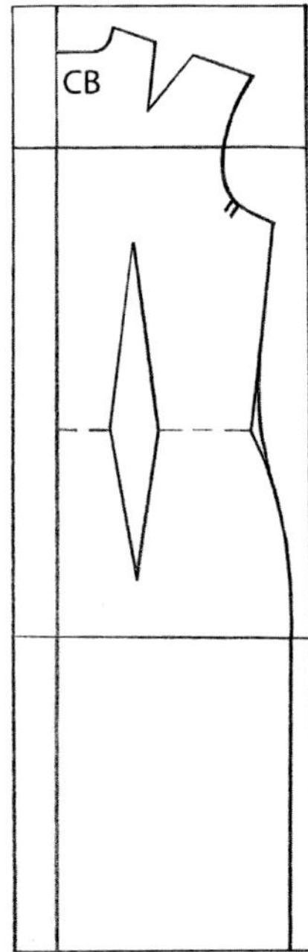

- Smooth the waistlines at the side seams so that they are not coming to a point, but have a smooth curve.

*True the darts that open on seams by following the directions in the Appendix for Trueing Darts.

Check List for Fit and Correct Amount of Ease

- Prior to pinning the pieces together to check for fit, trim the excess muslin down to 1″ seam allowance.
- Pin your trued muslin together, including all darts, side seam, and shoulder seam and place back on the dress form.

Ease Checklist

- At side seam/armhole intersection = ½″ (1.3 cm) per front and back (1″ (2.5 cm) total per side)
- At bust front = ⅛″–¼″ (0.3–0.6 cm)
- At back shoulder blade = ⅛″–¼″ (0.3–0.6 cm)
- At waist = ¼″ (0.6 cm) per front and back (½″ (1.3 cm) total per side)

After Trueing

- Fit Check:
- Pin the bodice to the dress form at neckline, shoulder seam, waistline at center front and center back, and side seam.
- Pin the front and back together at the side seams from the hip level line to hem.
- Pin the darts closed and check the waistline shape for a smooth curve.
- Using your flexible straight grid ruler, place the ruler on its edge and measure from the waistline to the hip level line for front and back side seams from hip level line to waistline. The measurements should be the same.
    - If the measurements are off, then adjust the back side seam to match the front side seam.
    - If the measurements off by are more than ⅝″ (1.6 cm), then you will need to check the drape to correct for this.
- Leaving the side seams pinned, draw the hemline in.
    - Mark the desired length of the skirt at the CB and draw a line parallel to the hip level line across to CF.
- Front and back grainlines should hang straight without twisting or pulling.
- Shoulder seams should align with each other and darts should align.
- Side seams should be the same length.
- The armhole is a smooth fat oval shape.
- Cross-grains should be parallel to the floor.
- Side seam should align with the side seam of the dress form.
- Darts are pinned shut to vanishing points.
- Darts are smooth without twisting.

How to Draft the Basic Sheath Dress

The basic sheath dress combines the fitted bodice and fitted skirt, removing the waistline seam to create a sheath sloper with a single combined dart per half of the front and back (two darts total in the front and two darts total in the back).

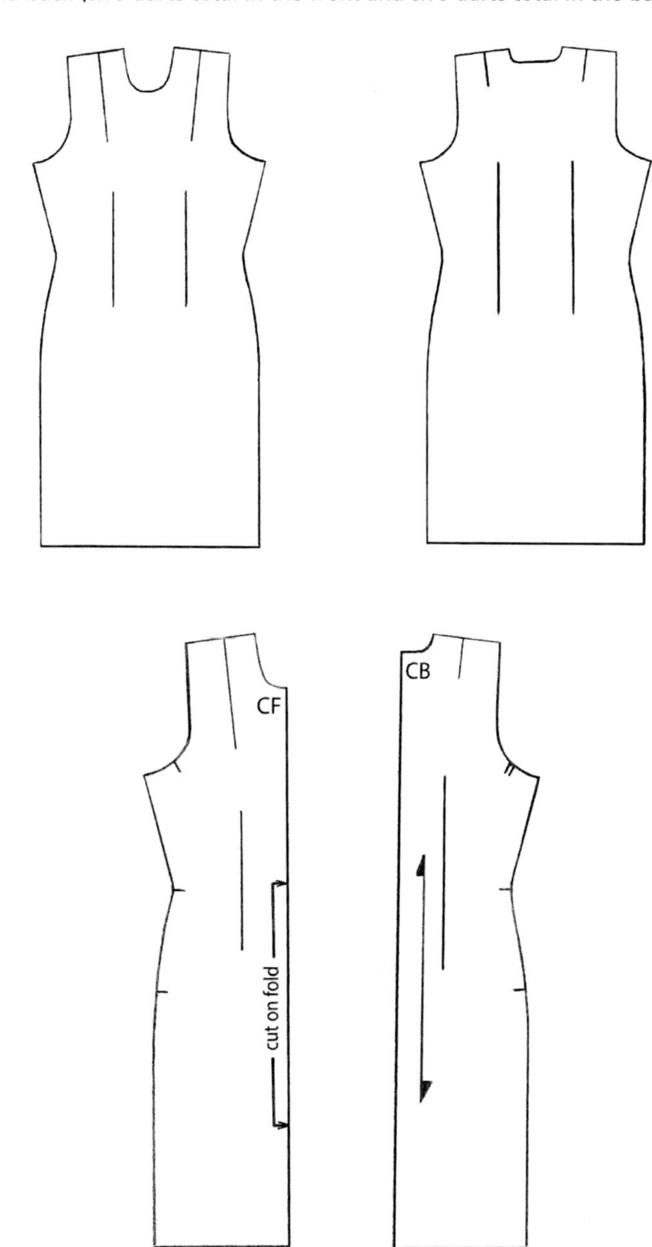

Anatomy of the Basic Sheath Dress

Front

- Use copies of your drafted Basic Bodice Front (with either a side seam bust dart or shoulder dart, and a waist dart), and your drafted Basic Skirt Front. (The Basic Skirt pattern should have 1.5"–2" (3.8–5.1 cm) of total ease at the hipline. If the skirt was drafted without this ease, add it to the side seams prior to drafting the Basic Sheath Dress. Divide the total ease by the number of seams and add that measurement to each seam.)

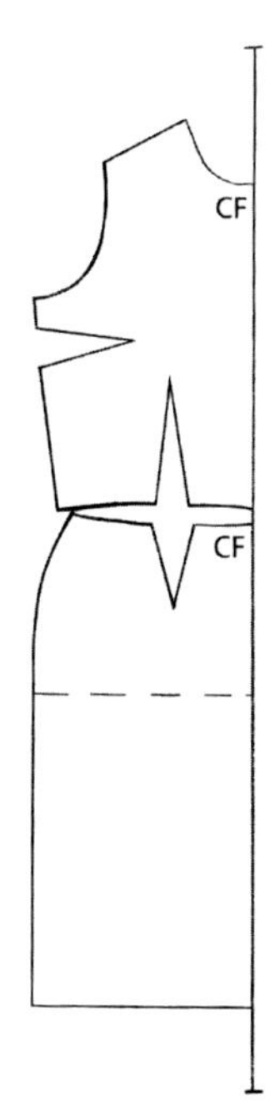

- On a large piece of paper, long enough to trace the bodice and skirt connected, draw a straight line down the right hand side of the page. Line up the center fronts of the bodice and skirt against this line.

Note: If the width of the bodice waistline is wider than the skirt waistline, then you will need to slash and spread the dart on the skirt waistline. Follow these instructions:

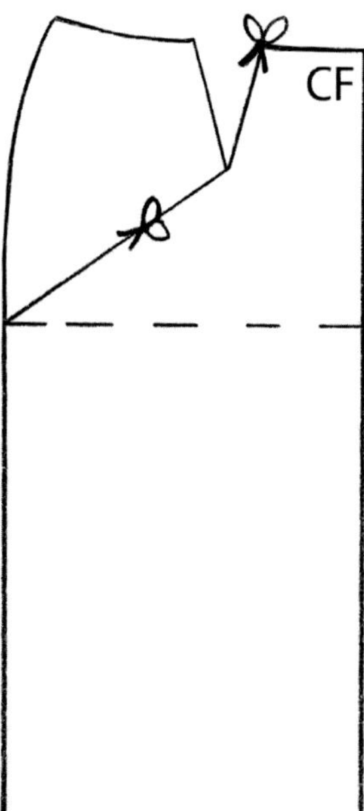

- Draw a line from the tip of the Skirt Front dart to the hipline at the side seam.
- Slash down the leg of the dart closest to the center front, continuing down the drawn line to but not through the side seam.

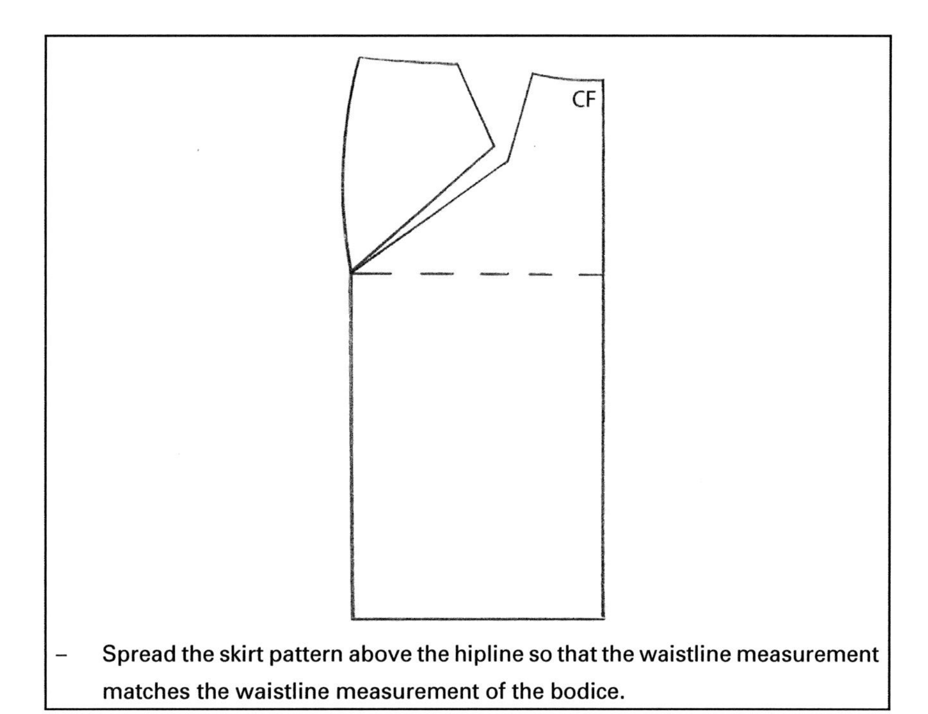

- Spread the skirt pattern above the hipline so that the waistline measurement matches the waistline measurement of the bodice.

- Pin the bodice front and skirt front to the paper along the line drawn on the right hand side joining the waistlines at the side seam. (The waistlines at the center front may not line up.)
- Trace the pattern – including darts, grainline, and labels.

Back

- Use copies of your drafted fitted Basic Bodice Back and drafted Basic Skirt Back. (The Basic Skirt pattern should have 1.5″–2″ [3.8–5.1 cm] of ease at the hipline. If the skirt was drafted without this ease, add it to the side seams prior to drafting the Basic Sheath Dress. Divide the total ease by the number of seams and add that measurement to each seam.)

Note: If the width of the bodice waistline is narrower than the skirt waistline, then you will need to slash and spread the dart on the bodice waistline. Follow these instructions:

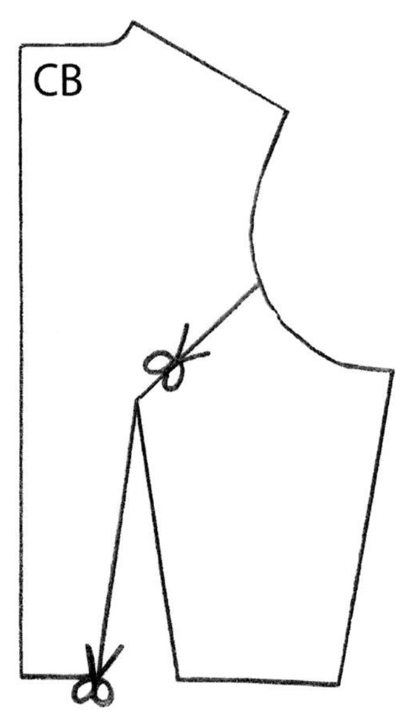

- Draw a straight line from the tip of the Bodice Back dart to the armscye.
- Slash up the leg of the dart closest to the center back, continuing up the drawn line to but not through the armscye.

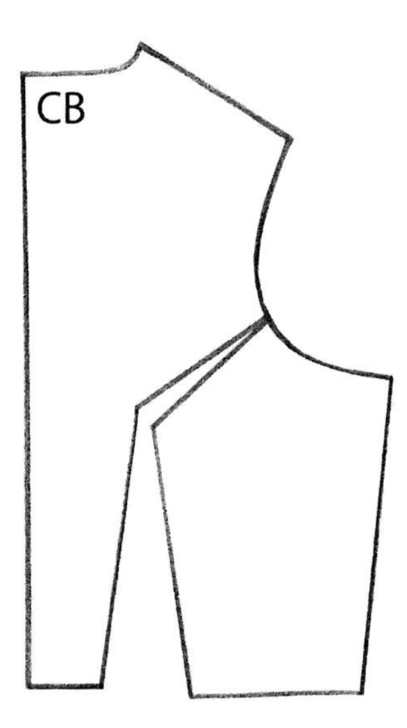

- Spread the bodice pattern at the waistline so that the bodice waistline measurement matches the waistline measurement of the skirt.

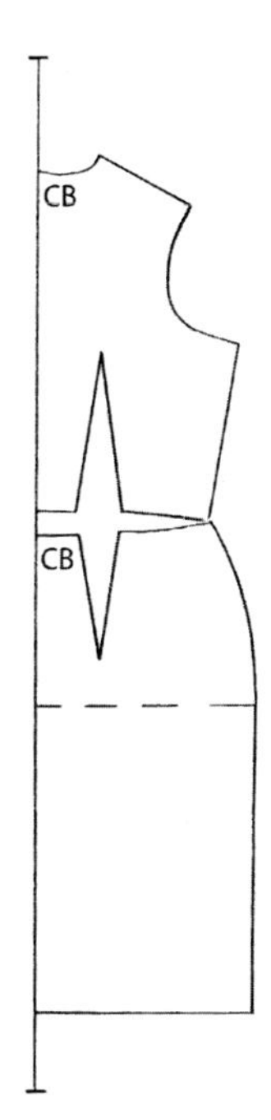

- On a large piece of paper with a straight line drawn down the left-hand side of the page, line up the center backs of the bodice and skirt against this line.
- Pin the Bodice Back and Skirt Back to the paper along the line drawn on the left hand sidc joining the waistlines at the side seam. (The waistlines at the center back may not line up.)
- Trace the pattern – including darts, grainline, and labels.

Creating the Double-Ended Dart for Front and Back

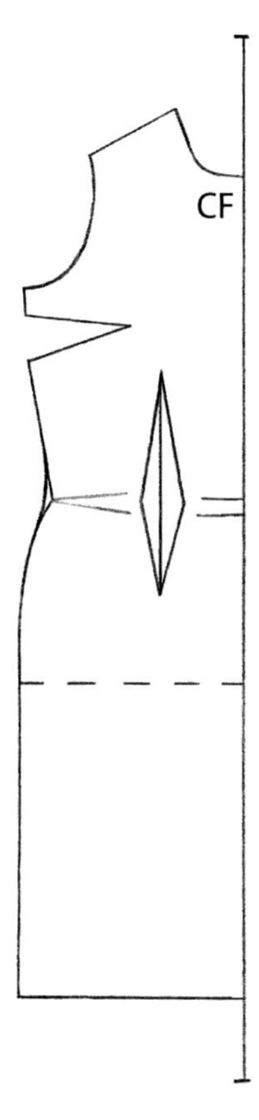

- For the front double-ended waist dart, measure the width of the dart at the waistline.
- Divide this measurement in half to determine the center line of the dart. Place a mark in the center of the opening on the waistline.
- Using your straight ruler, draw a line from the center point marking at the waistline equal to the length of the original dart.
- From the tips of the darts (the vanishing points), draw in the dart legs with lines connecting the vanishing points to the markings at the waistline.

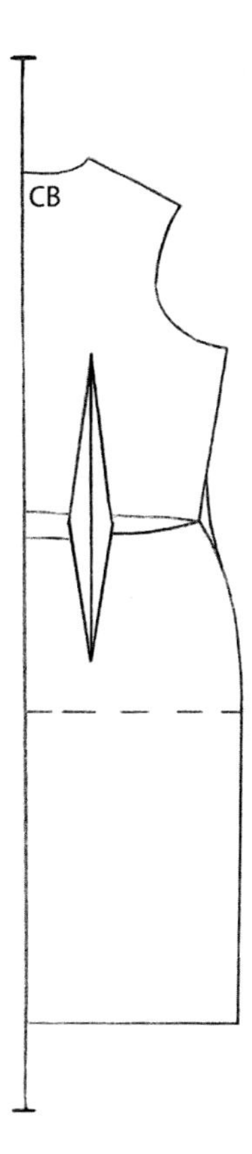

- For the back double-ended waist dart, measure the width of the dart at the waistline.
- Divide this measurement in half to determine the center line of the dart. Place a mark in the center of the opening on the waistline.
- Using your straight ruler, draw a line from the center point marking at the waistline equal to the length of the original dart.
- From the tips of the darts (the vanishing points), draw in the dart legs with lines connecting the vanishing points to the markings at the waistline.
- Smooth the waistline at the side seam so that it is not coming to a point, but is a smooth curve.

Chapter 9: Pants

How to Draft the Basic Pant

The Basic Pant is fitted through the hips, through the waist with shaping darts, and has a slightly tapered leg. These pants are designed to have a side seam opening.

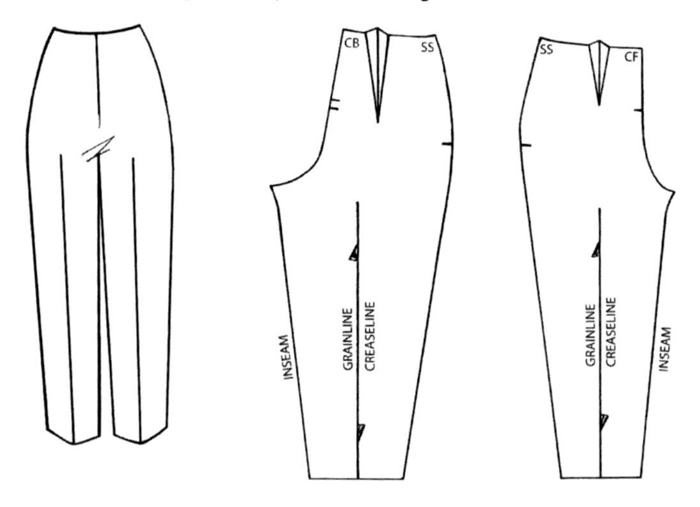

Anatomy of the Basic Pant

Measurements Needed:			
Inseam:	Waist to Above Knee:	Waist:	Hip Front:
Outseam:	Waist to Below Knee:	Hip:	Hip Back:
Crotch Depth:	Waist to Mid Knee:	Hip Point:	Bust Pt to Bust Pt:

(To get the Waist to Mid Knee measurement, subtract the Waist to Above Knee measurement from the Waist to Below Knee measurement and divide that number by 2. Then add that number to the Waist to Above Knee measurement.)

DOI: 10.4324/9781003022619-9

Note

- Add 1″ (2.5 cm) of ease to the crotch depth measurement.

Directions

- Paper size = Height of the paper should allow for the Outseam measurement + 4″ (10.2 cm), and width should allow for ½ Hip measurement + 14″ (35.6 cm).

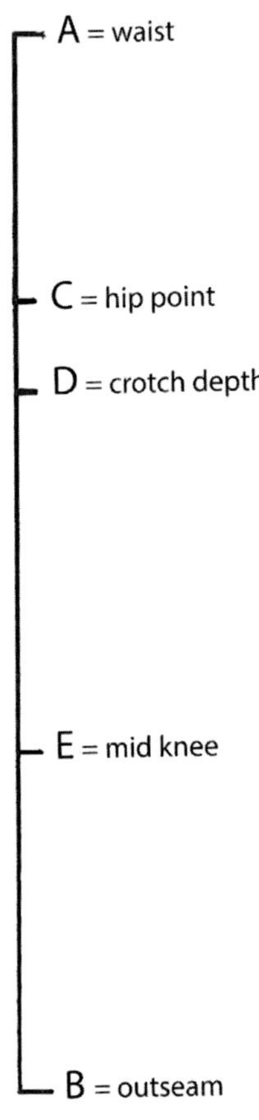

- Down the CENTER of the paper, draw a vertical line A-B, where A-B = the Outseam measurement.
- From A, measure down on the A-B line to new point C, where A-C = Hip Point measurement.
- From A, measure down on the A-B line to new point D, where A-D = Crotch Depth measurement.
- From A, measure down on the A-B line to new point E, where A-E = Waist to Mid Knee measurement.
- From point D, draw a horizontal line out across the paper perpendicular to the vertical center line A-B.

Pants

BACK: (LEFT side of the A-B line)

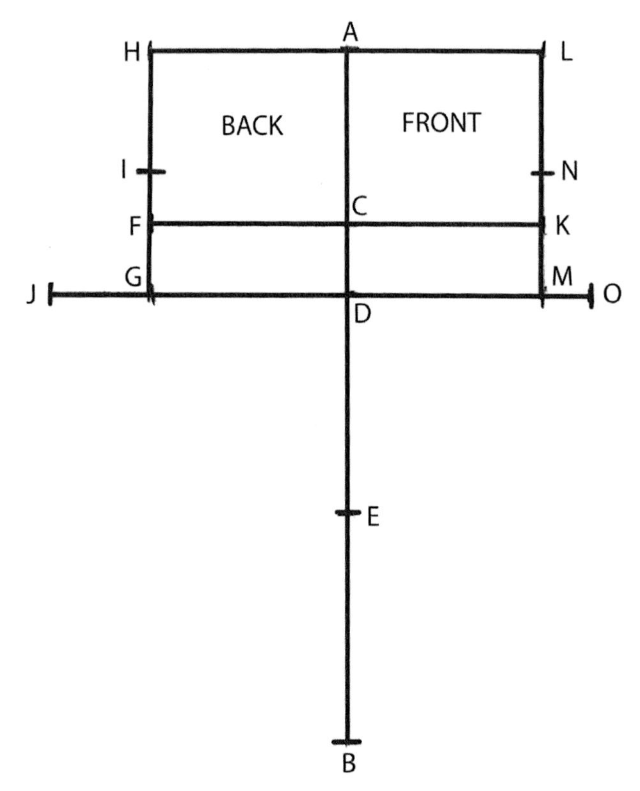

- Working on the left side of vertical line A-B, from C, draw a perpendicular line horizontally out to point F, where C-F = ½ Back Hip measurement + ¼" (0.6 cm) for ease.
- To the left of A and D, extend horizontal lines out from the A-B line to connect D to G and A to H where D-G and A-H = C-F.
- Connect G to H with a vertical line crossing through point F.
- Measure the distance between points G and H, divide this in half, and mark new point I.
- Extend line D-G to the left of point G to new point J, where G-J = ⅛ Total Hip measurement.

FRONT: (RIGHT side of the A-B line)

- Working on the right side of vertical line A-B, from C, draw a perpendicular line horizontally out to point K, where C-K = ½ Front Hip measurement + ¼" (0.6 cm) for ease.
- To the right of A and D, extend horizontal lines out from the A-B line to connect A to L and D to M where A-L and D-M = C-K.
- Connect L to M with a vertical line crossing through point K.
- Measure the distance between points M and L, divide this in half, and mark new point N.
- Extend line D-M to the right of point M to new point O, where M-O = Total Hip measurement.

Adding Darts

(*See DART CHART below to determine dart widths.)

Back Dart: (LEFT side of the A-B line)

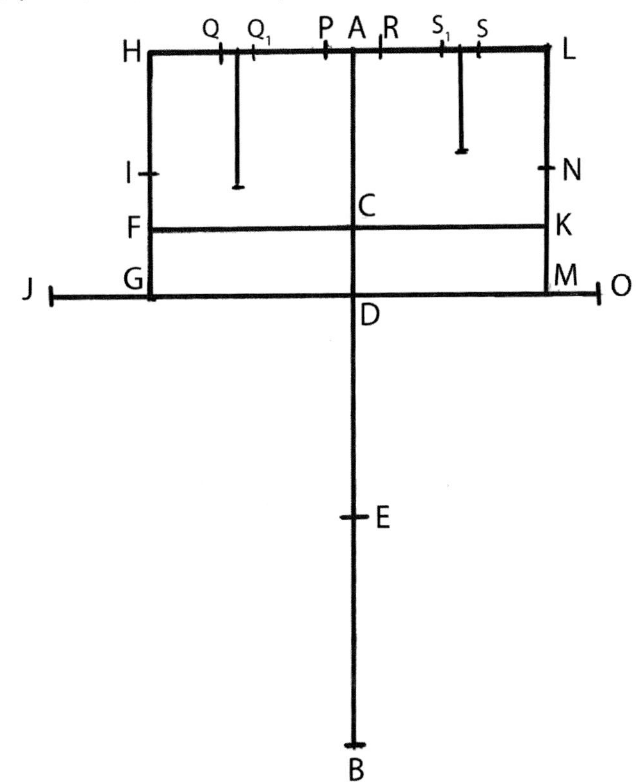

- From H, measure out to new point P, where H-P = ¼ Waist measurement + dart measurement from the Dart Chart (or 1½″ (3.8 cm)) + ¼″ (0.6 cm) for ease. (If you used the Dart Chart, and you find that the location for P is at or past A, then use a smaller dart measurement making sure to use the same measurement for the Front dart.)
- From H, measure to new point Q, where H-Q = 3″ (7.6 cm). (Q marks the top of the first leg of the dart.)
- For the other leg of the dart, measure over from Q to Q_1, where Q_1 = 1½″ (3.8 cm) (or your dart measurement from the Dart Chart).
- Mark the center of the dart between Q and Q_1 and draw a vertical line to a point 6″ down from the waistline.

Front Dart: (RIGHT side of the A-B line)

(*See Dart Chart below to determine dart widths.)

- From L, measure out to new point R, where L-R = ¼ Waist measurement + dart measurement from chart (or 1½″ (3.8 cm)) + ¼″ (0.6 cm) for ease. (If you used the Dart Chart, and you find that the location for P is at or past A, then use a smaller dart measurement that is equal to the Back dart measurement.)
- From L, measure to new point S, where L-S = 3″ (7.6 cm) or ½ Bust Point to Bust Point measurement. (S marks the top of the first leg of the dart.)

- For the other leg of the dart, measure over from S to S_1, where S_1 = 1½" (3.8 cm)(or your dart measurement from the Dart Chart).
- Mark the center of the dart between S and S_1 and draw a vertical line to a point 3" (7.6 cm) down from the waistline.

Crotch Depth Adjustments
Back: (LEFT side of the A-B line)

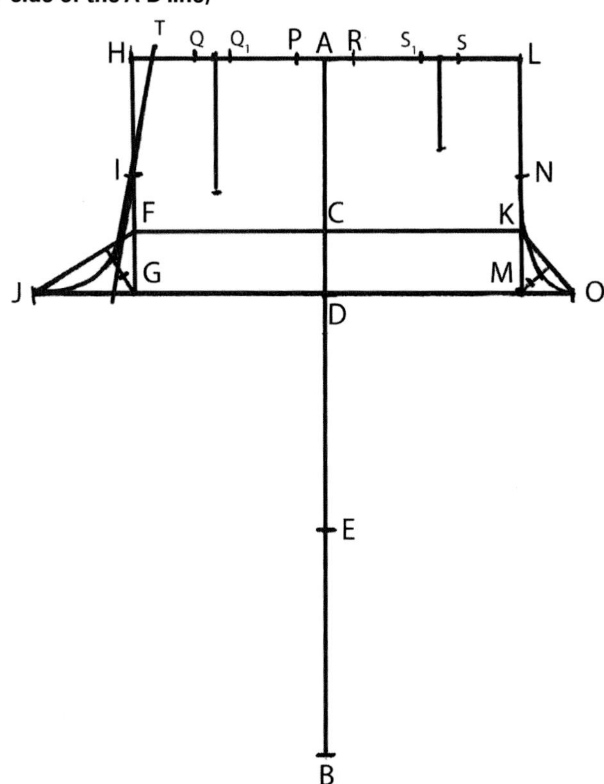

- From H, mark point T at ¾" (1.9 cm) in toward Q, and ¼" (0.6 cm) up from line A-H.
- From point T, draw a straight line to line J-G crossing through point I.
- Connect point F to point J with a diagonal line.
- Making a right angle, draw a line perpendicular to the F-J line to point G.
- Divide the new line into three equal lengths and mark the point closest to line F-J.
- Using your curved ruler with the straight end toward J, draw a line connecting I-J using the new point as a through point.

Front: (RIGHT side of the A-B line)

- Connect point K to point O with a diagonal line.
- Making a right angle, draw a line perpendicular to K-O to point M.
- Divide the new line into three equal lengths and mark the point closest to line K-O.
- Using your curved ruler with the straight end toward N, draw a line connecting N-O using the new point as a through point.

Waistlines
Back and Front:

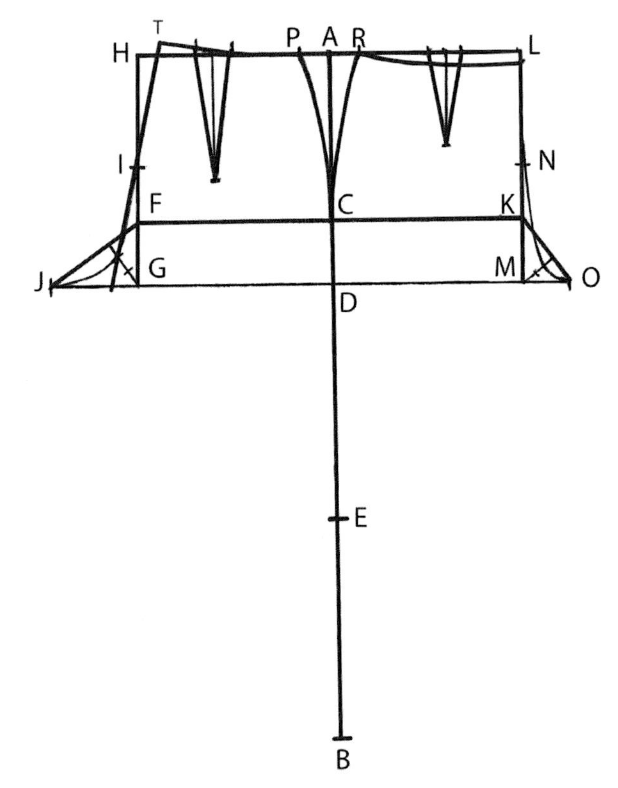

- Using your curved ruler with the straight end toward T, connect T to P, keeping the line perpendicular at the center back (point T) to keep a smooth line across the center front waistline.
- From L, on the L-M line, mark a point ¼″ (0.6 cm) down.
- Using your curved ruler with the straight end toward the new dropped point, draw a line from R to the new point keeping the line perpendicular at the center front (new dropped point) to keep a smooth line across the center front waistline.

(You may need to extend the length of the crotch depth depending on how the fullness of the figure is distributed. If the figure is more full in the front stomach area, you will want to add length to the front crotch depth by extending up from point L [not to be confused with crotch extension in the inseam area].

If the figure is more full in the back area, you will want to add length to the back crotch depth by extending up from point T [not to be confused with crotch extension in the inseam area]).

Darts

- Using your straight ruler, draw the legs of your darts from the adjusted waistlines to the dart points.

Outseams Above Hip Point

- Using your curved ruler with the straight edge down toward C and the curved edge up at R, draw the hip curves in from R to a point above C where the curve naturally fades out, close to, or at C, and then from P to the same vanishing point above, or at C. (The vanishing point of the hip curve will depend on the difference between the waist and hip measurement of the figure measured. The larger the difference between the waist and hip will result in a more abrupt curve from the waist. The less the difference between the waist and hip will result in a more gradual curve from the waist.)

Pant Legs

- Draw a horizontal line across the paper through B perpendicular to line A-B to create the ankle line.

Back:

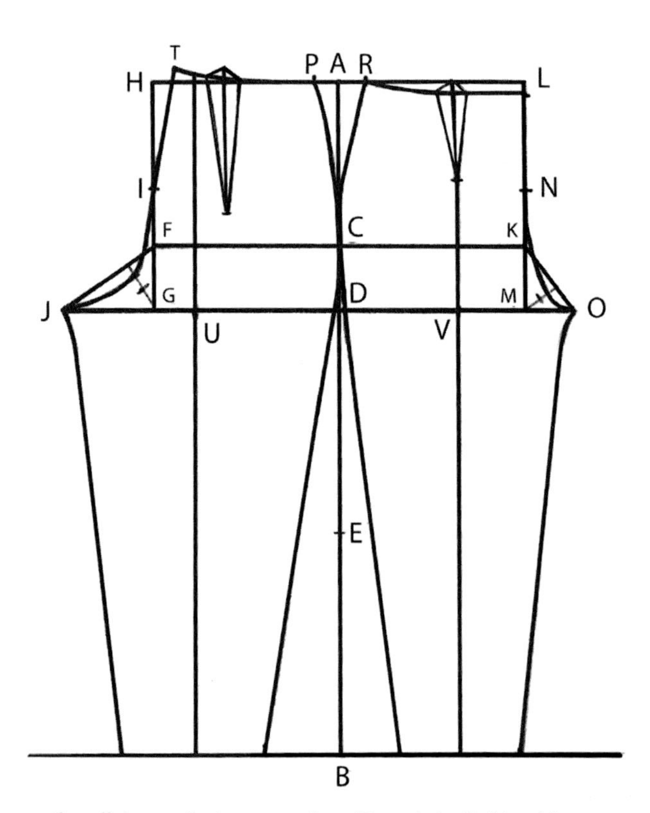

- Measure the distance between points D and J, divide this measurement in half, add ¼″ (0.6 cm) for ease and mark new point U with U closer to J.
- Draw a vertical line through U perpendicular to D-J from the waistline to the ankle line. (This line is your creaseline and grainline.)

Front:

- Measure the distance between points D and O, divide this measurement in half, add ¼″ (0.6 cm) for ease and mark new point V with V closer to O.
- Draw a vertical line through V perpendicular to D-O from the waistline to the ankle line. (This line is your creaseline and grainline.)

Outseams and Inseams
Back

- For a traditional trouser leg, at the ankle line, measure out 5″ (12.7 cm) to either side of creaseline and mark each point.
- For the Outseam, draw a straight line from the ankle point to point D and then connect to the hip point at point C with a slight curve.
- For the Inseam, using either your straight ruler or your curved ruler (with the straight edge at the ankle line and the curved edge at J), draw a line from the ankle line to J.

Front

- For a traditional trouser leg, at the ankle line, measure out 4″ (10.2 cm) to either side of creaseline and mark each point.
- For the Outseam, draw a straight line from ankle point to point D and then connect to the hip point at point C with a slight curve.
- For the Inseam, using either your straight ruler or your curved ruler (with the straight edge at the ankle line and the curved edge at O), draw a line from the ankle line to O.

(Pant legs can have varying fullness at the ankle depending on the style desired. Adjust as needed.)

*True the darts at the waistline by following the directions in the Appendix for Trueing Darts.

Labeling

- Label the pant legs, adding matching notches at the following locations: a single notch at N to indicate the Center Front, a double notch at I to indicate the Center Back, and a matching notch at C to match the Fronts and Backs to each other at the side seams.

Dart Chart

*To estimate the amount you need for darts, subtract your waist measurement from your hip measurement.

- If the difference is 11″ (27.9 cm) or more, use 2″ (5.1 cm) darts.
- If the difference is 9″ to 11″ (22.9–27.9 cm), use 1½″ (3.8 cm) darts.
- If the difference is 7″ to 9″ (17.8–22.9 cm) use 1″ (2.5 cm) darts.
- If the difference is less than 7″ (17.8 cm) use ½″ (1.3 cm) darts.

Chapter 10: Waistbands

How to Draft Waistbands

- **The rectangular waistband** is the most traditional style waistband as long as the waistline is at the natural waist and the waistband does not exceed 1¼″ (3.2 cm) in width. It is cut with an underlap, and can have a self-facing that is cut in one with the waistband.
- The common width for a finished waistband is 1¼″ (3.2 cm), but should not exceed 2″ (5.1 cm). If the waistband exceeds 2″ (5.1 cm), then it would need to be shaped to accommodate the curving of the figure (see later for the Shaped or Contoured Waistband).

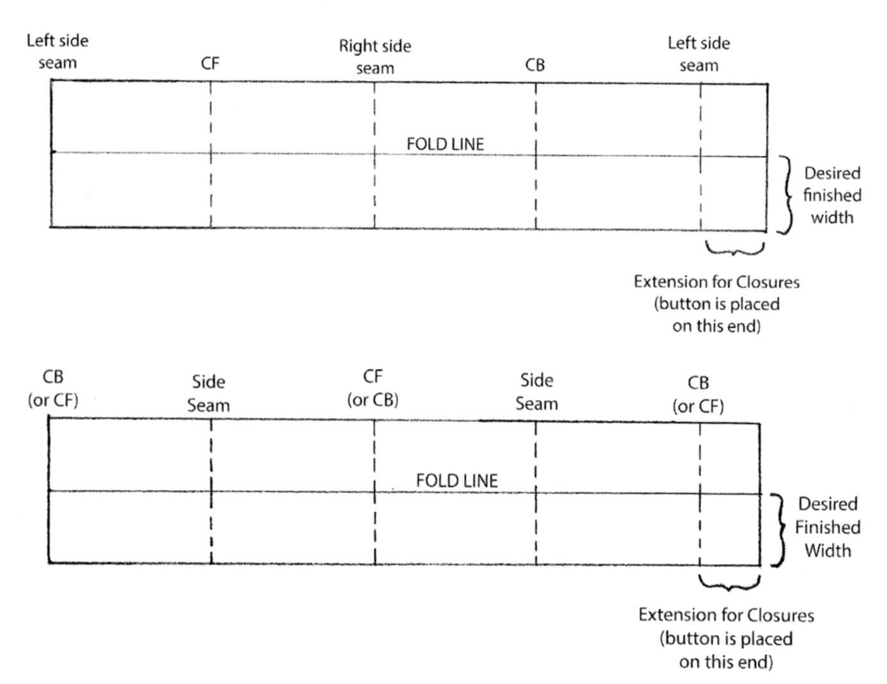

- To create the **Rectangular Waistband**, you will need the waist measurement of the garment you are applying the waistband to + 1½″ (3.8 cm) underlap. (The underlap measurement can vary depending on your closure needs.) You do

DOI: 10.4324/9781003022619-10

not need to add ease because it was added in the draping or drafting of the garment and the waistband is using those measurements.

- When creating the pattern for a self-faced rectangular waistband, you will need to double the finished waistband width measurement as indicated in the diagram.
- To create your rectangular waistband, you will need your original garment sloper for your pants or skirt.
- Before measuring, close any darts if there are any.
- Measure the sloper from the center front to the side seam. Save this measurement.
- Then measure the sloper from the side seam to the center back. Save this measurement also.
- Using the saved measurements, draw a rectangle the desired finished width and a length equal to SS to CF, CF to SS, SS to CB, and CB to SS + the length of the underlap on one length edge.
- This will give you a rectangular waistband with a side seam opening.

- **The Shaped or Contoured Waistband** is used on a skirt or pant with a lowered waistline or if the waistband exceeds 2″ (5.1 cm) in width. You must use a contoured waistband because a rectangular one will not fit the body and will gap.
- To create the shaped or contoured waistband, you will need your skirt or pant pattern. For this example, the skirt pattern will be shown.

Contoured Waistband

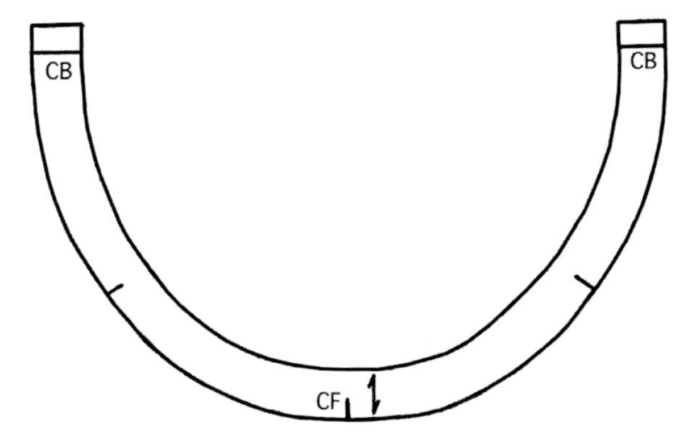

Drafting the Contoured Waistband

- Trace the top of the skirt pattern from the hip point up onto another layer of craft paper.
- Make sure you mark the dart legs, the dart tips, the center front and center back, and side seams.
- Remove your skirt pattern after you have traced it and have marked your lines, points, and labels.
- Draw in the darts using the markings you have made on the new paper.

Waistbands

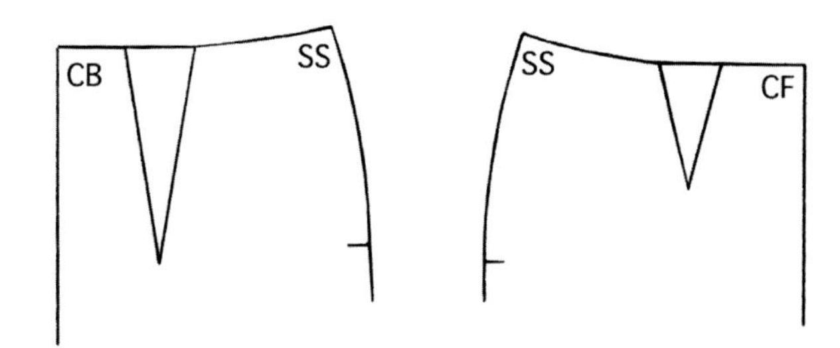

- Measure down from the waist for the depth of the waistband. For this example, the waistband will measure 1.5″ (3.8 cm) wide. The waistline is curved so you need to make sure that the line you draw is parallel to the upper curved line and measures 1.5″ (3.8 cm) in depth. The final shape of the new waistband should be the same curve as the original waistline.

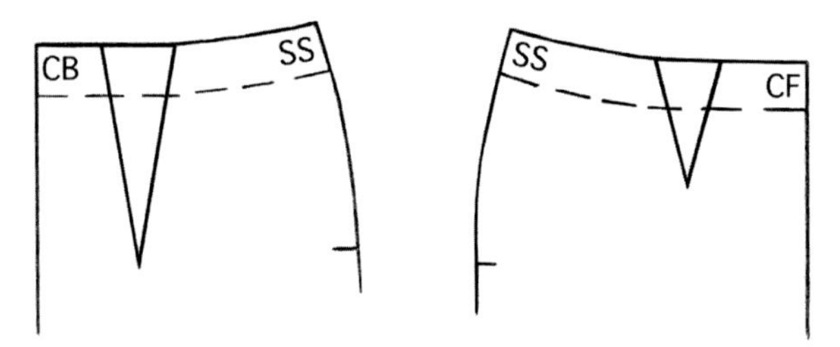

- You should now cut along the traced lines to separate the waistband from the skirt.

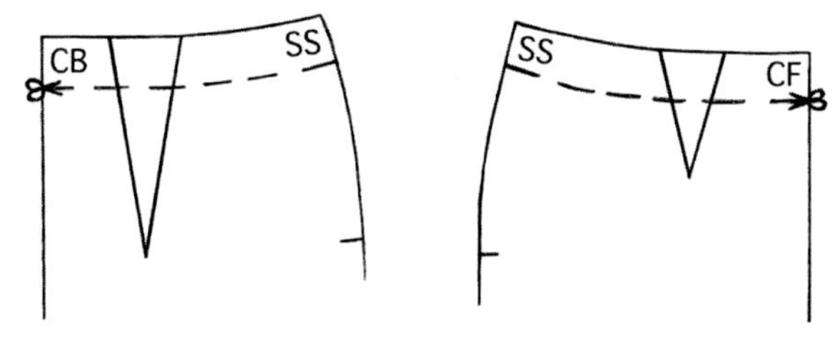

- Label the side front and the side back pieces.
- Cut along the dart lines; separating the waistband into six individual pieces: a center front, a dart section, and a side front, as well as a center back, a dart section, and a side back.

- You can discard the two dart sections.
- Use clear tape to tape the two front pieces (center front and side front) and the back pieces (center back and side back) together.

- Use clear tape and tape the side front to the side back for one continuous piece.

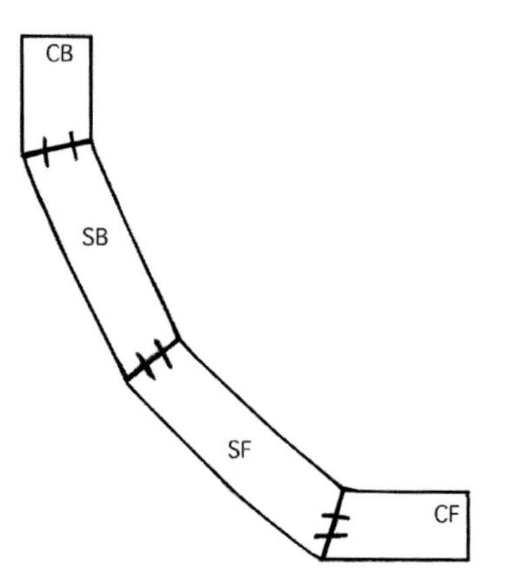

- Using another clean layer of craft paper, pin your taped waistband pieces on the paper.
- Trace the waistband onto the paper, transferring the markings for center front, center back, and side seams.

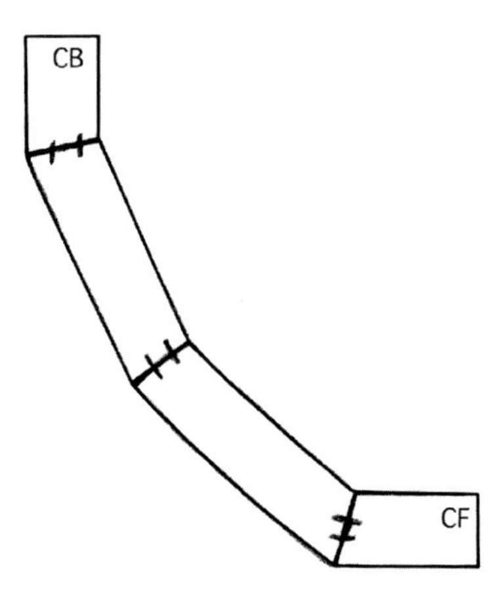

- Remove the taped waistband from the new paper.
- On the new paper pattern, add a 1″ (2.5 cm) extension from the center back for a closure.
- Smooth out the angles on the pattern to create smooth curves.
- Draw on the grainline with the center front as cut on fold or you can create the entire pattern and cut as one.

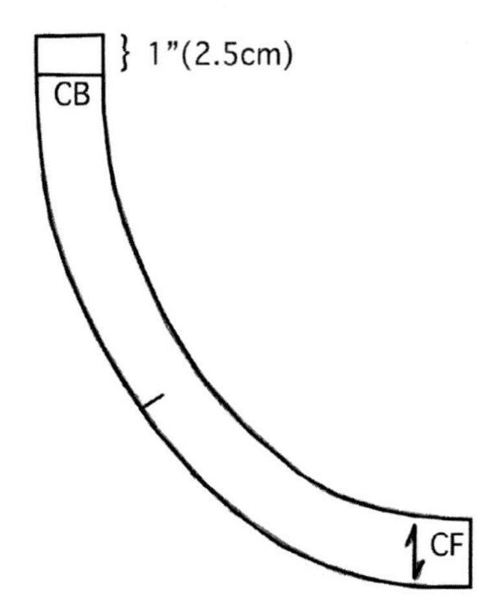

Chapter 11: Sleeves

The Basic Set-in Sleeve fits smoothly into the armscye and is tapered to the wrist.

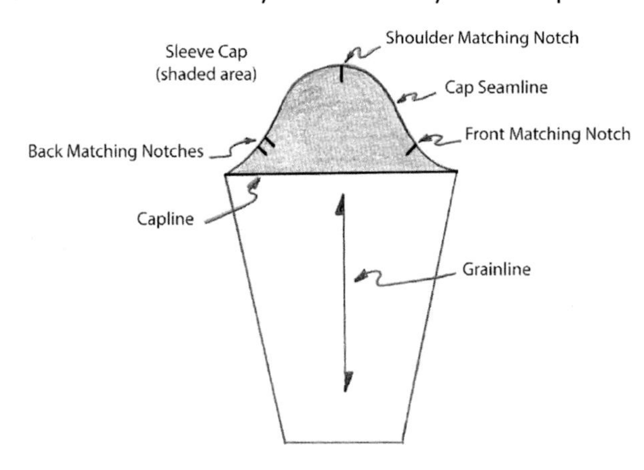

Anatomy of the Basic Set-in Sleeve

How to Draft a Set-in Sleeve

Measurements Needed

Armscye Front: (taken from bodice sloper):
Armscye Back: (taken from bodice sloper):
Total Armscye Measurement (Armscye Front + Armscye Back):
Desired Length of sleeve from shoulder (if full length, use Shoulder to Wrist measurement):
Sleeve opening (at desired length of sleeve):

Notes

– Sleeve cap ease = the difference between the sleeve cap measurement and total armscye measurement from the bodice sloper. The sleeve cap seamline should be slightly larger than the bodice sloper to create the ease necessary to cup the sleeve over the arm when stitching it in. The ease should be about ½″–1″ (1.3–2.5 cm) but no more than 1″ (2.5 cm) otherwise you will have gathers on the sleeve cap rather than a smooth, set-in sleeve.

Length of paper = desired sleeve length + 4″ (10.2 cm)
Width of paper = Total Armscye measurement + 4″ (10.2 cm)

DOI: 10.4324/9781003022619-11

NOTE: It is standard to place single matching notches on the front of a sleeve and armscye, and double matching notches on the back of a sleeve and armscye.

Method A

This method is used if there is 1" (2.5 cm) or less difference between the Armscye Front and Armscye Back measurements taken off of the bodice sloper.

Directions

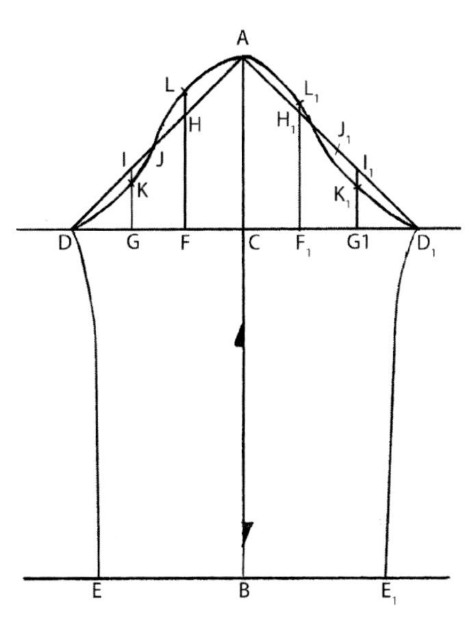

Method A

- Draw vertical line A-B down the middle of the length of the paper, where A-B = the desired sleeve length.
  (For a cap sleeve, the length = ¼ the Total Armscye measurement. The average is about 4"–4½" [10.2–11.4 cm].)
- From A, measure along the A-B line to new point C, where C = ¼ the Total Armscye measurement.
- From C, draw a line perpendicular to line A-B extending in both directions to the edges of paper.
- From point B, draw a line perpendicular to line A-B extending in both directions.

BACK: (LEFT side of line A-B)

- Using your straight ruler and starting at point A, angle your ruler diagonally along the left side of the perpendicular line where A-D = ½ of the Total Armscye measurement. Labelss point D.
- On the line to the left of B, mark point E, where E = ½ the measurement of the Total Sleeve Opening.
- Using either your straight ruler or your curved ruler (with the straight edge at E and the curved edge at D), draw a line from D to E. D-E is your underarm seam.
- Divide line C-D into three equal sections marking new points F and G.

- From F, draw a line perpendicular to line C-D extending up to line A-D and mark new point H on the A-D line.
- From G, draw a line perpendicular to line C-D extending up to line A-D and mark new point I on the A-D line.
- Divide the distance between H and I in half and mark new point J.
- From I, on line G-I, mark new point K, where K is ¼" (0.6 cm) toward G.
- Extend line H-F up ¼" (0.6 cm) to new point L.
- Using your curved ruler, and flipping it as necessary, draw a curved line from A-L-J-K-D.
- When drawing the curve, make sure that you have a flat section at point A by drawing a horizontal line for ¼" (0.6 cm). This will keep the armscye curve from having a sharp V-shaped point at the shoulder seam.

  =This side represents the BACK of your sleeve. It is important to mark your pattern. Place a double matching notch on the A-L-J-K-D line 2.5" (6.4 cm) from D.

FRONT: (RIGHT side of line A-B)

- Using your straight ruler and starting at point A, angle your ruler diagonally along the right side of the perpendicular line where A-D_1 = ½ of the Total Armscye measurement. Label point D_1.
- On the line to the right of B, mark point E_1, where E_1 = ½ the measurement of the Total Sleeve Opening.
- Using either your straight ruler or your curved ruler (with the straight edge at E_1 and the curved edge at D_1), draw a line from D_1 to E_1. D_1-E_1 is your underarm seam.
- Divide line C-D_1 into three equal sections marking new points F_1 and G_1.
- From F_1, draw a line perpendicular to line C-D_1 extending up to line A-D_1 and mark new point H_1 on the A-D_1 line.
- From G_1, draw a line perpendicular to line C-D_1 extending up to line A-D_1 and mark new point I_1 on the A-D_1 line.
- Divide the distance between H_1 and I_1 in half and mark new point J_1. (This point is to mimic the Back instructions but will not actually be used.)
- From I_1, on line G_1-I_1, mark new point K_1, where K_1 is ¼" (0.6 cm) toward G_1.
- Extend line H_1-F_1 up ⅜"(1cm) to new point L_1.
- Using your curved ruler and flipping it as necessary, draw a curved line from A-L_1-K_1-D_1. (Your curved line should not go through J_1 on this side.)
- When drawing the curve, make sure that you have a flat section at point A by drawing a horizontal line for ¼" (0.6 cm). This will keep the armscye curve from having a sharp V-shaped point at the shoulder seam.

  =This side represents the FRONT of your sleeve. It is important to mark your pattern. Place a single matching notch on the A-J_1-L_1-D_1 line 2.5" (6.4 cm) from D_1.
- True the underarm seam.

(See below for underarm seam alterations if the underarm seams of D-E and D_1-E_1 are not the same measurement.)

Method B

This method is used if there is 1″ (2.5 cm) or more difference between the Armscye Front and Armscye Back measurements taken off of the bodice sloper.

Directions

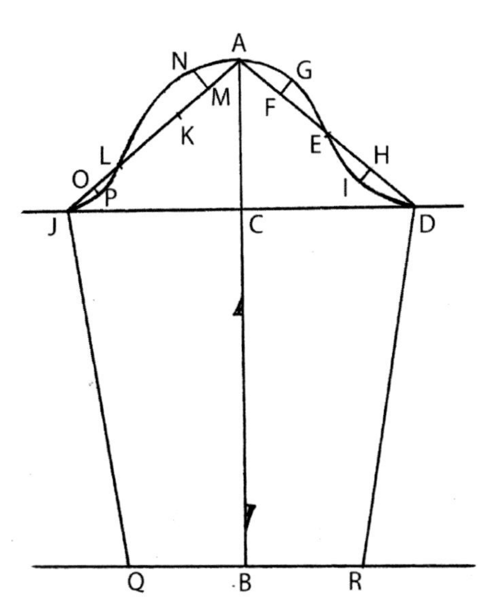

Method B

- Draw vertical line A-B down the middle of the length of the paper where A-B = the desired sleeve length.
  (For a cap sleeve, the length = ¼ the Total Armscye measurement. The average = 4″–4½″ [10.2–11.4 cm]).
- From A, measure along the A-B line to new point C, where C = ¼ the Total Armscye measurement + 1″ (2.5 cm).
- From C, draw a line perpendicular to line A-B extending in both directions to edges of paper.
- From point B, draw a line perpendicular to line A-B extending in both directions.

FRONT: (RIGHT side of line A-B)

- Using your straight ruler and starting at point A, angle your ruler diagonally along the right side perpendicular line where A-D = ½ of the Total Armscye measurement. Label point D.
- Divide the distance between point A and point D in half and mark the new point E.
- Divide the distance between point A and point E in half and mark the new point F.
- From point F, draw a perpendicular line up from line A-D ⅝″ (1.6 cm) and mark new point G.
- Divide the distance between point E and point D in half and mark new point H.

- From point H, draw a perpendicular line in from line A-D ⅝″ (1.6 cm) and mark new point I.
- Using your curved ruler and flipping it as necessary, draw a curved line from A-G-E-I-D.
- When drawing the curve, make sure that you have a flat section at point A by drawing a horizontal line for ¼″ (0.6 cm). This will keep the armscye curve from having a sharp V-shaped point at the shoulder seam.
  =This side represents the FRONT of your sleeve. It is important to mark your pattern. Place a single matching notch on the A-G-E-I-D line 2.5″ (6.4 cm) from D.

BACK: (LEFT side of line A-B)

- Using your straight ruler and starting at point A, angle your ruler diagonally along the left side perpendicular line where A-J = ½ of the Total Armscye measurement. Label point J.
- Divide the distance between point A and point J into three sections and mark the new points K and L.
- Divide the distance between point A and point K in half and mark the new point M.
- From point M, draw a perpendicular line up from line A-J ¾″ (1.9 cm) and mark new point N.
- Divide the distance between point J and point L in half and mark new point O.
- From point O, draw a perpendicular line in from line A-J ¼″ (0.6 cm) and mark new point P.
- Using your curved ruler and flipping it as necessary, draw a curved line from A-N-L-P-J.
- When drawing the curve, make sure that you have a flat section at point A by drawing a horizontal line for ¼″ (0.6 cm). This will keep the armscye curve from having a sharp V-shaped point at the shoulder seam.
- On the line to the left of B, mark point Q, where Q = ½ the measurement of the Total Sleeve Opening.
- On the line to the right of B, mark point R, where R = ½ the measurement of the Total Sleeve Opening.
- Using either your straight ruler or your curved ruler (with the straight edge at Q, and then at R, and the curved edge at D, and then at J), draw a line from D to R and J to Q. D-R and J-Q are your underarm seams.
  =This side represents the BACK of your sleeve. It is important to mark your pattern. Place a double matching notch on the A-N-L-P-J line 2.5″ (6.4 cm) from J.
- True the underarm seam.

(See below for underarm seam alterations if the underarm seams of J-Q and D-R are not the same measurement.)

***Underarm Seam Alterations ***

If, after following the instructions as in the previous section, the two underarm seams are not the same length, then proceed as follows:

Method A

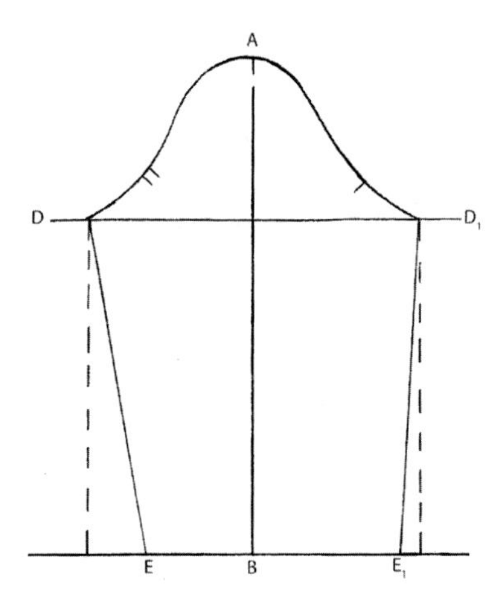

- From D, draw a vertical line down to the E-E_1 line so that the new line is perpendicular to E-E_1. Where the vertical line intersects line E-E_1, mark new point M.
- From D_1, draw a vertical line down to the E-E_1 line so that the new line is perpendicular to E-E1. Where the vertical line intersects line E-E_1, mark new point M1.
- Measure the distances between M-E and M_1-E_1. Subtract the smaller number from the larger number. Divide that number by 2.
- Shift both points E and E_1 that distance to the left, if D-E is the longer length of the underarm seams.
- Shift both points E and E_1 that distance to the right, if D_1-E_1 is the longer length of the underarm seams.
- Draw new underarm seam lines to these new points.

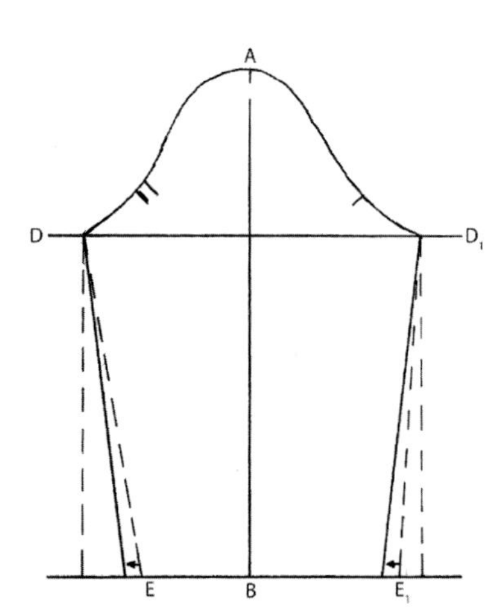

Method B

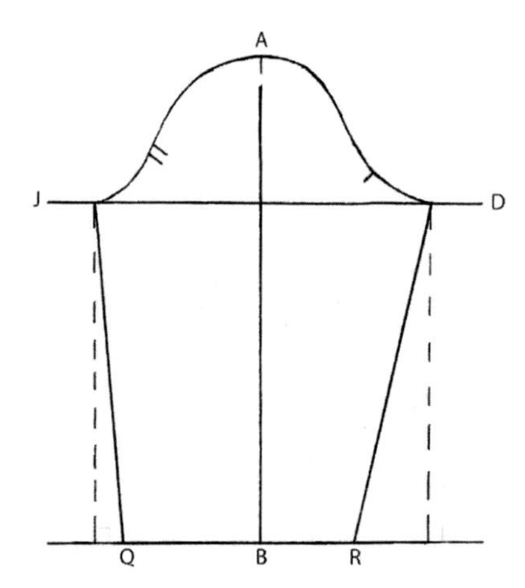

- From J, draw a vertical line down to the Q-R line so that the new line is perpendicular to Q-R. Where the vertical line intersects line Q-R, mark new point S.
- From D, draw a vertical line down to the Q-R line so that the line is perpendicular to the Q-R line. Where the vertical line intersects line Q-R, mark new point T.
- Measure the distances between S-Q and T-R. Subtract the smaller number from the larger number. Divide that number by 2.
- Shift both points Q and R that distance to the left, if J-Q is the longer length of the underarm seams.
- Shift both points Q and R that distance to the right, if D-R is the longer length of the underarm seams.
- Draw new underarm seam lines to these new points.

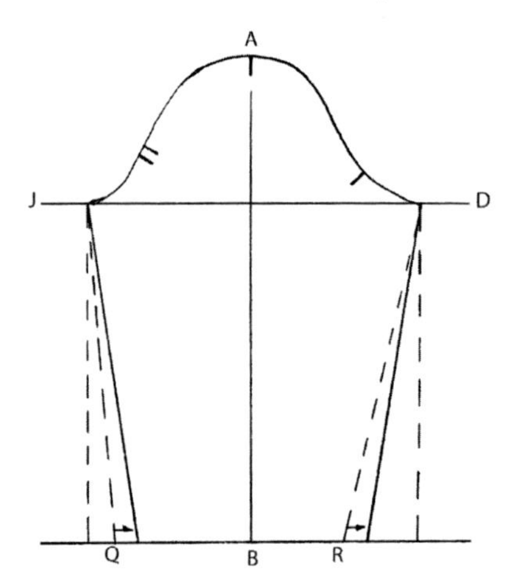

Creating Alternate Looks With Sleeves

The following sleeve shapes are just some of the optional designs that can be created from the Basic Set-in sleeve.

Some of the sleeve shapes are achieved using the Slash and Spread Method.

The slash and spread method involves drawing lines onto a copy of the original pattern, cutting on that line, and then spreading the pattern until the desired fullness is achieved.

*Always use copies of the original pattern just in case an error occurs. This will prevent you from having to redraft a new original.

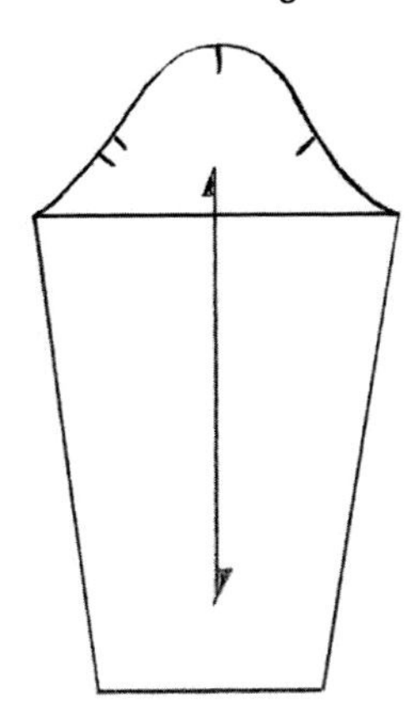

Cap Sleeves

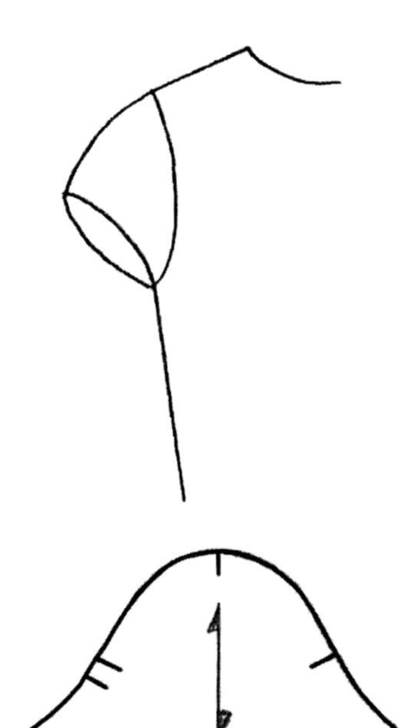

Cap Sleeve

- The basic sleeve can be converted to a cap sleeve by removing the underarm length and only using the area above the capline.
- A cap sleeve can have minimal underarm length but then you should scoop the hem up at the center.

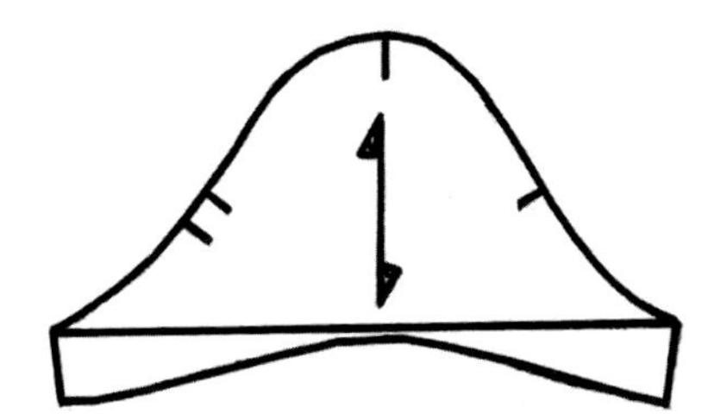

Sleeves

Short Sleeves

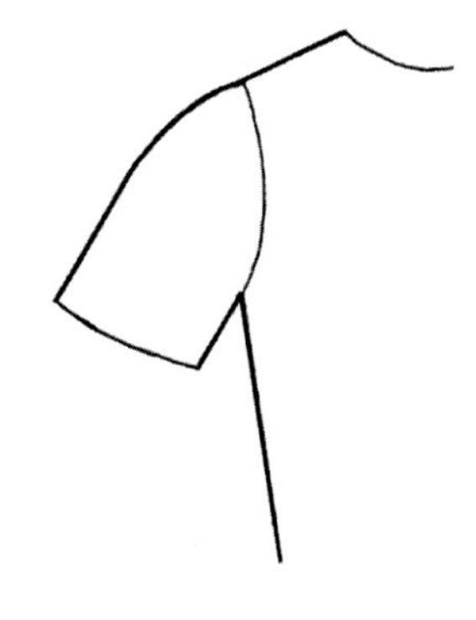

Short Sleeve

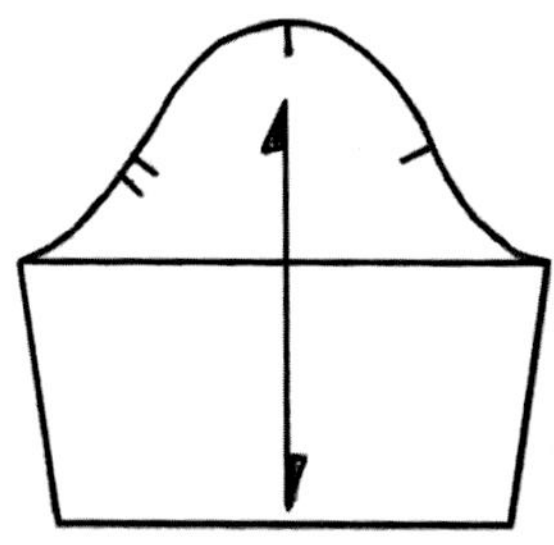

- The basic sleeve can be converted to a short sleeve by changing the length and then cutting the sleeve off at this desired length.
- In order to maintain a straight hem, you should also straighten the underarm seams so they no longer taper but are perpendicular to the hem. Make sure that the underarm seams are equal lengths.

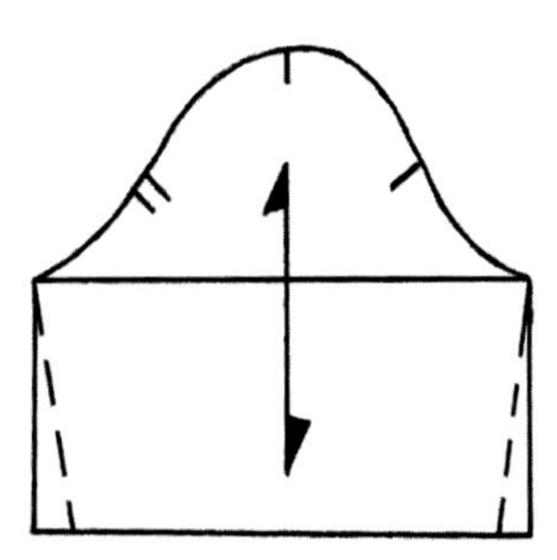

Puff Sleeves – Gathered at the Hem

This version of the puff sleeve fits smoothly into the armscye and has added fullness at the hem. It can be gathered into a cuff or elastic, if desired. If the sleeve is not gathered at the hem, then it would be considered a Bell Sleeve.

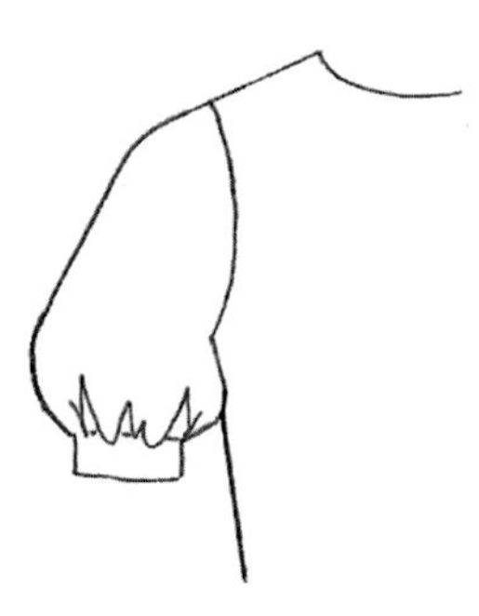

Puff Sleeve Gathered at the Hem

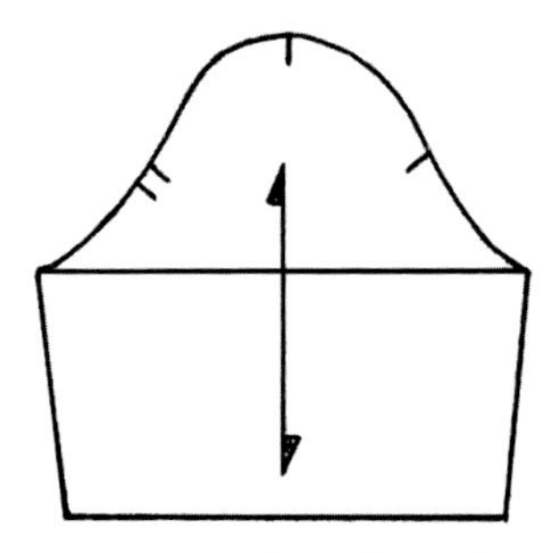

- Alter the basic sleeve pattern to make a short sleeve.

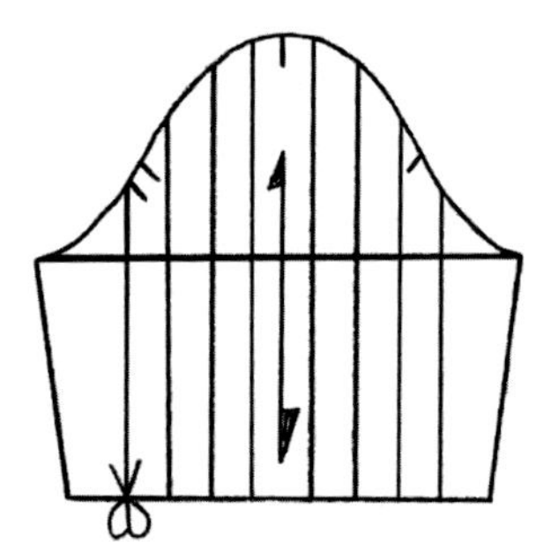

- Draw slash lines parallel to the grainline, but straddle the center of the sleeve cap where the shoulder seam matching notch lies (you do not want to cut through your matching notches), from the hem to the sleeve cap seamline.
- From the hem, cut to but not through the sleeve cap seamline.

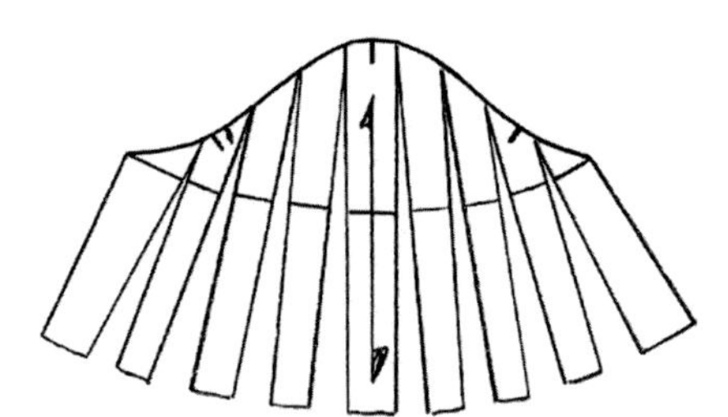

- Start by pinning the center strip to your paper so that you have enough room on either side to expand the pattern. Spread the sleeve from the center out, continuing to pin with an even amount of spread on either side of center.
- Trace the pattern along the sleeve cap seamline and underarm seams. Before tracing the hemline, you should decide how much extra puff you would like, if any. If you drop the hem seamline more than what is indicated by the spread of the pattern, then you will have more puff.

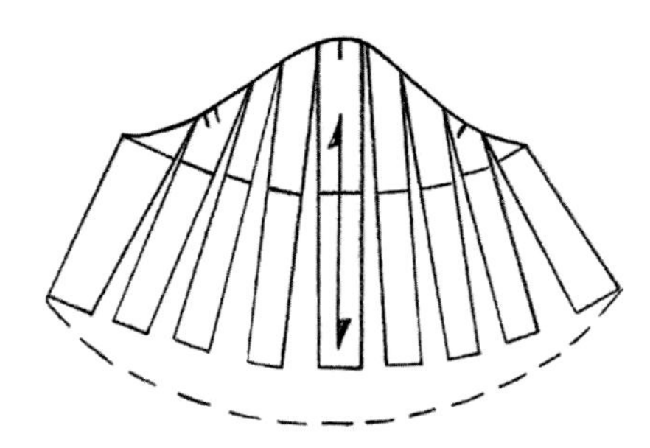

Sleeves

- Using your curved ruler, draw in a new bottom hemline keeping the hem curve smooth and even.

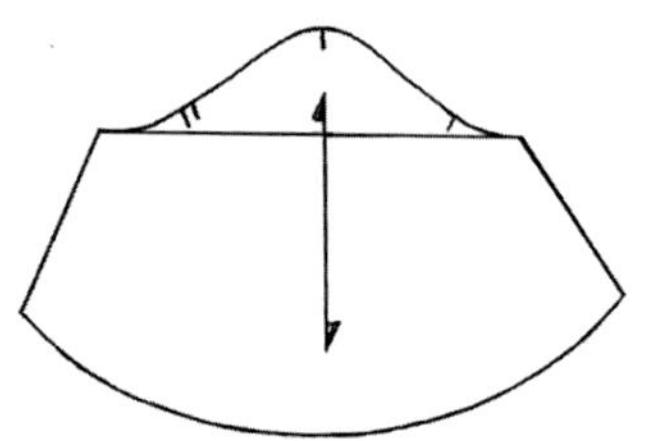

- Transfer matching notches and grainline.
- Remove the slashed pattern and cut out the new pattern.
- Add labels, drawing in a new capline, and include matching notches and grainline.

Puff Sleeves – Gathered at the Cap

This version of the puff sleeve has added fullness at the cap and tapers into a fitted hem.

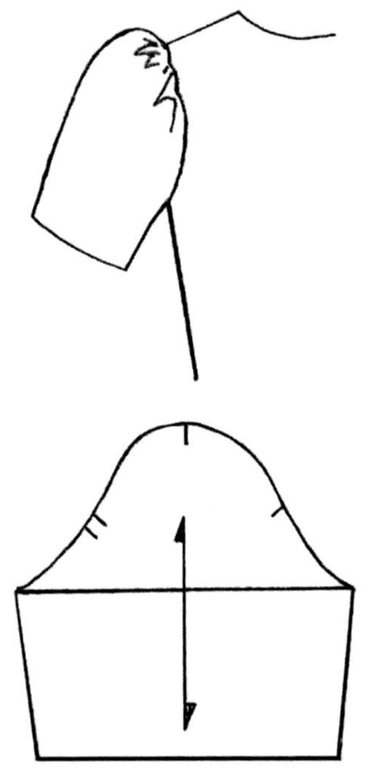

Puff Sleeve Gathered at the Cap

- Alter the basic sleeve pattern to make a short sleeve.

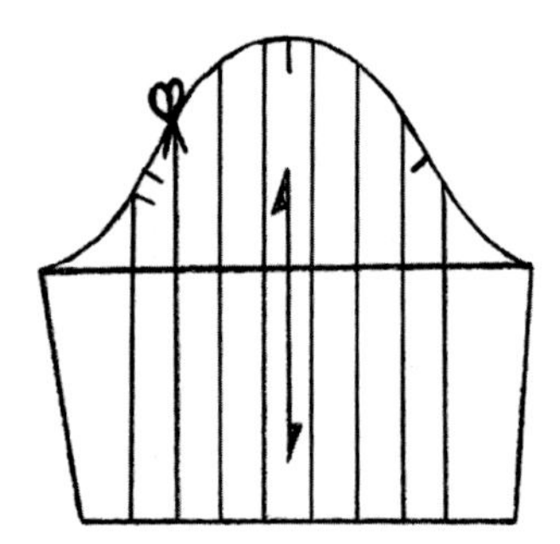

- Draw slash lines parallel to the grainline, but straddle the center of the sleeve cap where the shoulder seam matching notch lies (you do not want to cut through your matching notches), from the hem to the sleeve cap seamline.
- From the sleeve cap seamline, cut to but not through the hem.

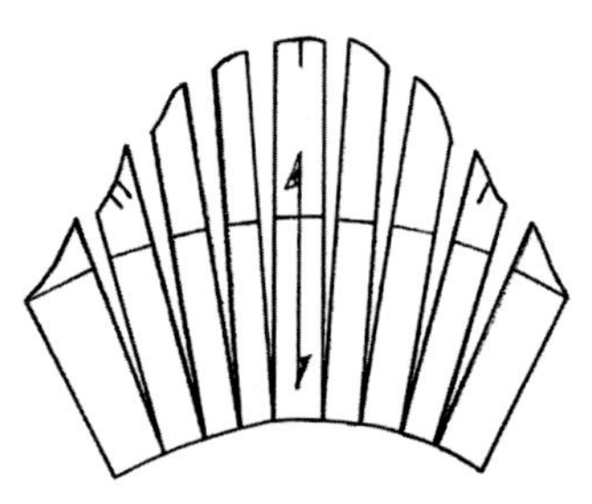

- Start by pinning the center strip to your paper so that you have enough room on either side to expand the pattern. Spread the sleeve from the center out, continuing to pin with an even amount of spread on either side of center.
- Trace the pattern along the hem and underarm seams. Before tracing the cap seamline, you should decide how much extra puff you would like, if any. If you increase the cap seamline more than what is indicated by the spread of the pattern, then you will have more puff.

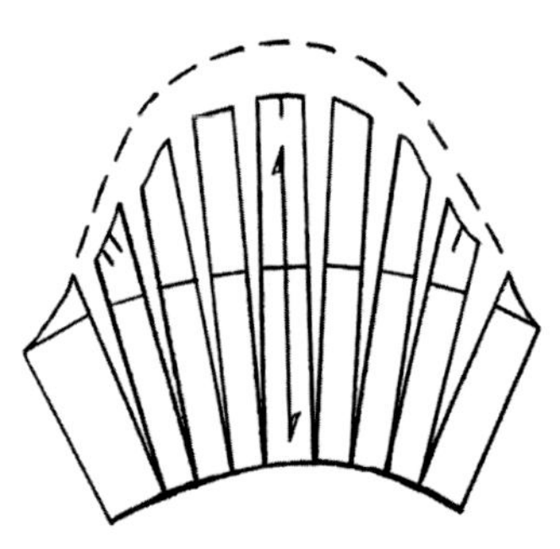

- Using your curved ruler, draw in a new cap seamline keeping the curve smooth and even.

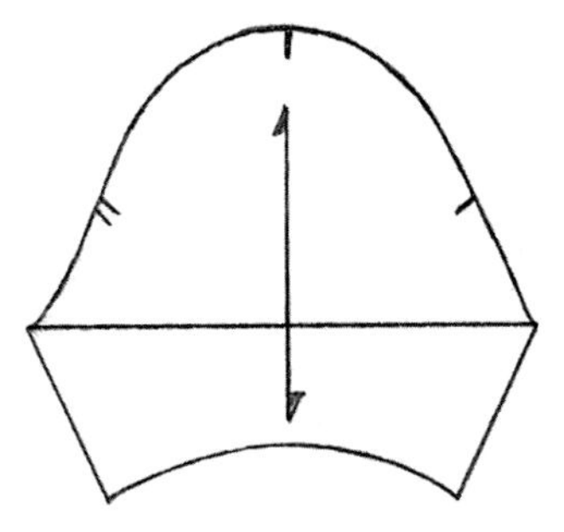

- Transfer matching notches and grainline.
- Remove the slashed pattern and cut out the new pattern.
- Add labels, drawing in a new capline, and include matching notches and grainline.

Puff Sleeves – Fullness at the Cap and at the Hem

This version of the puff sleeve has added fullness at the cap and at the hem. It can be gathered into a cuff or elastic, if desired.

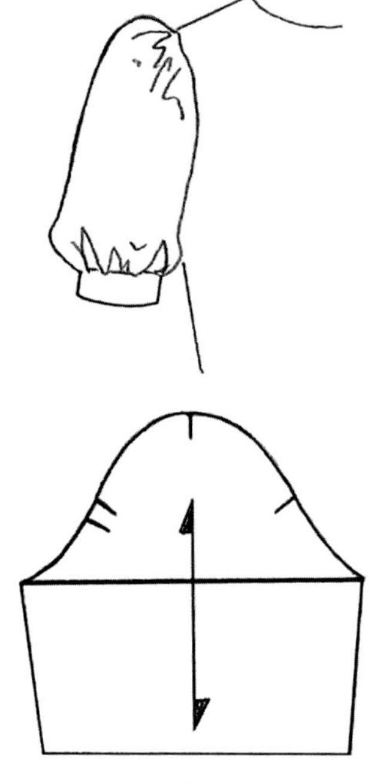

Sleeve with Fullness at the Cap and Hem

- Alter the basic sleeve pattern to make a short sleeve.

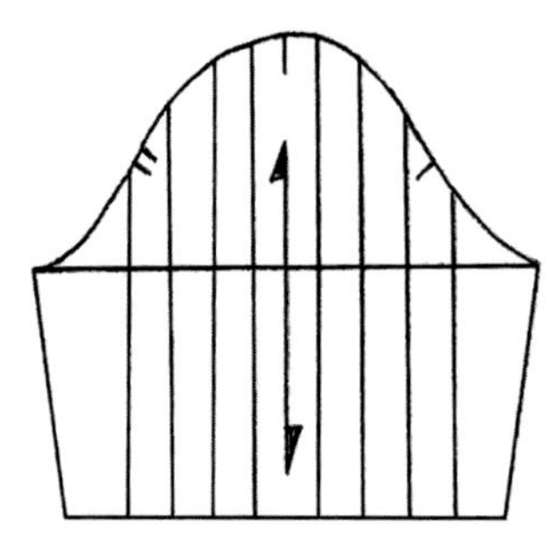

- Draw slash lines parallel to the grainline, but straddle the center of the sleeve cap where the shoulder seam matching notch lies (you do not want to cut through your matching notches), from the hem to the sleeve cap seamline.

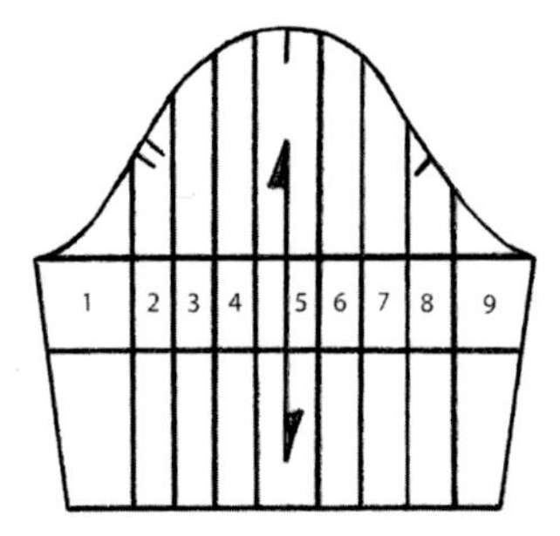

- Draw a horizontal line across the sleeve parallel to the capline, but below it about 3" (7.6 cm).

- Number each section in order (you will be cutting through the pattern, creating separate pieces – this allows you to put them back in the correct order).

- On the paper you will be tracing the new pattern onto, draw a horizontal line significantly wider than the original sleeve pattern.

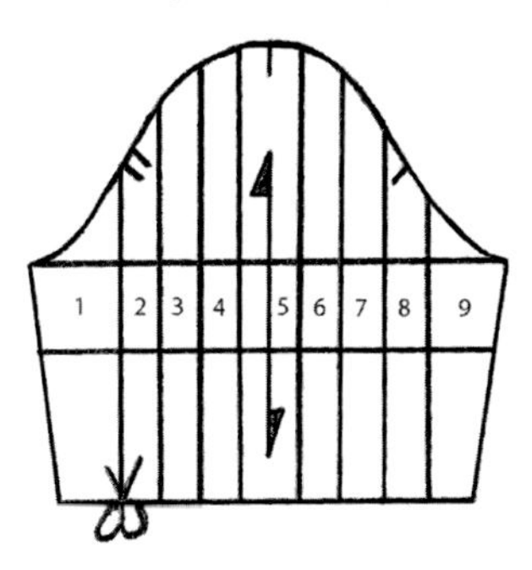

- Slash the pattern all the way through from hem to cap.

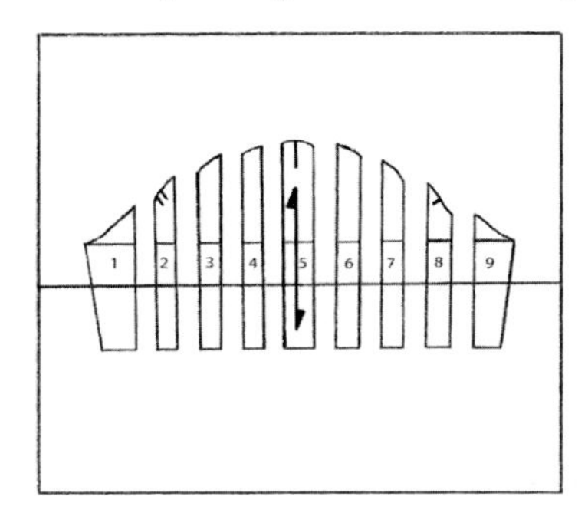

- With the horizontal line of the slashed strip matching the underneath paper's horizontal line, pin the center strip to your paper so that you have enough room on either side to expand the pattern. Spread the sleeve from the center out, continuing to pin with an even amount of spread on either side of center.

Sleeves

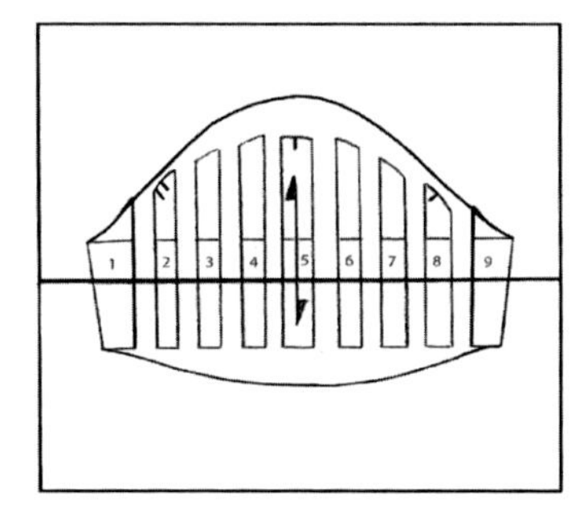

- Trace the underarm seams.
- To increase the amount of puff at the cap and at the hem, increase the height of the cap above the shoulder notch and, using your curved ruler, blend the curve down to the underarm seams. Then drop the hem at the center line and, using the curved ruler, blend the curve up to the underarm seams.

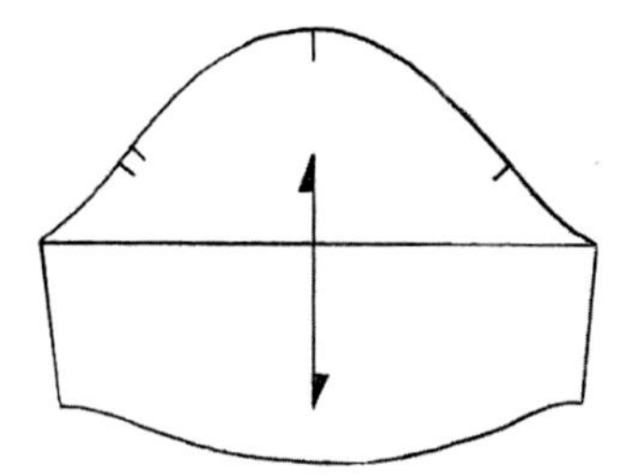

- Transfer matching notches and grainline.
- Remove the slashed pattern pieces and cut out the new pattern.
- Add labels, drawing in a new capline, and include matching notches and grainline.

Bishop Sleeve

The Bishop sleeve fits smoothly into the armscye and blouses out over a fitted cuff or into elastic at the wrist. If the sleeve is not gathered at the hem, then it would be considered a Bell Sleeve.

Bishop Sleeve

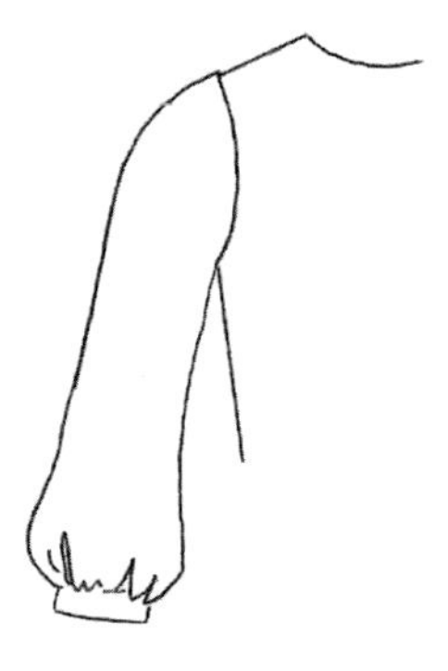

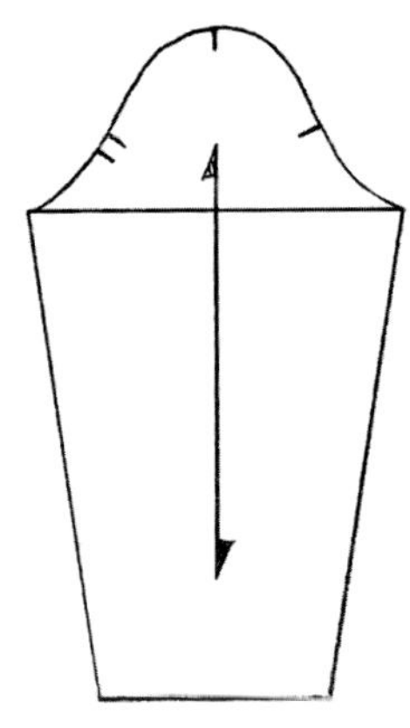

- Use a copy of the basic sleeve at full length.

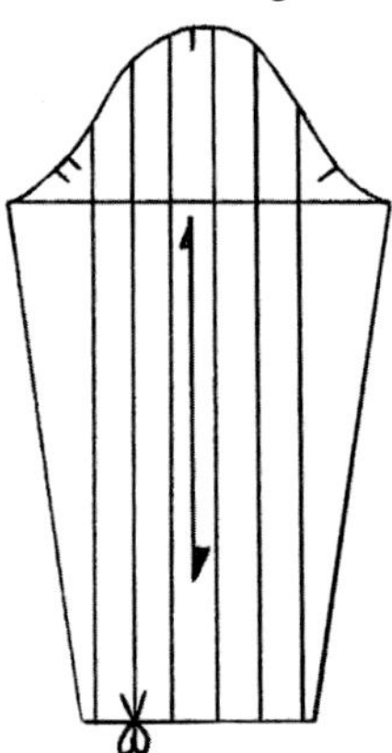

- Draw slash lines parallel to the grainline, but straddle the center of the sleeve cap where the shoulder seam matching notch lies (you do not want to cut through your matching notches), from the hem to the sleeve cap seamline.
- From the hem, cut to but not through the sleeve cap seamline.

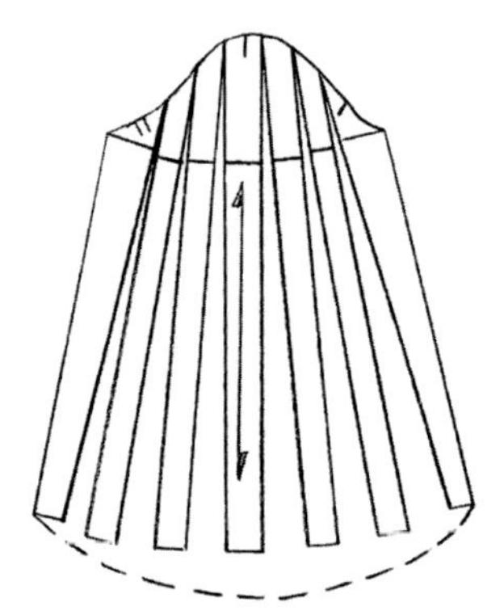

- Start by pinning the center strip to your paper so that you have enough room on either side to expand the pattern. Spread the sleeve from the center out, continuing to pin with an even amount of spread on either side of center.
- Trace the pattern along the cap and underarm seams. Before tracing the hem, you should decide how much extra puff you would like, if any. If you drop the hem more than what is indicated by the spread of the pattern, then you will have more puff.
- Using your curved ruler, draw in a new hemline keeping the curve smooth and even.

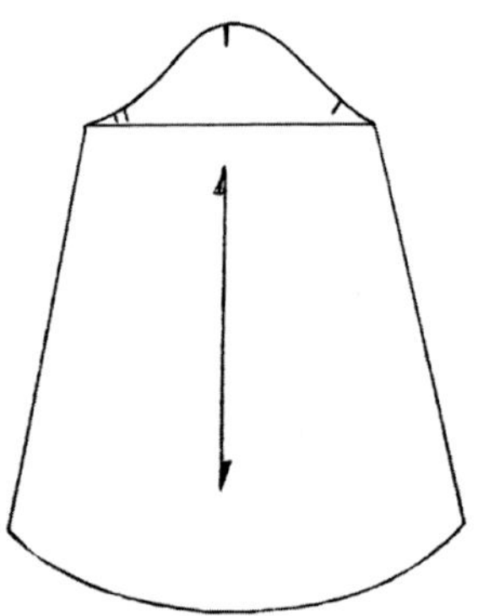

- Transfer matching notches and grainline.
- Remove the slashed pattern and cut out the new pattern.
- Add labels, drawing in a new capline, and include matching notches and grainline.

Leg-of-Mutton Sleeve

The Leg-of-Mutton Sleeve is a full-length sleeve that has an exaggerated puff at the cap and then fits smoothly down the arm.

The method of alteration used for this style sleeve is different than previous methods. The previous methods slashed and spread across the entire pattern, while this method only alters the top of the pattern. This method allows for fullness to be distributed along the cap yet maintains the fitted section below the elbow.

Leg-of-Mutton Sleeve

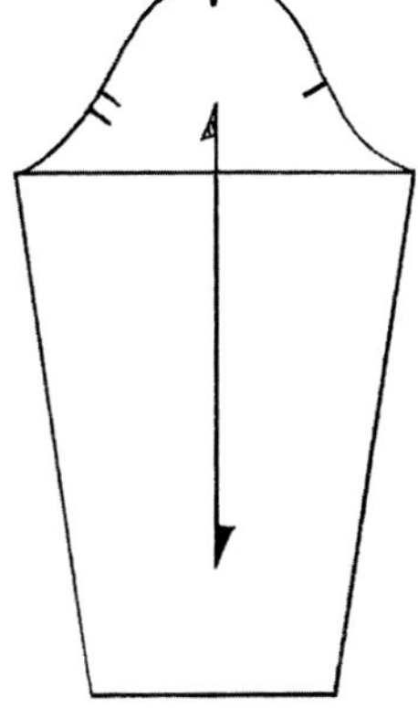

- Use a copy of the basic sleeve at full length.

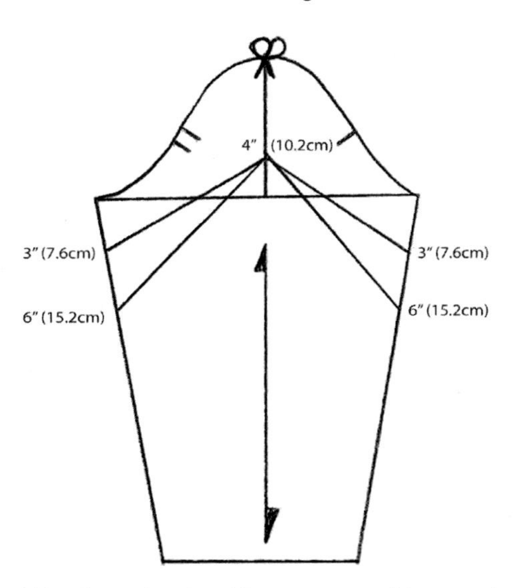

- Draw a vertical line from the shoulder seam matching notch to the capline that is parallel to, or matches the grainline.
- From the shoulder seam matching notch at the top of the capline seam, mark a point 4" (10.2 cm) down on the vertical line.
- On both of the underarm seams, make marks 3" (7.6 cm) down and 6" (15.2 cm) down from the capline.

- Draw diagonal lines connecting the 4″ (10.2 cm) mark to the 3″ (7.6 cm) and 6″ (15.2 cm) marks on both underarm seams.
- Cut from the top of the sleeve at the shoulder seam matching notch, down to the 4″ (10.2 cm) mark, then continue diagonally, to but not through, the underarm seams of the sleeve.

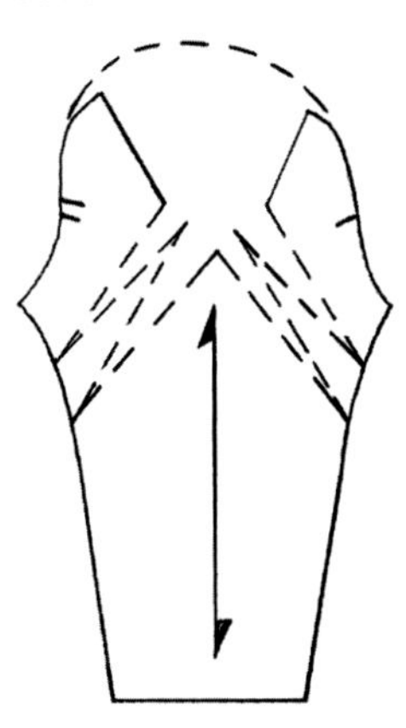

- Spread the upper section of the sleeve 4–8″ (10.2–20.3 cm) crosswise and raise the cap 1½–3″ (3.8–7.6 cm), depending on how full a sleeve is desired. (A leg-of-mutton sleeve with moderate fullness will have about a 4″ [10.2 cm] spread crosswise and 1½″ [3.8 cm] higher cap. A leg-of-mutton sleeve with significant fullness will have about an 8″ (20.3 cm) spread crosswise, and a 3″ [7.6 cm] higher cap.)
- Trace the rest of the pattern.

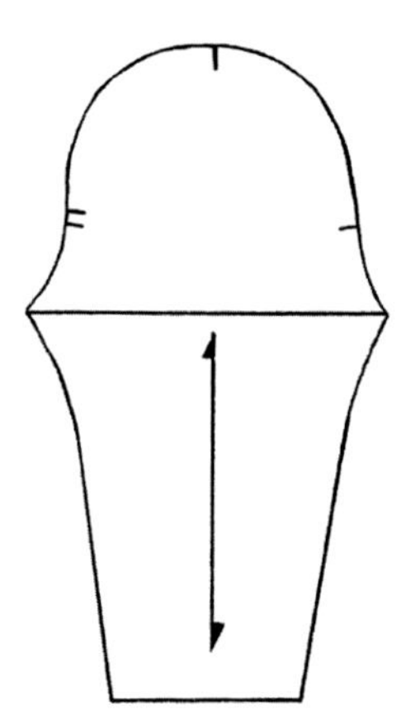

- Transfer matching notches and grainline.
- Remove the slashed pattern and cut out the new pattern.
- Add labels, drawing in a new capline, and include matching notches and grainline.

Circular Sleeves

Circular sleeves are made similarly to circular skirts, except that the waist circumference measurement is now the armscye circumference measurement, and you need to move the location of the armscye opening in order to allow the sleeve to fall more evenly.

The two versions shown in the following section give options of where the armscye opening could be to create the two different looks.

For Sleeve A

Sleeve A

- Determine the desired sleeve length of the sleeve. Add seam allowance. This measurement is the length of A-B.
- The length of A-B = the radius of the outer circle.
- Draw a circle with this radius.
- Draw two lines through the center of the circle. One from top to bottom, and then the other horizontally from side to side, making sure that the lines intersect the center of the circle and are perpendicular to each other.

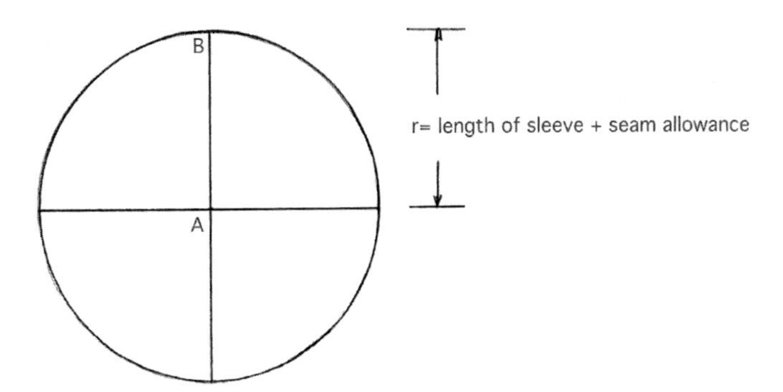

- Measure the front and back armscyes on your bodice pattern. Add them together for the total armscye measurement. This will equal the circumference of the armscye. Subtract ⅜″ (1 cm) from this measurement to account for stretch on the bias of the sleeve.
- Use this formula to determine the radius:

  radius = circumference or total armscye measurement – ⅜″ (1 cm)

  2 x 3.14
- Using the radius measurement that you just found, draw the armscye circle starting at A and going up toward B. The circle should rest on the horizontal center line.

Sleeves

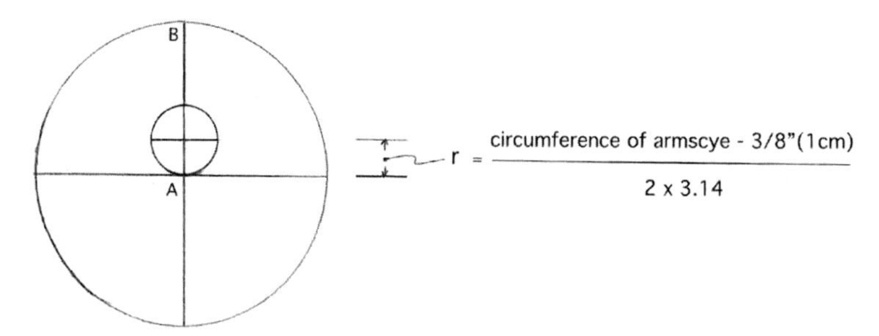

- The inner circle will be cut out but make sure to add matching notches on the large circle. The top notch lines up with your side seam, and the bottom notch lines up with your shoulder seam.

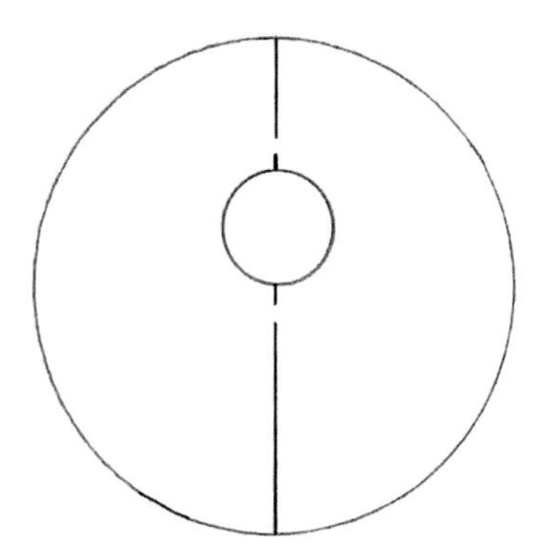

For Sleeve B

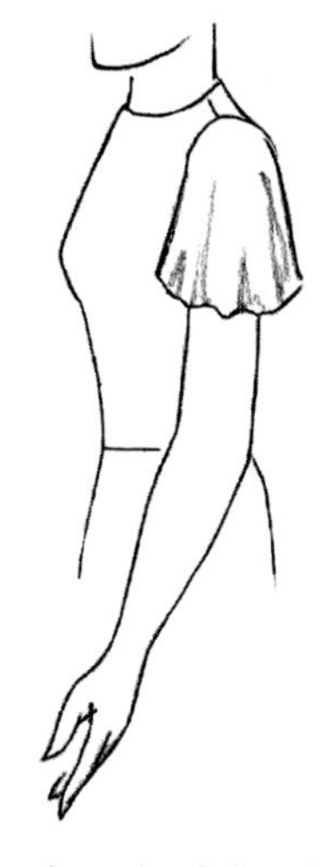

Sleeve B

- Determine the desired sleeve length of the sleeve. Add seam allowance. This measurement is the length of A-B.
- The length of A-B = the radius of the outer circle.
- Draw a circle with this radius.
- Draw two lines through the center of the circle. One from top to bottom, and then the other horizontally from side to side, making sure that the lines intersect the center of the circle and are perpendicular to each other.

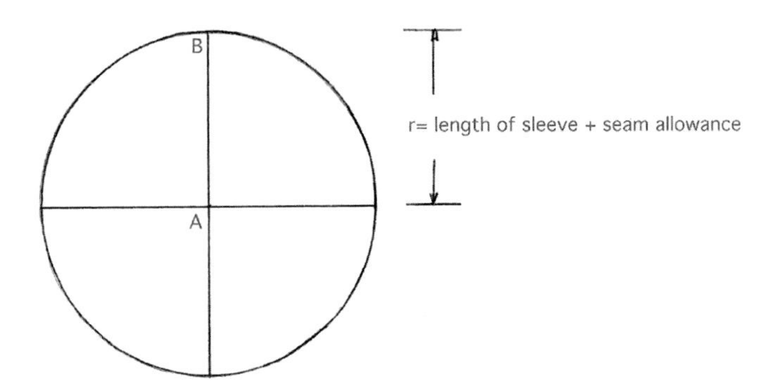

- Measure the front and back armscyes on your bodice pattern. Add them together for the total armscye measurement. This will equal the circumference of the armscye. Subtract ⅜″ (1 cm) from this measurement to account for stretch on the bias of the sleeve.
- Use this formula to determine the radius:

$$\text{radius} = \frac{\text{circumference or total armscye measurement} - \frac{3}{8}''\ \text{(1 cm)}}{2 \times 3.14}$$

- Gently fold the top edge of the circle down to meet point A. Crease the fold line at the outer edges of the circle.

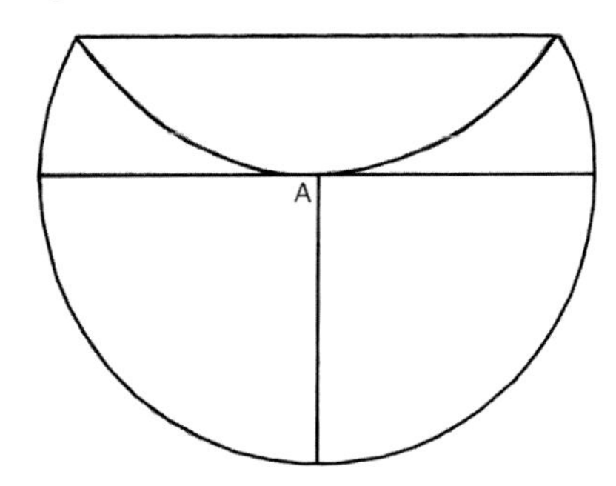

- From these creases, draw in the fold line with your pencil and straight ruler.
- Where the fold line and the vertical center line intersect is the center of the armscye circle.
- Using the radius measurement that you found for the armscye, draw the armscye circle with the center at the intersection point.

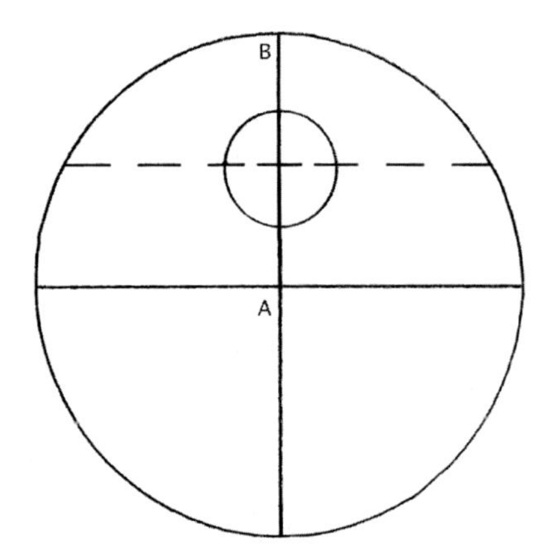

- The inner circle will be cut out but make sure to add matching notches on the large circle. The top notch lines up with your side seam, and the bottom notch lines up with your shoulder seam. Be aware that the notches seem to line up counter-intuitively, but if they go in upside down a different look will result.

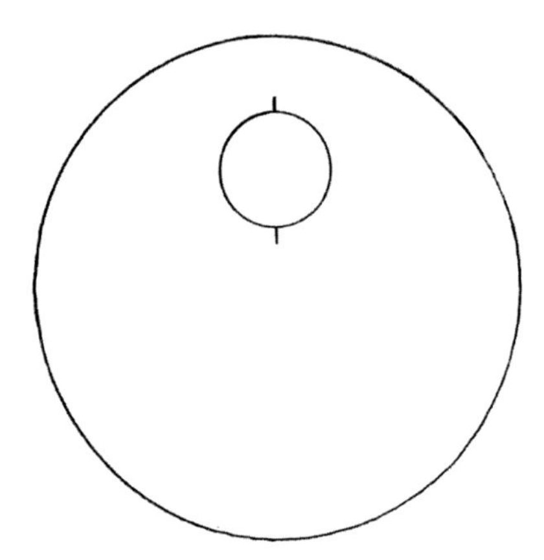

Chapter 12: Collars

How to Draft Collars

There are three types of basic collars: the flat, the partial roll, and the full roll. These types refer to how the collar lies along the neckline. The flatter the collar, the more the pattern curves at the neckline. The full roll collar pattern is straight and stands up against the back of the neck. The partial roll pattern is slightly curved at the neckline and stands less than the full roll but more than the flat.

The collar style is determined by the shape of the outer edge. There are many styles of collars including the Peter Pan, Sailor, or Mandarin (also known as the Military, Chinese, or Nehru), for example.

There are two characteristics of collars: convertible or nonconvertible. The convertible collar can be worn with the neckline open or closed. The nonconvertible collar can only be worn closed.

There are two methods for converting collar patterns from their originals: slash and spread, and slash and compress.

Slash and spread, and alternately, slash and compress, consists of lines drawn on the pattern that are cut to flare out or overlap to change the shape of the garment. If you slash and spread, the pattern will expand in an area creating flare on the finished garment. If you slash and compress, the pattern will shrink in an area creating a narrower look on the finished garment.

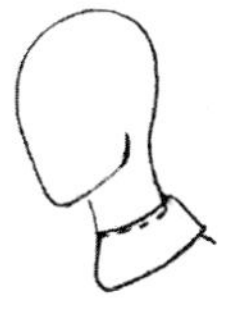

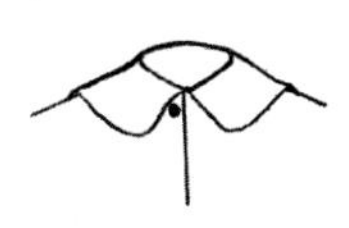

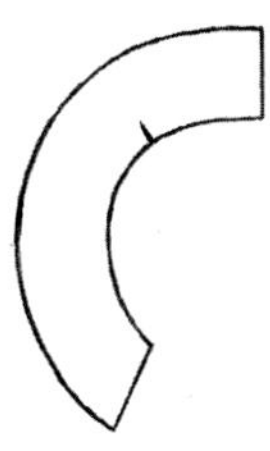

Flat Collar

DOI: 10.4324/9781003022619-12

Collars

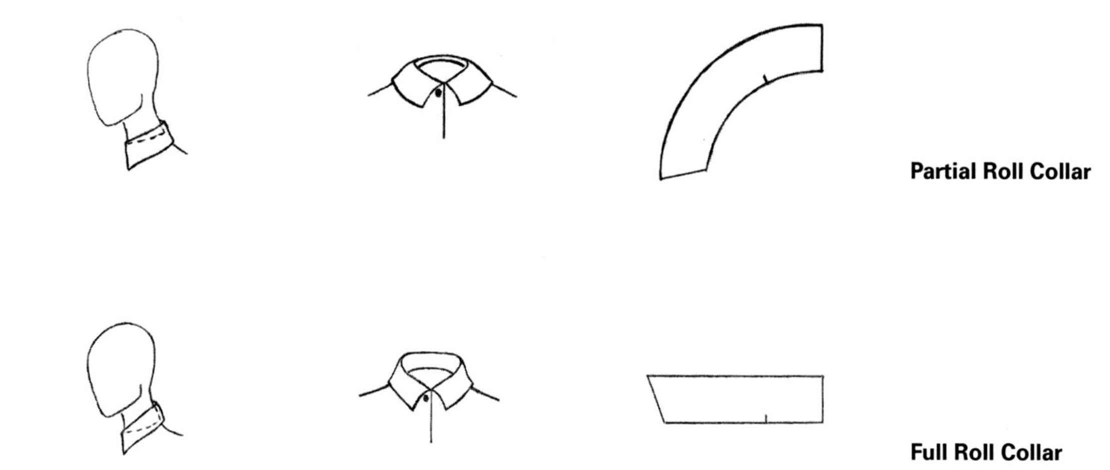

Types of Collars Determined by the Shape of the Neckline Edge

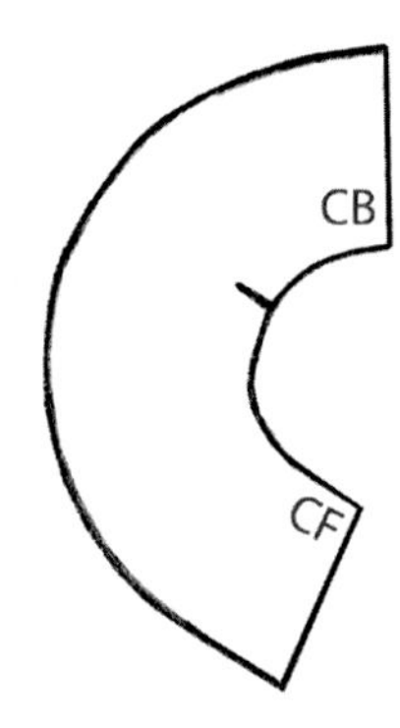

Flat: the shape of the collar is the most curved of the styles and lays against the body.

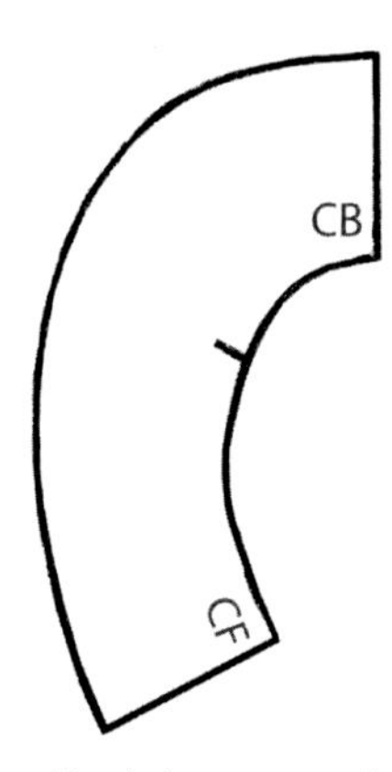

Partial-roll: the shape of the collar is less curved and has a gentle roll at the back of the neckline.

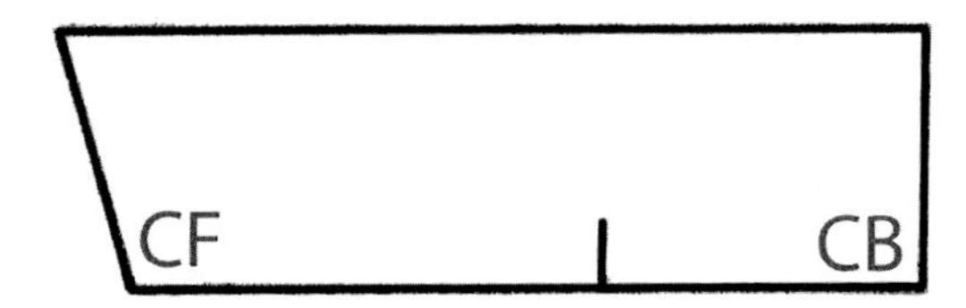

Full-roll: the shape of the collar is straighter and has the most roll at the back of the neckline. The Straight Full-Roll collar stands up at the back neckline, folds, and rolls down and covers the neckline seam. The collar roll ends at the seam line at the back and does not hang down over the bodice back.

Styles of Collars Determined by the Shape of the Outer Edge

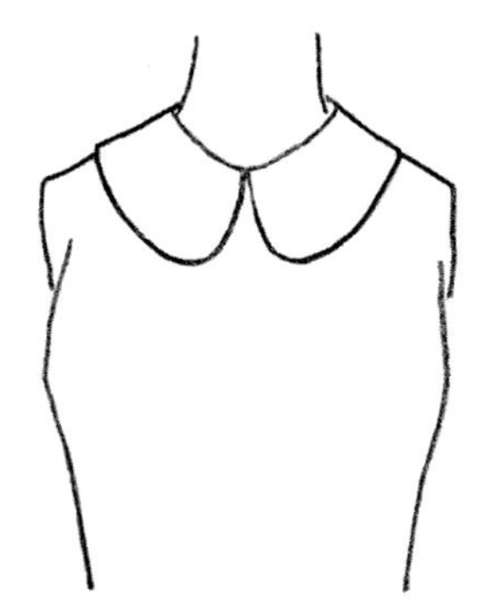

Peter Pan – a flat collar with a curved outer edge frequently found on children's clothing.

Bertha – a flat collar that looks like a shawl.

Collars

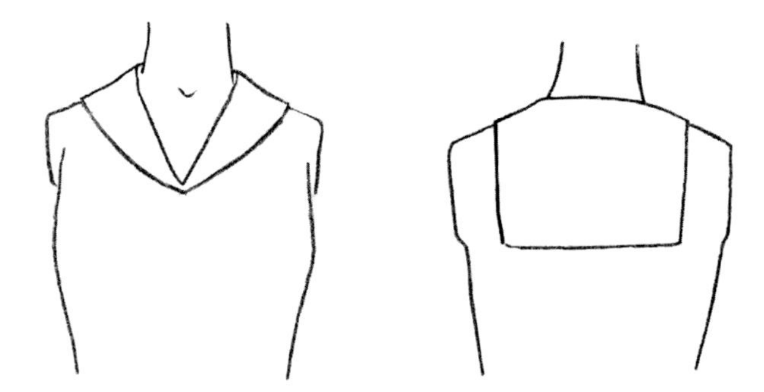

Sailor – a flat collar with a long point at the front and a squared off back edge.

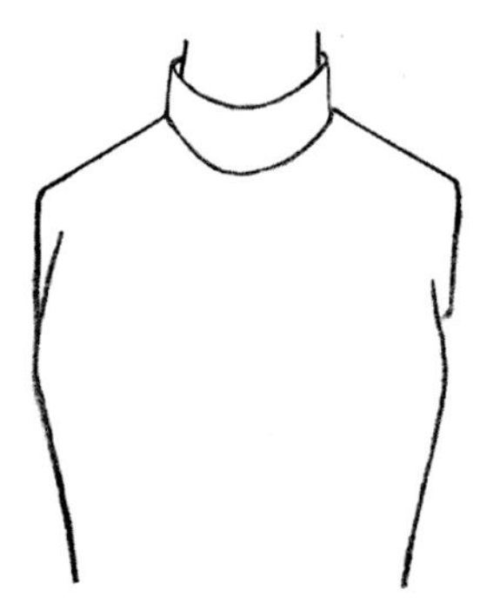

Mandarin, Military, Chinese, or Nehru – a stand collar with no roll.

Note

- Make sure that the shoulder seam marking (matching notch) is clearly drawn on each pattern because when sewing the collar, it sometimes has the unfortunate potential to go in with the neckline on the outer edge and the outer edge on the neckline. It should also be noted that the distance from the center back to the shoulder seam matching notch is shorter than the distance from the shoulder seam matching notch to the center front.

Flat Collars

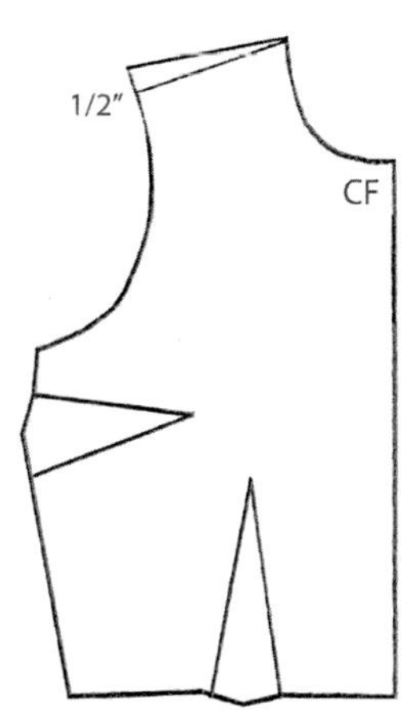

- Using copies of the bodice front and bodice back slopers, place a mark ½" (1.3 cm) down the armscye from the shoulder seam on the bodice front sloper.
- Draw a line from the neckline to the new shoulder seam marking.

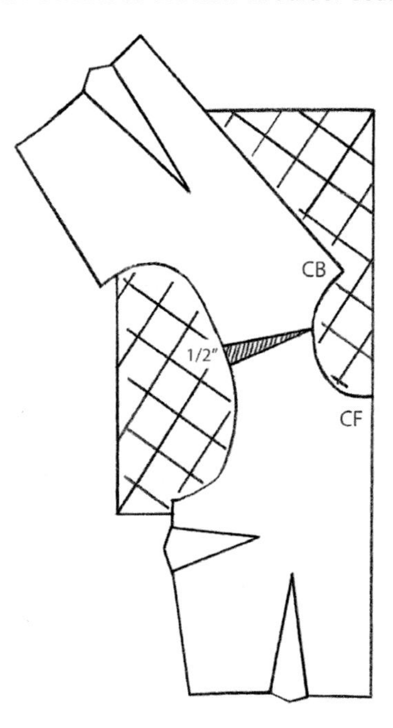

- Place a piece of paper large enough to create the collar under the bodice front sloper and pin the bodice front sloper to the paper.
  (If the bodice back sloper shoulder seam has a dart, close it with tape and then pin the sloper up against the bodice front sloper so that the neckline is smooth and the back bodice shoulder seam is aligned with the new shoulder seam line. Do not flatten the dart, but allow it to tent up from the table.)

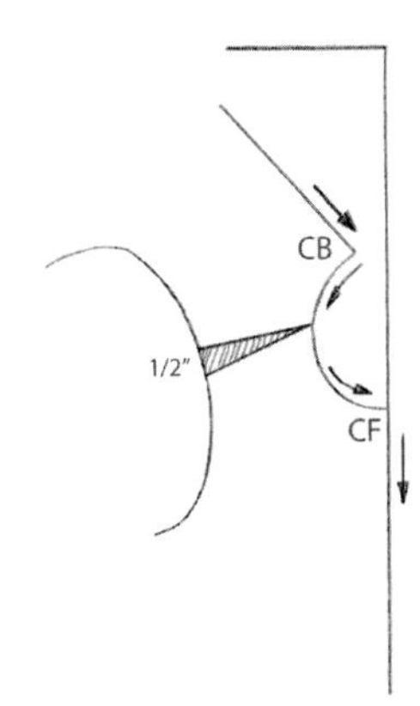

- Trace around the center back, neckline, and center front of the bodice slopers.
- Mark the shoulder seam with a matching notch.

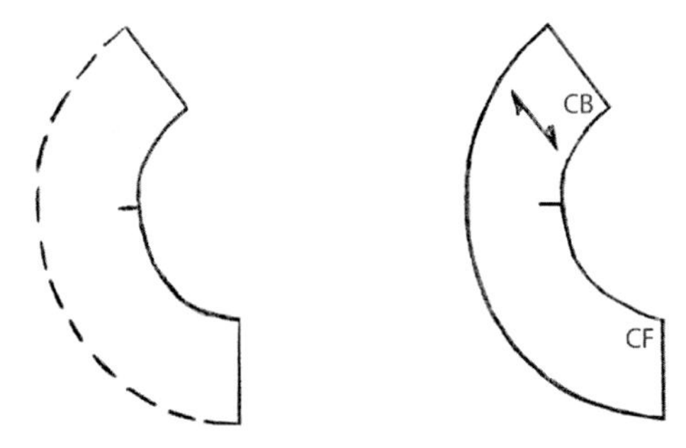

- Remove the slopers and draw the collar shape at about 3" (7.6 cm) width, or the width desired.
- Add a grainline marking that is parallel to the center back.
- Add markings to the collar.

Note

- It is important that the shoulder seam lines on the slopers overlap the ½" (1.3 cm) or the outer edge of the flat collar will ripple in that location. By overlapping the shoulder seams, a small amount of roll is created at the neckline.

Full-Roll Collars

- Full-Roll Straight Collar:
- Using copies of the bodice front sloper and the bodice back sloper, and using the grid ruler, stand the ruler on edge and bend it to get the measurements of the bodice front neckline and the bodice back neckline.

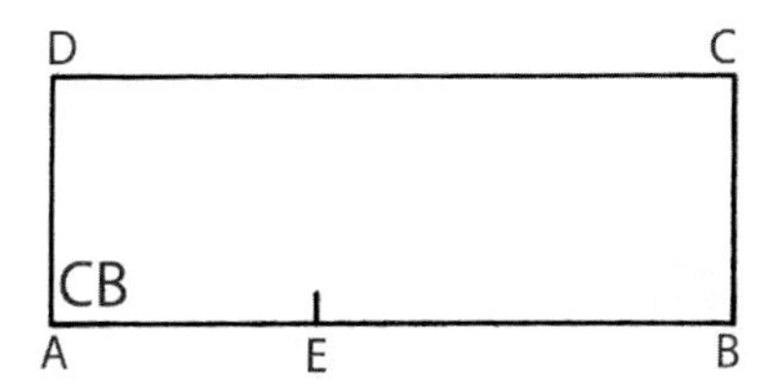

- Add the two measurements together and draw a rectangle 2½″ (6.4 cm) tall by the total neckline measurement. You should have a rectangle ABCD.
- From A, measure out and mark new point E along the A-B line where A-E equals the bodice back neckline measurement and E-B equals the bodice front neckline measurement (A-D is the center back of the collar). E will match to the shoulder seam on the sloper.

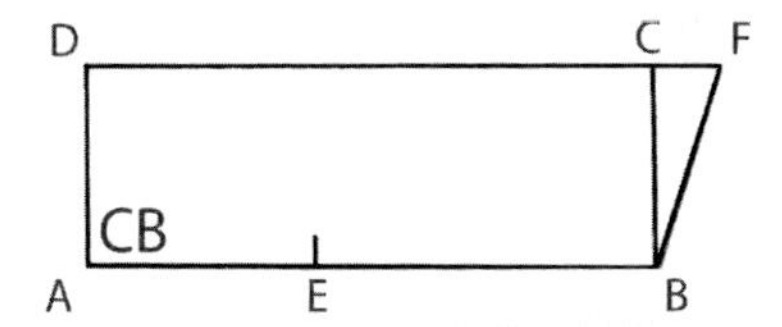

- From C, measure out to new point F to create the collar point. This point is often 1″ (2.5 cm) but will vary based on the design of the collar.
- Connect C to F and B to F with your ruler.

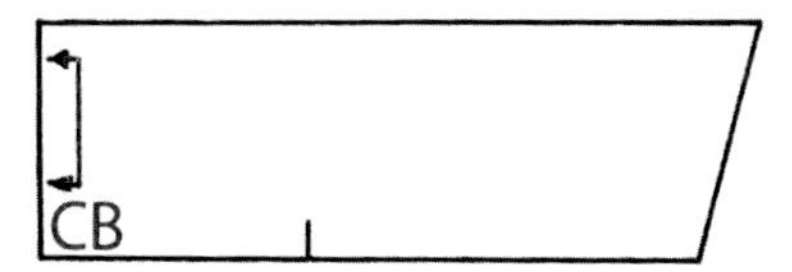

- Add labels to the collar with center back as cut on fold (although this may be different and on cross-grain for certain designs).

Full-Roll Convertible Collar

*-This collar looks very much like the Full-Roll Straight Collar but the convertible collar fits better at the neck.

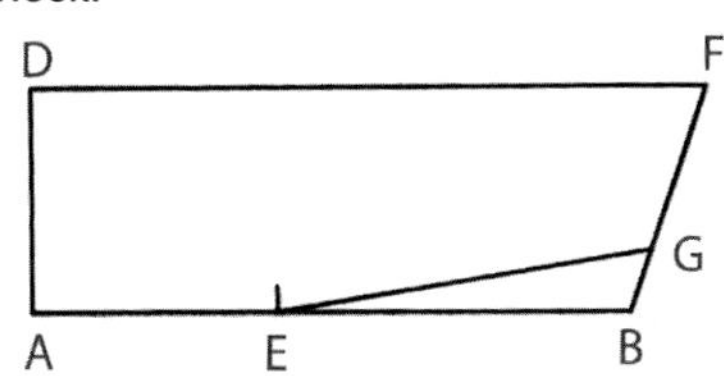

- Using a copy of the Full-Roll Straight Collar, mark a point perpendicular up from B at ½″ (1.3 cm).

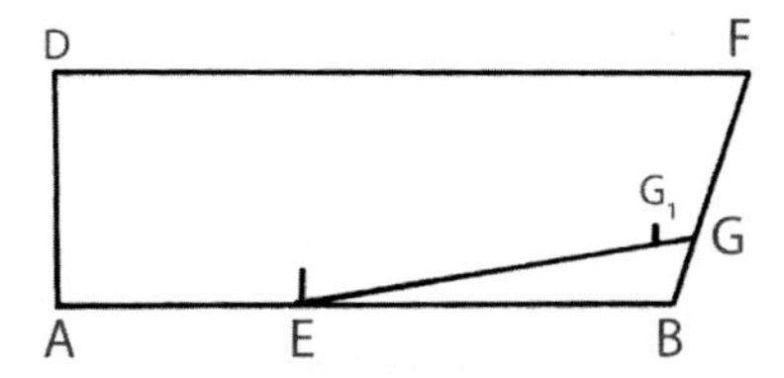

- Draw a line from E to new point G through the ½″ (1.3 cm) point.

- Check the length of the new E-G line and if it is longer than the bodice front neckline measurement, then mark a new point G_1 at that length on the E-G line.

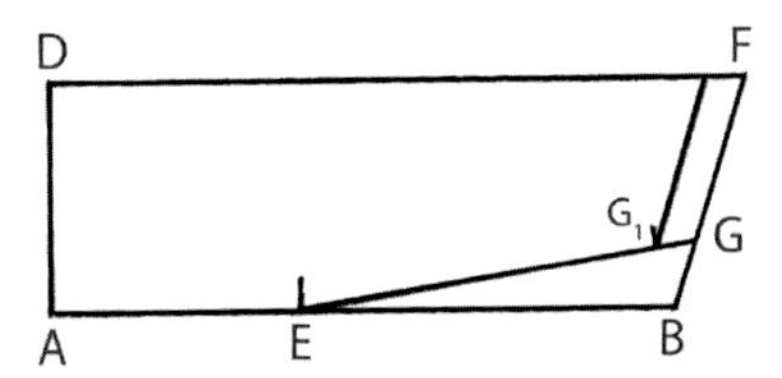

- Draw a line parallel to the B-F line from G_1 to the F-D line.

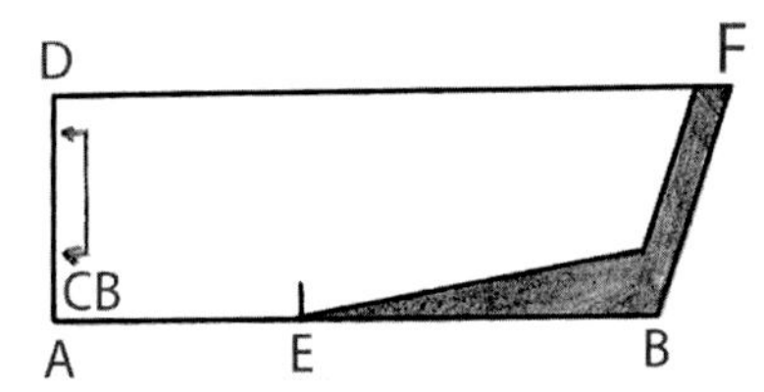

- Cut away the area outside of the new shape (the new shape is your Full-Roll Convertible Collar).

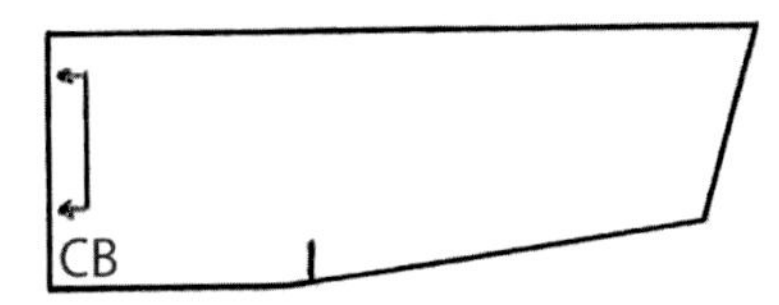

- Add labels to the collar with center back as cut on fold, and E as your shoulder seam matching notch.

Stand Collar

*-These collars consist of only the stand and the fall has been removed. This collar is also known as a Chinese, Mandarin, Military, or Nehru collar. The Chinese collar is interfaced and made on the bias with a slight gap in the center front. The Military collar usually has a gap of 1–1½" (2.5–3.8 cm) in the center front. A plain stand collar overlaps at center front and closes with a button or other closure.

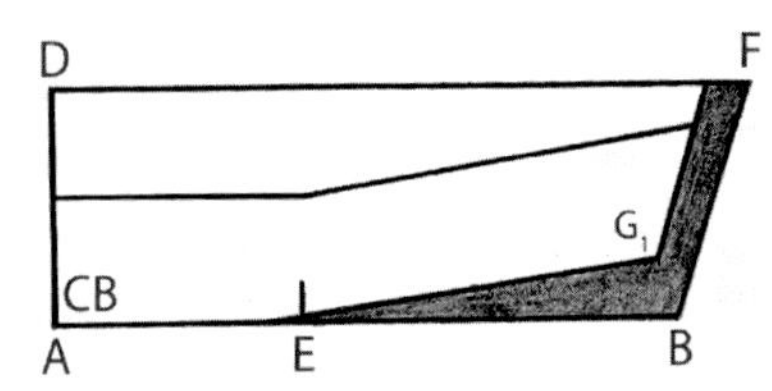

- Using a copy of the Full-Roll Straight Collar, make the adjustments for a Full-Roll Convertible Collar.
- Determine the height of the stand collar (usually 1–1½" [2.5–3.8 cm]) and draw a line parallel to the neckline at this height, following the shape of the adjusted neckline.

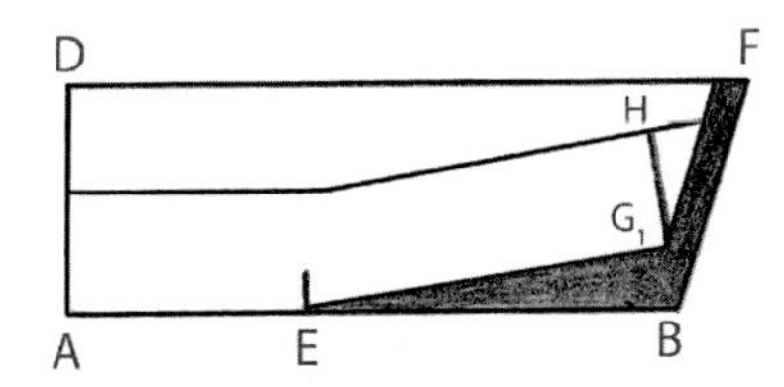

- From G_1, draw a line up perpendicular to the adjusted line to H.
- This new shape is your stand collar.
- Curve the angles to smooth the lines.

- Add labels to the collar with center back as cut on fold, and B as your shoulder seam matching notch.

Partial-Roll Collar

*-These collars have a roll between a Full-Roll Collar and a Flat Collar.

Note

- The Partial-Roll Collar can be drafted from either the Full-Roll Collar or the Flat Collar using the slash and spread method or conversely, the slash and compress method.
- You may use as many slashes in the pattern as you like: less slashes are easier to control, but more slashes allow for a smoother curve.
- It is important to create very smooth curves after making the adjustments.

From the Full-Roll Collar

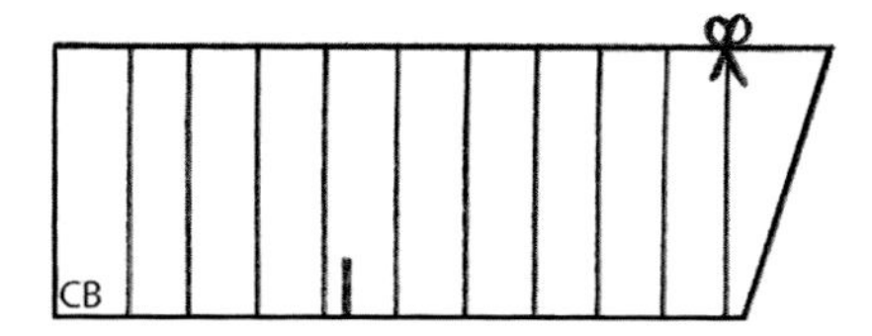

- Using a copy of the Full-Roll Straight Collar, draw lines perpendicular to the neckline and outer edge at evenly spaced points between the center back and the center front, taking care to avoid the matching notch for the shoulder seam.
- Using the slash and spread method, cut along the lines from the outer edge to but not through the neckline.

Collars

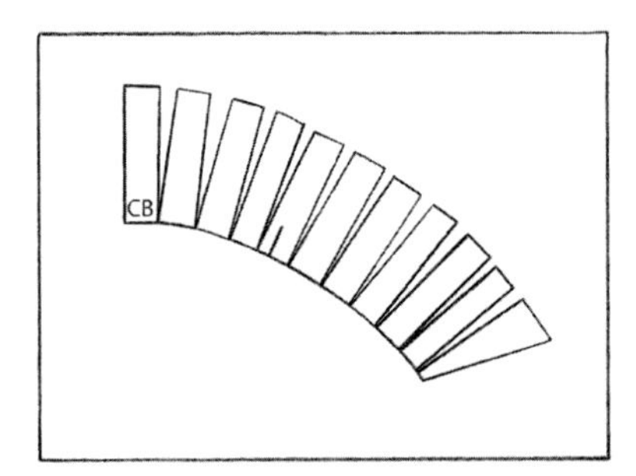

- Pin to a sheet of paper and spread the outer edge of the collar to make a gentle neckline curve.
- Draw the new collar and adjust the curves to be smooth.

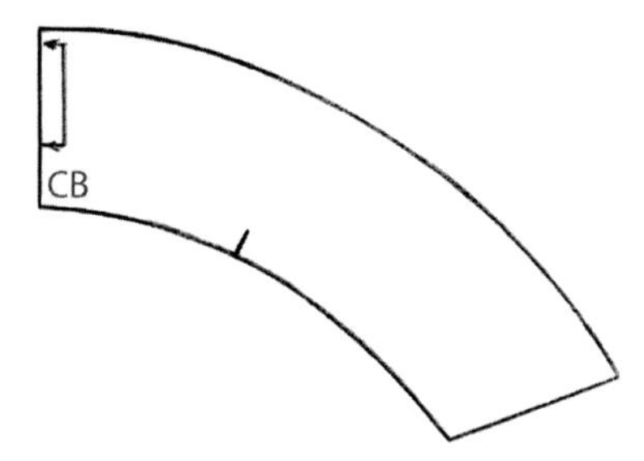

- Add labels to the collar with center back as cut on fold, and as your shoulder seam matching notch.

From the Flat Collar

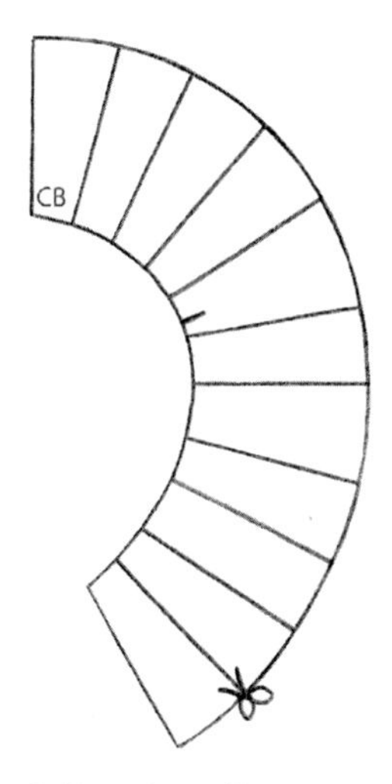

- Using a copy of the Flat Collar, draw lines perpendicular to the neckline and outer edge at evenly spaced points between the center back and the center front, taking care to avoid the matching notch for the shoulder seam.
- Using the slash method, cut along the lines from the outer edge to but not through the neckline.

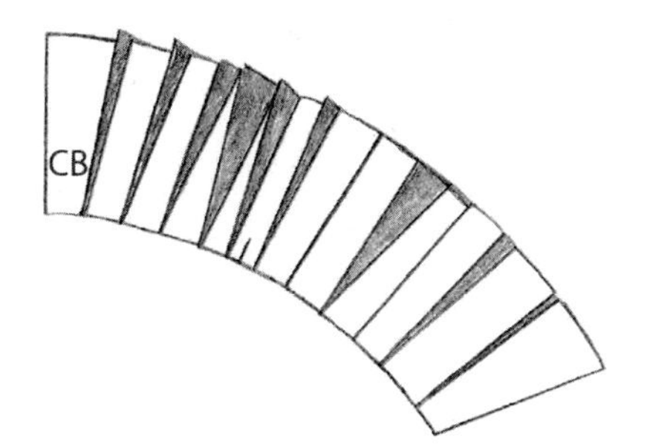

- Pin to a sheet of paper and overlap the outer edge of the collar to make a gentle neckline curve.
- Draw the new collar and adjust the curves to be smooth.

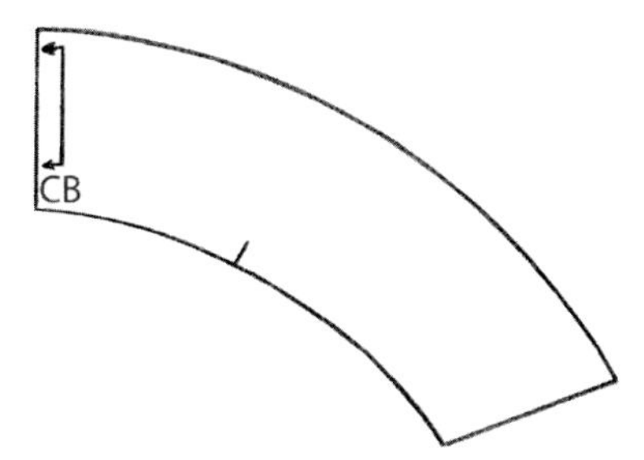

- Add labels to the collar with center back as cut on fold, and your shoulder seam matching notch.

Chapter 13: Cuffs

How to Draft Cuffs

There are many types of cuffs, but the two that will be covered in this chapter are straight cuffs and shaped cuffs. The straight cuff (also known as the single button shirt cuff) can have the facing included – which is what is represented in the following instructions. The shaped cuff follows the shape of the wrist end of the sleeve pattern. After tracing, the cuff can be flared by using the slash and spread method.

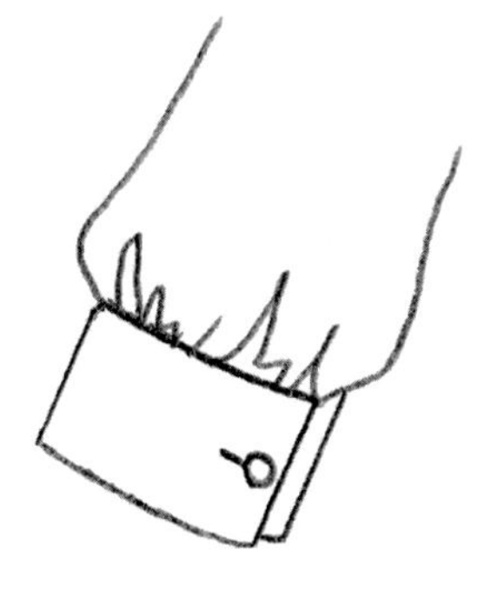

Straight Cuff

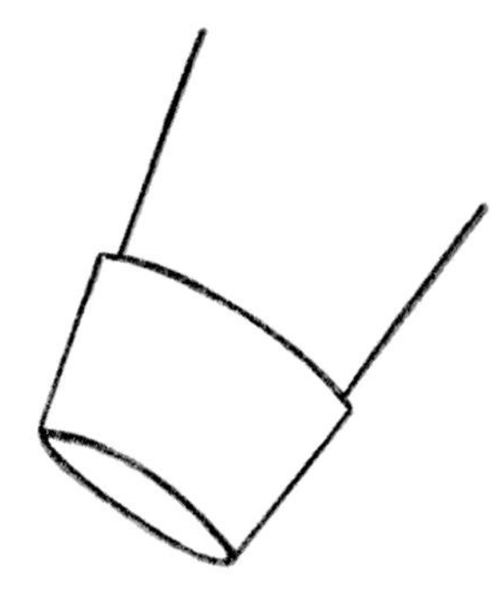

Shaped Cuff

DOI: 10.4324/9781003022619-13

What is Needed for a Straight Cuff

Wrist measurement ____________

Tracing Wheel

Paper about 12"x 12" in size

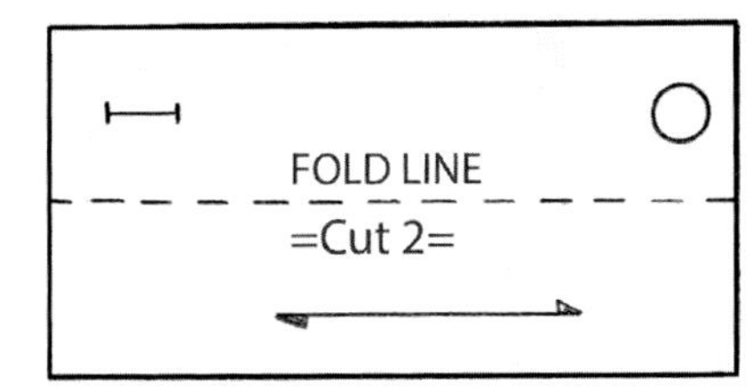

Single-Button Straight Cuff

(This cuff pattern has the facing included.)

- Draw a rectangle where the length = 2" (5.1 cm) longer than wrist measurement, and width = 2–3" (5.1–7.6 cm) when finished. It will be between 4–6" (10.2–15.2 cm) wide when flat and unfolded. (The width for the cuff is a recommendation and can be adjusted according to the desired width based on the design.)
- Draw in a fold line along the halfway point of the width.
- The grainline should follow the length of the cuff.
- Label the cuff with instructions to "Cut 2".
- The placement of the button and buttonhole on the cuff should be centered between the outer edge of the length and the fold line, but the spacing for the edge of the buttonhole and center of the button should correspond to the instructions in the chapter on Buttons and Buttonholes and is determined by the size of the button.

What is Needed for a Shaped Cuff

Sleeve Sloper

Tracing Wheel

Paper to fit under the sloper where the cuff is to be located and large enough to make the cuff the desired width

Push pins, pencil, and ruler

Shaped Cuffs

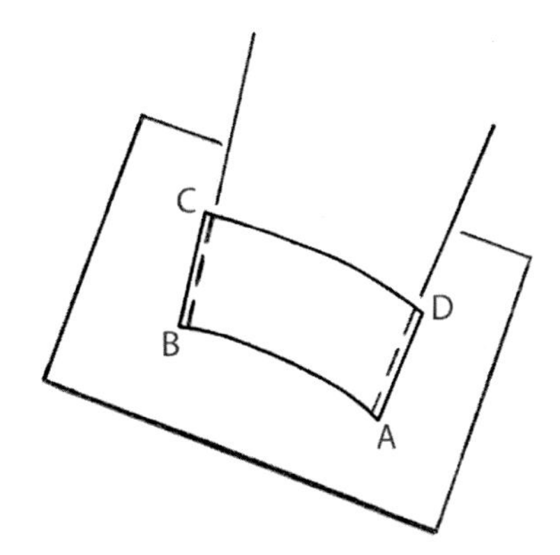

- Lay the sleeve sloper pattern down over the paper and pin in place.
- Trace line A-B which is the edge of the sleeve.

Cuffs

- Measure out from the underarm seam sleeve edges ⅛″ (0.3 cm) to create ease for the cuff. (More than ⅛″ [0.3cm] may need to be added depending on the thickness of the fashion fabric.)
- Measure up from the edge the desired size of the cuff and trace that line C-D parallel to line A-B.
- Remove the sleeve sloper pattern from the paper.

Additional Flare

- If you desire additional flare to your cuff, make a copy of your shaped cuff, then draw lines perpendicular to the wrist edge on the new copy.
- From the upper edge, cut to but not through the wrist edge.

- Place the slashed copy onto a new piece of paper and pin it down with the desired amount of flare included.

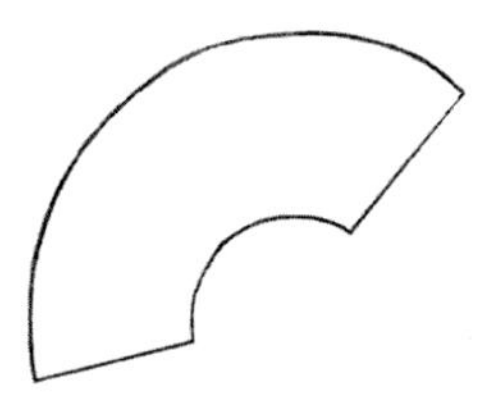

- Trace the new cuff.

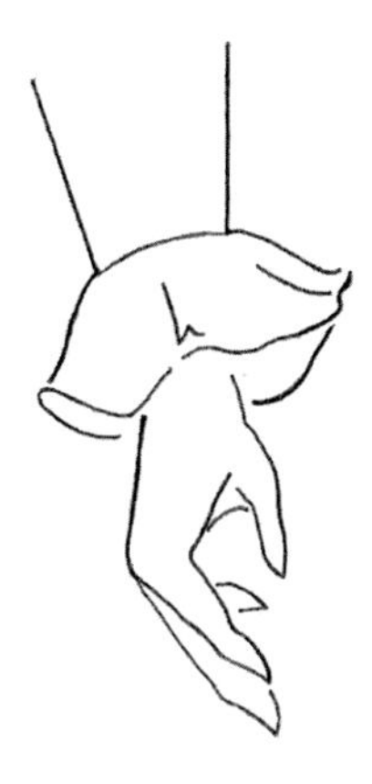

Cuff with Additional Flare

Chapter 14: Facings

How to Draft Neckline and Armscye Facings

Facings are sections of fabric that are fitted and shaped to a garment and, after stitching them in, create a finished edge. The following instructions are for garments with sleeves and garments without sleeves. Facings for garments with buttons and buttonholes will be discussed in the chapter on Buttons and Buttonholes.

Facings can vary in width due to preference, but are usually between 2–3″ (5.1–7.6 cm) wide.

NOTE: Due to the similarities between the shoulder seams and the center front and center back, it is important to recognize that the center front and center back have corners at right angles and that the shoulder seam corners are not at right angles.

- When labeling the facing patterns, there should be a matching notch located at the shoulder seam. Do not place the matching notch directly in the center of the seam, but off-set it so that it is less likely to create an upside-down connection when stitching.
- The grainlines for the facings should follow the center front and center back seam lines. This is so that the facing pieces and the bodice don't have conflicting grainlines which would cause the garment to be ill-fitting and uncomfortable.

What is Needed for a Fitted Facing for the Neckline on a Garment with Sleeves

Bodice Front Sloper

Bodice Back Sloper

Paper to fit under the slopers where the facing is to be located and large enough to make a facing 2–3″ (5.1–7.6 cm) wide

Push pins, pencil, and ruler

DOI: 10.4324/9781003022619-14

Facings

Front Neck Facing

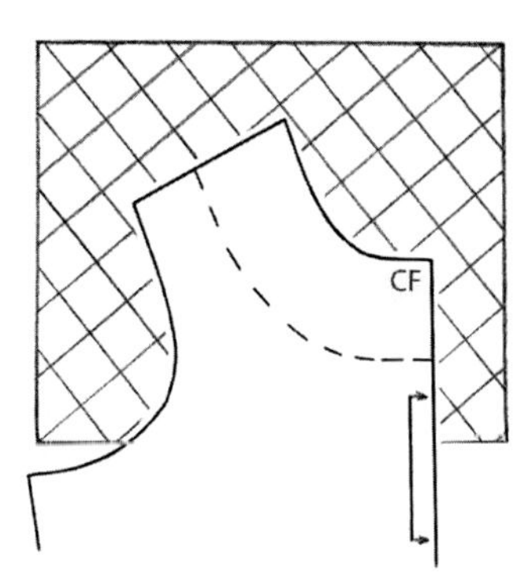

- Lay the sloper pattern down over the paper to trace on and pin in place.
- Trace the neck edge, shoulder seam, and center front.
- There should be a right angle at the center front point.
- Center front may be cut on fold depending on the original pattern.
- The grainline should follow the center front line if it is cut on fold or if the pattern is on the straight of grain there.
- Remove the sloper pattern from the paper.
- Measure out from the neckline 2–3″ (5.1–7.6 cm) and create a curve that follows the traced line.

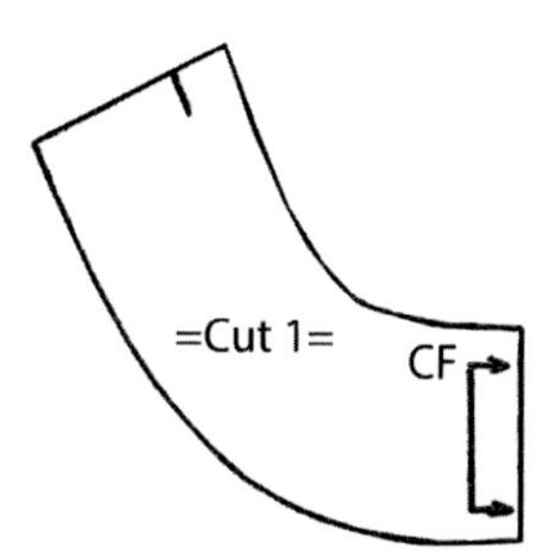

- Place a matching notch on the shoulder seam. The matching notch will assist when stitching because the center back and shoulder seam look similar. Note that there is a right angle at center and not at the shoulder seam.
- Add the grainline and labels.

Back Neck Facing

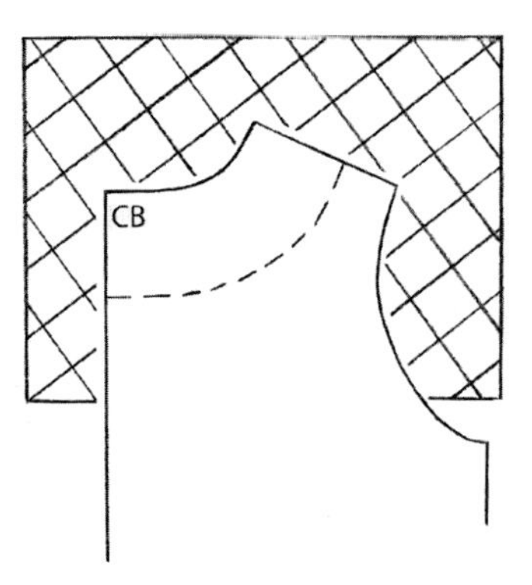

- Lay the sloper pattern down over paper to trace on and pin in place.
- Trace the neck edge, shoulder seam, and center back.
- There should be a right angle at the center back point.
- Center back may be cut on fold depending on the original pattern.
- The grainline should follow the center back line if it is cut on fold or if the pattern is on the straight of grain there.
- Remove the sloper pattern from the paper.
- Measure out from neckline 2–3″ (5.1–7.6 cm), whichever measurement you chose for the front, and create a curve that follows the traced line.

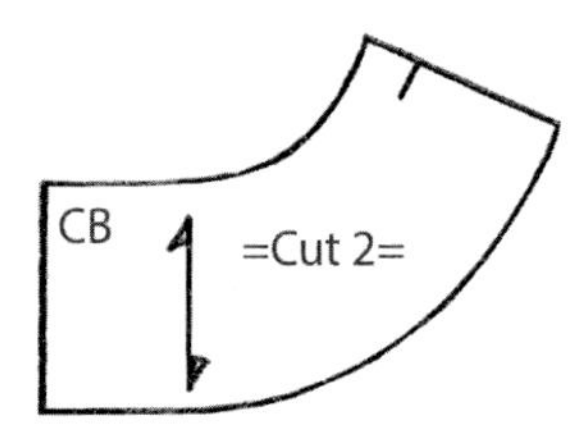

- Place a matching notch on the shoulder seam. The matching notch will assist when stitching because the center back and shoulder seam look similar. Note that there is a right angle at center and not at the shoulder seam.
- Add the grainline and labels.

Facing With Dart at Neckline or Shoulder

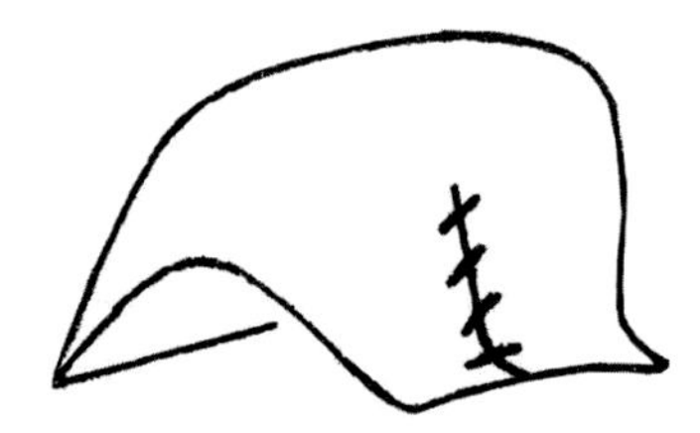

- If there is a dart within the area of the facing, fold the dart first and tape it shut without flattening the tip of the dart. (Allow the tip of the dart to rise up off the table.)
- Once the dart is closed, continue by following the previous directions.

What is Needed for a Shaped Armhole Facing

Bodice Front Sloper

Bodice Back Sloper

Paper to fit under the slopers where facing is to be located and large enough to make a facing 2" –2½" (5.1–6.4 cm) wide

Push pins, pencil, and ruler

Armscye Facing for Sleeveless Garment

NOTE: For a sleeveless garment, you may want to, or need to adjust the armholes of the bodice front and back slopers. Garments without sleeves should have less ease in them than those that have sleeves.

- To adjust the pattern, you will want to raise the side seam into the armhole ½" (1.3 cm). You will then take in the side seam ½" (1.3 cm) at the armhole and grade out to zero at the waistline.

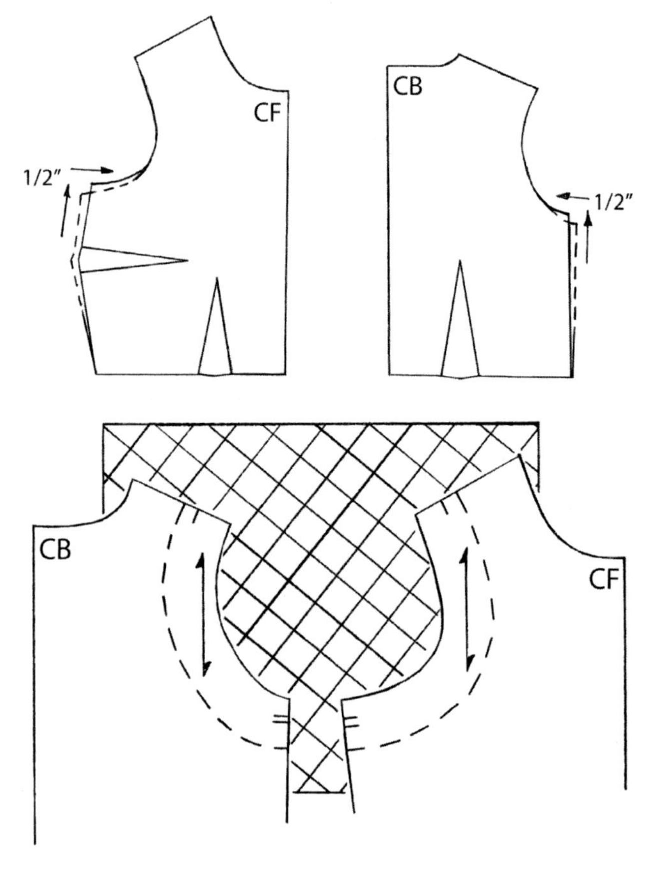

- Lay the sloper pattern down over paper to trace on and pin in place.
- The facing should measure about 2" (5.1 cm) wide
- Trace the armscye, shoulder seam, and side seam.

- The grainline should follow the bodice's grainline. This means that if the grainline on the original pattern is parallel to the center front or center back, then the facing's grainline is parallel to the center front or center back.
- Remove the sloper pattern from paper.
- Measure out from the armscye 2" (5.1 cm) and create a curve that follows the traced line.
- Place a matching notch on the shoulder seam and side seam.
- Make sure that you use a single notch and double notch to indicate the different locations because once the pattern is removed from the bodice, it can be difficult to differentiate the edges.
- Add the grainline and labels.

Shaped Facing for Armscye

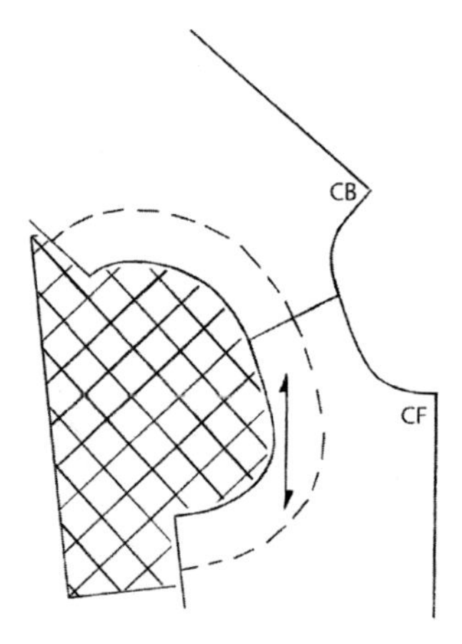

- Tape the bodice front sloper to the bodice back sloper together at the shoulder seam (or pin carefully with edges butting up to each other).
- Lay the sloper pattern down over paper to trace on and pin in place.
- Trace the armscye, and side seams.
- The grainline should follow the center front grainline.
- Remove the sloper pattern from the paper.
- Measure out from the armscye 2"–2½" (5.1–6.4 cm) and create a curve that follows the traced line.

- Place a matching notch on the side seam. The matching notch will assist when stitching because the center back and shoulder seam look similar. Note that there is a right angle at center and not at the shoulder seam.
- Add the grainline and labels.

Lowered Neckline All-in-One Facing

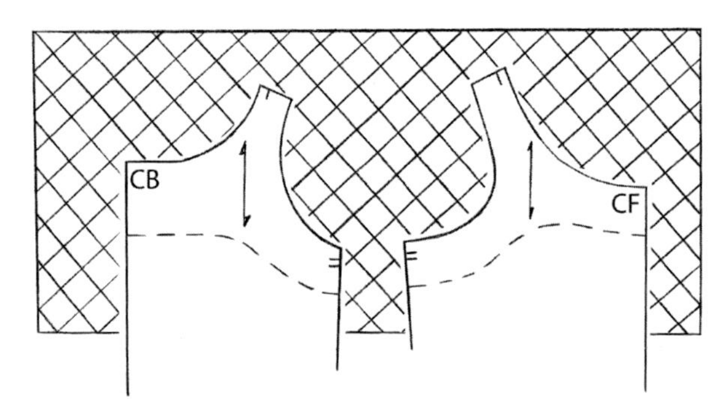

FRONT:

- Lay the sloper pattern down over the paper to trace on and pin in place.
- Trace the center front, neck edge, shoulder seam, armscye, and side seam.
  - There should be a right angle at the center front point.
  - Center front may be cut on fold depending on the original pattern.
  - The grainline should follow the center front line if it is cut on fold or if the pattern is on the straight of grain there.
- Remove the sloper pattern from the paper.
- Measure out from the neckline 2½″ (6.4 cm) and create a curve that follows the traced line making sure that there is also a gentle curve from the side seam to the front.
- Place differentiating matching notches on the shoulder seam and side seam.
- Add the grainline and labels.

BACK:

- Lay the sloper pattern down over paper to trace on and pin in place.
- Trace the center back, neck edge, shoulder seam, armscye, and side seam.
  - There should be a right angle at the center back point.
  - Center back may be cut on fold depending on the original pattern.
  - The grainline should follow the center back line if it is cut on fold or if the pattern is on the straight of grain there.
- Remove the sloper pattern from the paper.
- Measure out from the neckline 2½″ (6.4 cm) and create a curve that follows the traced line making sure that there is also a gentle curve from the side seam to the front. (The center back of the facing can be as wide as 4″ if desired.)
- Place differentiating matching notches on the shoulder seam and side seam.
- Add the grainline and labels.

NOTE: Reducing the size of the facing at the outer edge of the facing at the shoulder seams by 1⁄16″ (0.16 cm) and grading to zero at the neckline, and the facing at the outer edge of the underarm seams by 1⁄8″ (0.3 cm) and grading to zero at the armhole will reduce looseness and will create a better fit after stitching the finished garment.

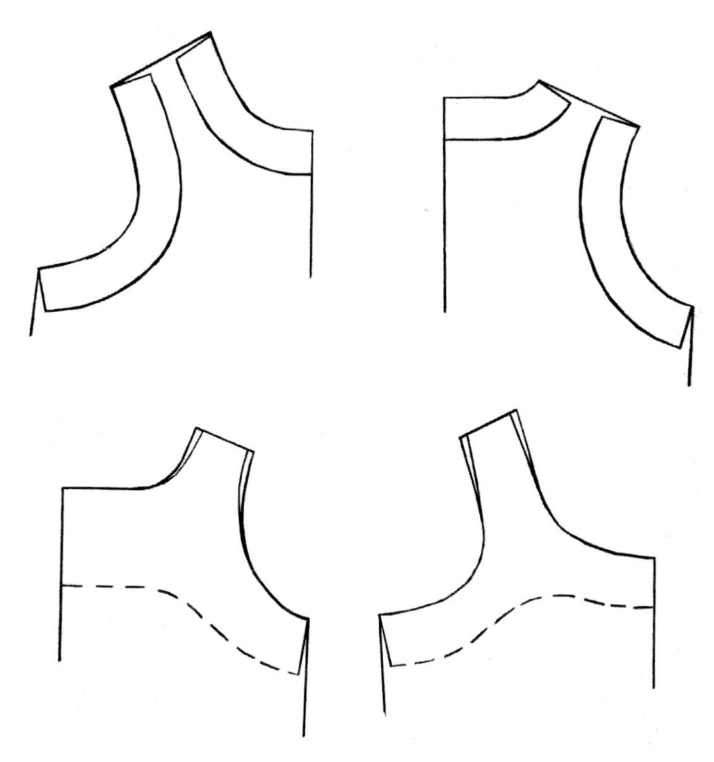

Chapter 15: Buttons and Buttonholes

Buttons and Buttonhole Closures

Buttons and buttonholes can be functional or decorative, but this chapter will focus on the functional aspects.

It is important that when placing buttons and buttonholes on a garment that an overlap is added and that center front or center back lines meet when the garment is buttoned or you will change the size and fit of the garment.

Buttonholes and Buttonhole Closures

Buttonhole Rule

- For women's garments, on the front, the buttonholes are placed on the right side of the body. For the back, the buttonholes are placed on the left side of the body. (Men's garments are the opposite.)

If the button is 3/4"(1.9cm)
then D = 3/4" (1.9cm) and
r = 3/8"(.9cm)

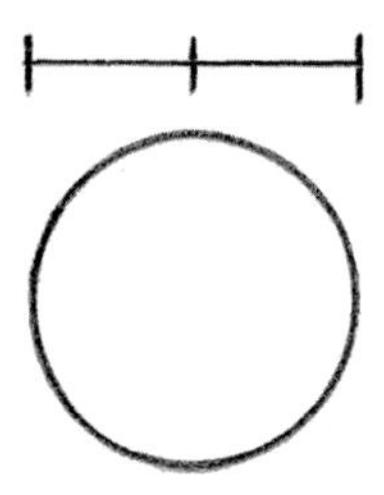

- The overlap on the garment is determined by the button size. It should equal the radius of the button + ¼" (0.6 cm).
- Fig 14–1 is an example of a flat button diameter and radius. If the button is a domed button you will need to add the height as well.

DOI: 10.4324/9781003022619-15

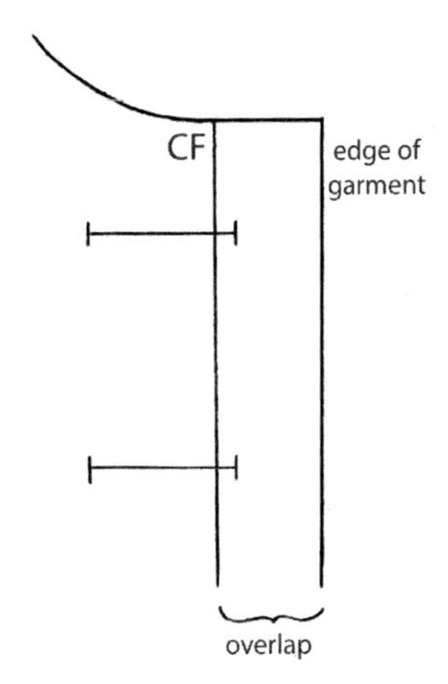

- The first button at the neckline is also determined by the button size. It should equal the radius of the button + ¼" (0.6 cm).
- For horizontal buttonholes, the buttonholes should be placed so they overlap the center front line. They should start at ⅛" (0.3 cm) from center front into the overlap and then extend into the body of the garment.
- The length of the buttonhole is equal to the width of the button + ⅛"(0.3 cm) for a flat button or if it is a domed button, you should add its height. (This is necessary to allow the button to pass through the buttonhole with ease.)

To Create the Overlap and Underlap

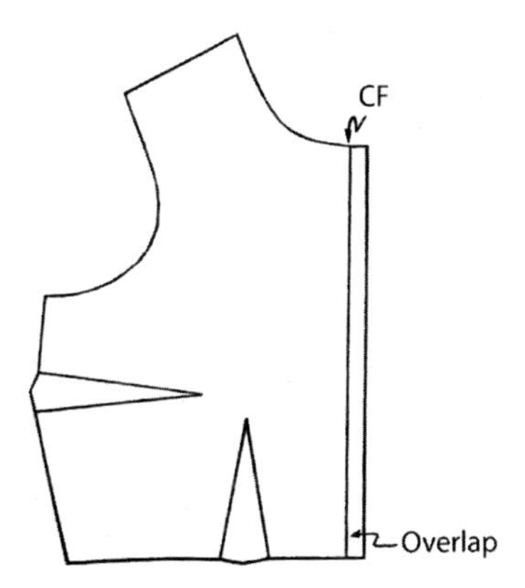

- Use a copy of your bodice front sloper.
- Using the measurement of your button, add an overlap to the right side of the bodice and an underlap to the left side of the bodice. Follow the guidelines listed previously for creating the correct overlap width.
- Using a buttonhole spacer, or by measuring, determine the center placement of the button locations. (Buttons are measured "on center" meaning that the distance is measured from the center of the button to the center of the next button.) It is suggested that a button be placed at the point of most stress, which is at the bust point line, otherwise you may experience a gap in the garment.

Facings for Garments With Buttons and Buttonholes

- There are two methods of creating a front facing for a garment with center front buttons and buttonholes. One method is an extension with the overlap and facing cut in one with the bodice front. The other method has a separate facing that extends to the armscye.

Cut-in-one Facing

What is Needed for a Cut-in-One Facing

Bodice Front Sloper with an overlap extension

Paper to fit under the sloper where the facing is to be located and large enough to make a facing 2" (5.1 cm) wide

Paper to fit under the slopers of the bodice front and facing

Push pins, pencil, and ruler

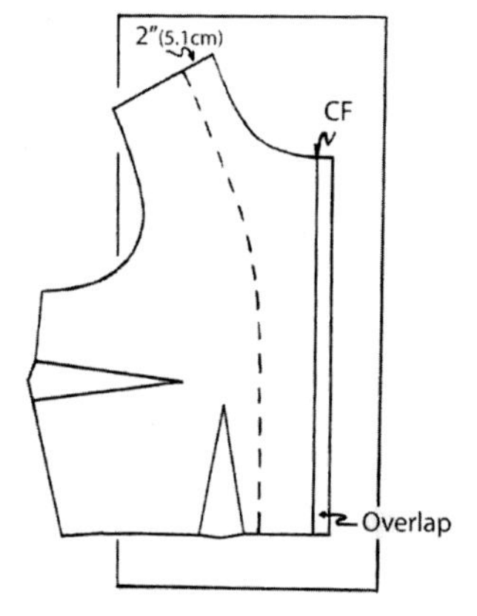

- Lay the sloper pattern down over the paper to trace on and pin in place.
- Trace the front overlap extension, neck edge, shoulder seam, and waistline up to, but not including, the waist dart.
- Using your tracing wheel and tracing paper, also trace the center front line.
- The grainline should follow the center front line.
- Remove the sloper pattern from the paper.
- Measure out from the neckline 2" (5.1 cm) along the shoulder seam and create a gently curved line with the section below the bust point parallel to the center front, being careful not to cross over into the waist dart.

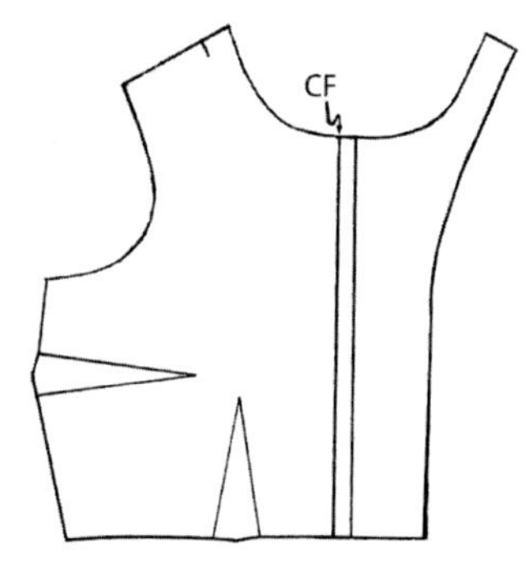

- Using a piece of paper large enough to trace the entire bodice and facing onto it, pin the bodice sloper to the paper and then align and pin the facing so that the overlaps line up.

- Trace the entire bodice front with facing.
- Add the grainline and labels.

Separate Facing for Opening With Button Overlap

What is Needed for a Separate Facing for an Opening With a Button Overlap

Bodice Front Sloper with an overlap extension

Paper to fit under the sloper where the facing is to be located and large enough to make a facing that extends to the armscye

Push pins, pencil, and ruler

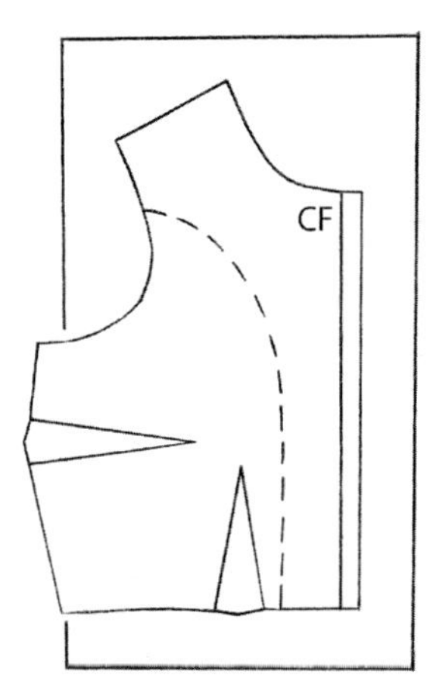

- Lay the sloper pattern down over the paper to trace on and pin in place.
- Trace the front overlap extension line, neck edge, shoulder seam, armscye, and the waistline up to, but not including, the waist dart.
- Using your tracing wheel and tracing paper, also trace the center front line.
- The grainline should follow the center front line.
- Remove the sloper pattern from the paper.

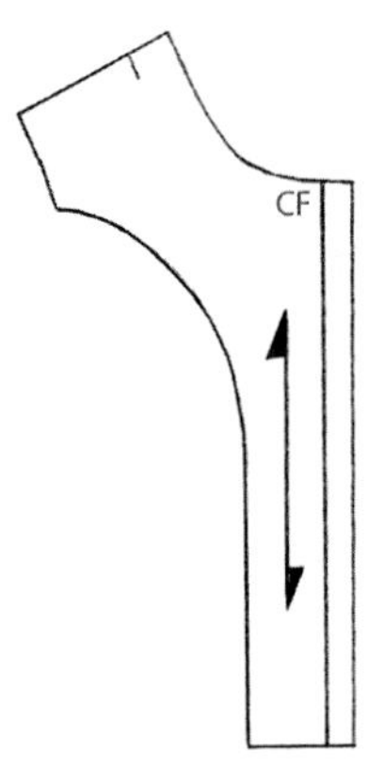

- Starting down from the shoulder seam onto the armscye about 3" (7.6 cm), draw a gentle curve down to the waistline with the section below the bust point parallel to the center front, being careful not to cross over into the waist dart.
- Trace the entire bodice front with facing.
- Add the grainline and labels.

Appendix

Labeling A Pattern

Labels are most conveniently written for the cutter when they are placed with the lettering written so that the top of the label is near the top of the pattern and written in the direction that the pattern is worn on the body.

- Include the following:
- What is the name of the piece (front, side front, side back, etc.)
- Who drafted the pattern – you may choose to use initials
- Date created
- How many to cut of fashion fabric, interfacing, lining, etc.
- Grainline or cut on fold
- Matching notches
- Darts, gathers, etc.
- Size made for or measurements used

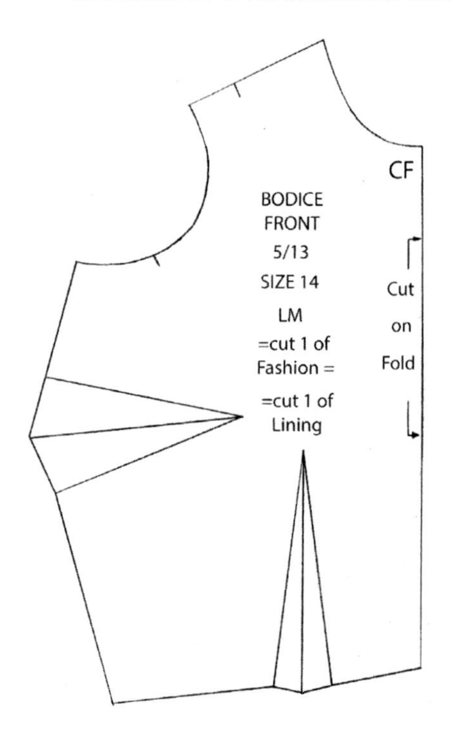

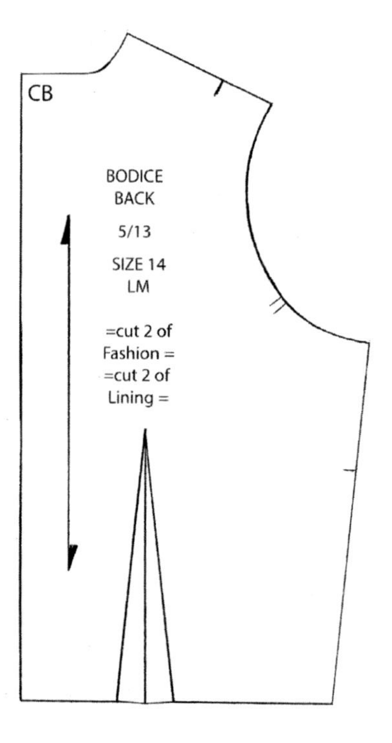

Trueing Darts

Trueing is a term used to describe the process of creating accuracy on a draped or drafted sloper. When the muslin is still on the dress form for a draped pattern, it may seem as if the sloper fits well and matches the other sections. It is only when the muslin is removed that the accuracy can be determined. Trueing can be done directly on the draped muslin pieces, or on craft paper.

Use the following instructions to true the darts for draped or drafted patterns. Trueing the dart adjusts the dart legs and center line so that it will lie smooth across the stitching line without a gap. This applies to all darts that have an end on a seam line rather than an interior dart like the double-ended dart in the sheath dress.

Note: After draping or drafting your pattern, and before cutting out all of your pattern, you need to true your darts. You will need to leave the paper surrounding the darts intact.

Note: For darts that lie horizontally, like side seam bust darts, the dart excess should be folded down. Vertical darts, like a shoulder dart, or a waistline dart either in a bodice, skirt, or pants – can be folded in the direction of your preference, but be consistent. If you press your shoulder bust dart toward center front, the other vertical darts, including those on your skirt or pants, should also get pressed toward center front. If you press your back waist dart toward center back then the darts on your skirt or pants should also get pressed toward center back.

*The following instructions are for trueing on craft paper.

For a Side Seam Bust Dart

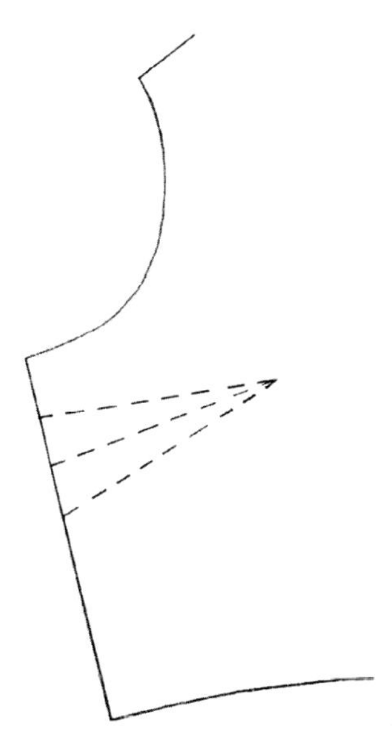

- Using the serrated tracing wheel and straight ruler, trace both legs and the center line of the dart. This is to perforate the lines on the paper and make it easier to fold.

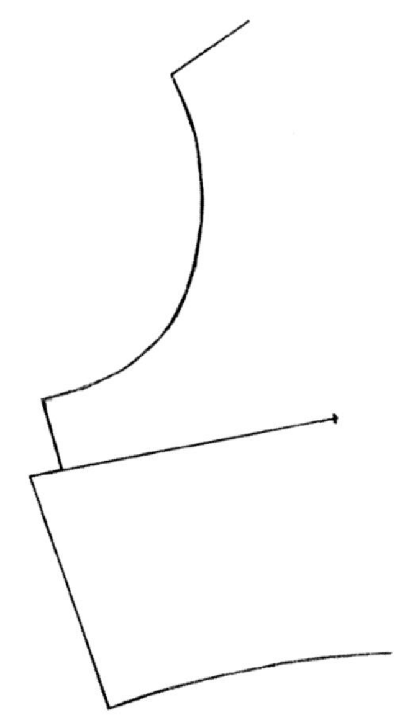

- Fold the dart along the legs so that the interior of the dart folds down on the center line and the two leg lines meet. (Refer to the previous note for guidelines on directions of the fold.) Be careful to let the apex of the dart create a three-dimensional bump where the bust would go. Don't try to flatten it.

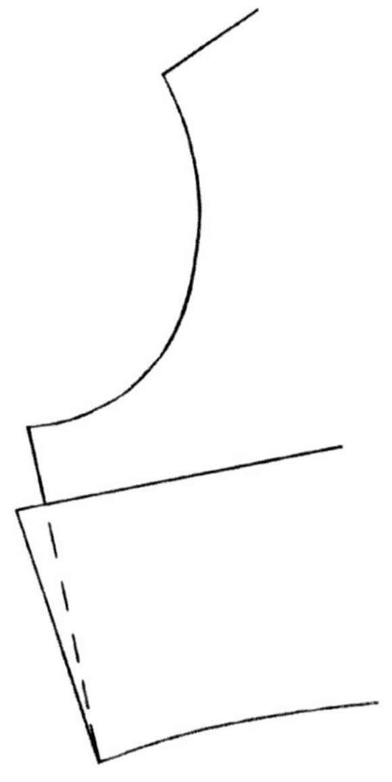

(Once the dart is folded, you may wish to use a small piece of tape to hold it together near the outer edge of the dart).

- Using your ruler and pencil, draw a line connecting the armscye/side seam point to the waistline/side seam point.

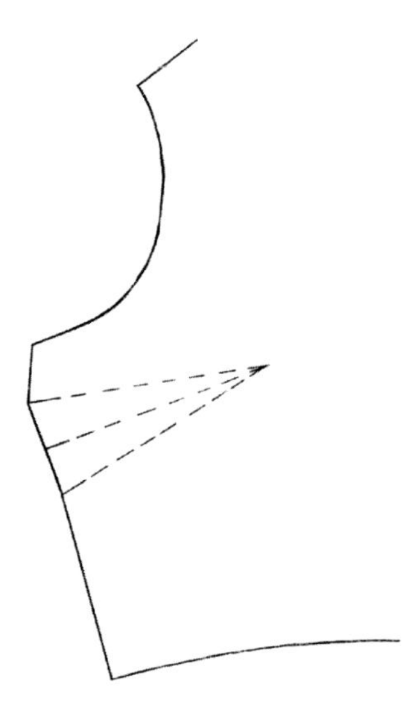

- You can now cut along this line.
- Open the dart and extend the dart lines to the new side seam.

For Shoulder and Waistline Bust Darts

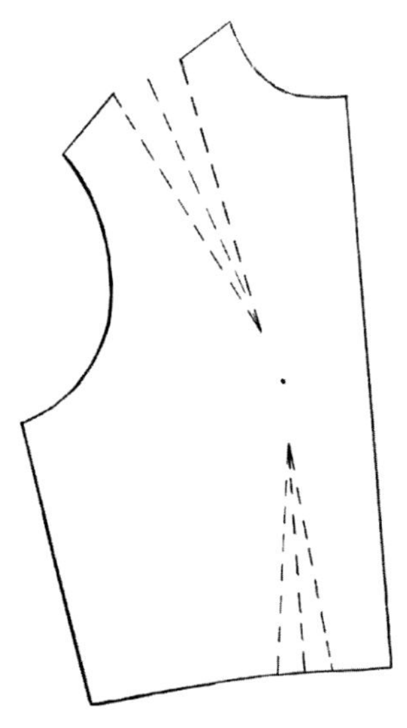

- Using the serrated tracing wheel and straight ruler, trace both legs and the center line of the darts. This is to perforate the lines on the paper and make it easier to fold.
- Fold the dart along the legs so that the interior of the dart folds on the center line and the two leg lines meet. (Refer to the previous note for guidelines on directions of the fold.) Be careful to let the apex of the dart create a three-dimensional bump where the bust would go. Don't try to flatten it.

  (Once the darts are folded, you may wish to use a small piece of tape to hold them together near the outer edges of the darts.)

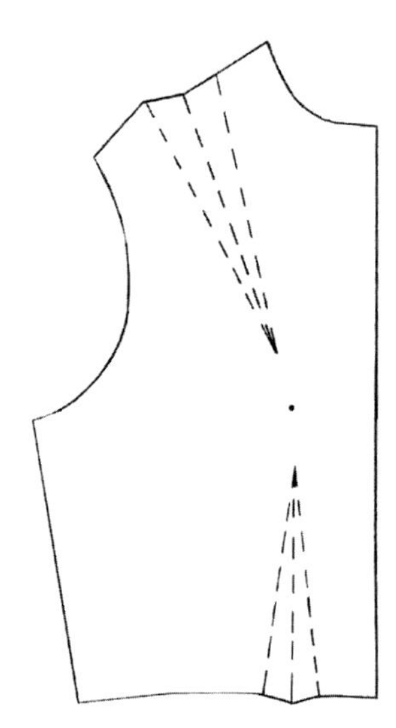

- You can now cut along the shoulder seam and waistline seam.
- Open the darts and extend the dart lines to the seam lines.

For Skirt or Pant Darts at the Waistline

(Skirt darts will be used for the diagrams.)

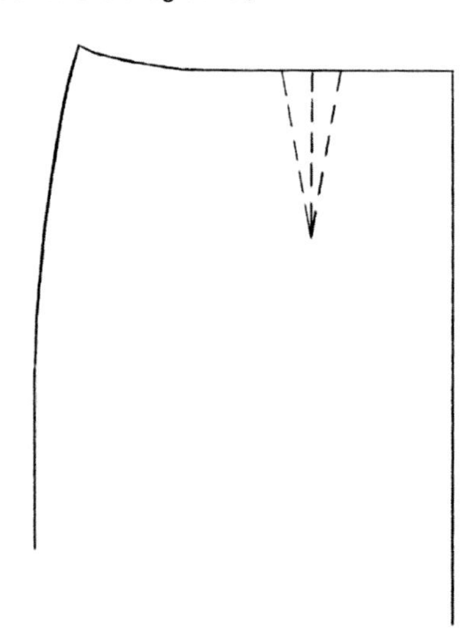

- Using the serrated tracing wheel and straight ruler, trace both legs and the center line of the dart. This is to perforate the lines on the paper and make it easier to fold.
- Fold your dart along the legs so that the interior of your dart folds on the center line and the two leg lines meet. (Refer to the previous note for guidelines on directions of the fold.) Be careful to let the apex of the dart create a three-dimensional bump. Don't try to flatten it.

  (Once the dart is folded, you may wish to use a small piece of tape to hold it together near the outer edge of the dart.)

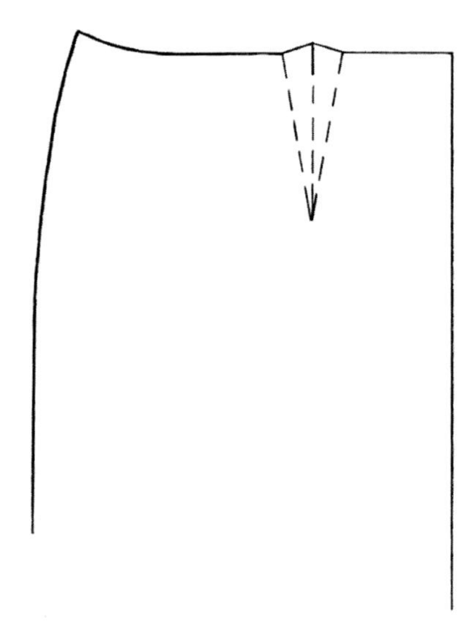

- You can now cut along the waistline.
- Open the dart and extend the dart lines to the waist seam.

FRACTION	DECIMAL
1/16	.0625
1/8	.125
3/16	.1875
1/4	.25
5/16	.3125
3/8	.375
7/16	.4375
1/2	.5
9/16	.5625
5/8	.625
11/16	.6875
3/4	.75
13/16	.8125
7/8	.875
15/16	.9375

Inches/cm Conversion Chart

INCHES In	CENTIMETERS cm	INCHES In	CENTIMETERS cm	INCHES In	CENTIMETERS cm
1	2.5	31	78.7	61	154.9
2	5.1	32	81.3	62	157.5
3	7.6	33	83.8	63	160
4	10.2	34	86.4	64	162.6
5	12.7	35	88.9	65	165.1
6	15.2	36	91.4	66	167.6
7	17.8	37	94	67	170.2
8	20.3	38	96.5	68	172.7
9	22.9	39	99.1	69	175.3
10	25.4	40	101.6	70	177.8
11	27.9	41	104.1	71	180.3
12	30.5	42	106.7	72	182.9
13	33	43	109.2	73	185.4
14	35.6	44	111.8	74	188
15	38.1	45	114.3	75	190.5
16	40.6	46	116.8	76	193
17	43.2	47	119.4	77	195.6
18	45.7	48	121.9	78	198.1
19	48.3	49	124.5	79	200.7
20	50.8	50	127	80	203.2
21	53.3	51	129.5	81	205.7
22	55.9	52	132.1	82	208.3
23	58.4	53	134.6	83	210.8
24	61	54	137.2	84	213.4
25	63.5	55	139.7	85	215.9
26	66	56	142.2	86	218.4
27	68.6	57	144.8	87	221
28	71.1	58	147.3	88	223.5
29	73.7	59	149.9	89	226.1
30	76.2	60	152.4	90	228.6

Inches/cm Conversion Chart

Appendix

Additional Resources

Amaden-Crawford, Connie, *The Art of Fashion Draping*, Fairchild Books, 5th Ed., 2018.

Hollen, Norma R. and Carolyn J. Kundel, *Pattern Making by the Flat-Pattern Method*, Macmillan Publishing Company, 7th Ed., 1993.

Ingham, Rosemary and Liz Covey, *The Costume Technician's Handbook*, Heinemann Drama, 3rd Ed., 2003.

Joseph-Armstrong, Helen, *Patternmaking for Fashion Design*, Pearson, 5th Ed., 2009.

Moore, Dorothy, *Pattern Drafting and Dressmaking*, Golden Press, 1971.

For help with sewing the mock-ups or any other sewing questions, I highly recommend the following book:

Reader's Digest New Complete Guide to Sewing, Reader's Digest Association, Inc., 2011.

Index

Page numbers in *italics* indicate a figure on the corresponding page.